3.50

CW01654161

The Best of Russian Cookery

Recipes from Russia and the Ukraine

NINA PETROVA

Drawings by Miriam Macgregor

B T Batsford Limited London

© Nina Petrova 1979

First published 1979
ISBN 0 7134 3297 7

Typeset by Tek-Art Ltd, London

Printed in Great Britain by
The Garden City Press Limited
Letchworth, Hertfordshire SG6 1JS
for the publishers
B T Batsford Limited
4 Fitzhardinge Street
London W1H 0AH

Ilana Canape
19th Feb. 1981 Birmingham

Contents

Introduction

My first book *Russian Cookery* was written because I realised there was room for a really good Russian cookbook. Also I was continually stopped in our Russian Orthodox church and elsewhere and asked for recipes and advice about cooking. I am still stopped and these requests continue.

My second book was written as a complement to my first book since it was impossible to include many recipes and only the basic ones survived. Ukrainian cooking is different from Russian cooking since it is a richer country and many fruits and vegetables are commonplace and grow locally whereas they may be difficult to get elsewhere. Hence Ukrainian cooking is more varied and exotic. I have left some of the Ukrainian names since they are rather fun.

Most modern Russian housewives have to work even when they have small children so there is far less good cooking than before the Revolution. However, the recipes survive.

In Russia, as in America, ingredients were mostly measured by volume rather than weight hence the Russian tumbler is equal to an American cup which equals 8 fluid ounces in imperial measure. Remember when trying new recipes to follow instructions.

Butter and sugar should be whipped properly, in a mixer for preference to save time and effort. Yeast baking becomes simple with a hook for this purpose.

It is possible to cheat a little when cooking however. You can use yoghurt instead of sour cream for sauces and soups. Cornflour or arrowroot can replace potato flour. Sweet-sour cucumbers in dill can be used instead of salted ones. Use cottage cheese instead of curd cheese when this is not available. But you have to first strain the cheese and then put it through a sieve to take out the lumps. Then weigh it since it contains a lot of liquid.

In America, farm cheese if fresh can be mixed with equal quantities of cottage cheese in a blender and used for cooking dishes in this book. There are many recipes using curd cheese since this is a favourite in Russia to this day and replaces meat sometimes. If olive oil or sunflower oil is missing from your cupboard substitute corn oil. A mixture of oil and butter is excellent for roasting.

You will find all the old recipes here and many new ones which I hope you will enjoy trying. I have to thank all those who contributed to the new recipes and especially to Count Leon Razumovsky who gave me several recipes which belonged to his late grandmother the Countess Maria Razumovskaia (née Princess Poniatowska). I hope you will enjoy these new dishes and remember that presentation is important. Always garnish if possible. For a dinner party lay the table with the best china and silver and use good colour schemes. Even simple food can taste delicious if cooked well and presented properly. You will get a reputation as an excellent hostess if you study these recipes and cook economically since Russian and Ukrainian cookery is basically peasant cooking and therefore cheap and easy to prepare. The cakes, however, fall into the category of *La Pâtisserie Fine*.

Finally may I wish you happy cooking and *bon appétit*.

Nina Petrova, London 1979

About the book

As an experienced cook the author realises that the majority of housewives, like herself, adapt recipes to their own preferences and that exact measures are unimportant to the ingredients themselves, except in the cakes section where the proportion of one ingredient to another does affect the result.

Zakuski

Zakuski is the Russian word for hors d'oeuvre. They can either be tiny open sandwiches served with vodka before a meal or take the form of a cold or hot dish served as a first course. For the open sandwiches use black, brown or grey (a mixture of white and rye flour) bread. There are many different spreads. Pâté, salted herring, smoked cod's roe, anchovies, caviar, smoked sausage and smoked salmon are among the most typical.

Other suggestions for zakuski are to be found elsewhere in the book. Pickled grapes, mushrooms, salted cucumbers and tomatoes (page 149) are usually served with vodka. Aubergines (egg plants) stuffed with vegetables (page 70) and cucumber or radishes in sour cream (page 69) also make excellent zakuski.

CAVIAR

The most famous Russian hors d'oeuvre is, of course, caviar. It should be served cold, and is usually garnished with lemon. It can also be eaten with blini (page 108). Red or black caviar is excellent on small slices of rye bread.

Caviar d'aubergines

serves 4

2 medium aubergines (egg plants)
1 onion
1 green pepper or
3 medium sized tomatoes
french dressing (see page 92)
salt to taste

Wash and score the aubergines, brush with oil and bake them in a dish in a moderate oven 180°C (350°F) Mark 4 for about 30 minutes or until tender. Cut them in half and remove all the pulp. Chop. Peel and chop the onion. Chop the pepper or tomatoes, removing the seeds from the pepper, if used. Chop all the ingredients together very finely on a wooden board. Transfer to a bowl and add french dressing and salt to taste.

This hors d'oeuvre is eaten all along the Mediterranean coast with slight variations.

Some like to cook the mixture but I prefer to keep the tomato and onion raw. This gives it a better flavour and retains the vitamins. However if you find the mixture too moist to spread on bread you can cook it slowly in a saucepan with the lid off so that the liquid is reduced. First of all skin the tomatoes by pouring boiling water over them.

Prepare small pieces of black bread and butter beforehand and allow guests or family to spread the mixture themselves. This zakuska should be chilled and served best with cold vodka drunk from little glasses at one gulp. Remember that men are very fond of this spread, so make enough!

Salted herring

serves 4

1 salted herring	DRESSING
¼ spanish onion or 1 hard boiled egg	2 tablespoons olive oil
slices of fresh or salted cucumber	1 tablespoon wine vinegar
	1 teaspoon made mustard

If you are unable to buy salted herring fillets from a delicatessen, prepare the whole salted herrings yourself in the following manner. Wash all the utensils thoroughly after use as the smell is very strong.

Soak the fish in cold water, cold milk or strong cold tea for about two hours to prevent it tasting too salty. Put the herring on a double sheet of greaseproof paper. Skin the fish, starting at the neck. Remove the stomach and the head with a sharp knife. Take out all the bones. Wash the fish under the cold tap and drain. Cut in slices about 25mm (1 in.) thick and arrange on a plate in the shape of the fish. Put the actual tail and head back in place, spreading out the gills so that the head is fairly flat.

This should be kept in the fridge till just before serving, as this improves the flavour. Serve with black bread and butter if possible.

DRESSING

Make the dressing from the oil, vinegar and mustard. Let the dressing soak into the fish before serving as it improves the flavour. It will also prevent the fish from becoming too dry if it is prepared in advance.

Garnish with slices of Spanish onion or hard boiled egg and fresh or salted cucumber. The yolk of the egg can also be sieved and used as decoration. Serve with potato salad (page 83) or Russian salad (page 83).

Salted herrings with sour cream

serves 4

2 salted herring fillets	1 sprig dill or parsley or ¼ onion or 2 spring onions
2-3 tablespoons sour cream	

Cut the fish in 25mm (1 in.) pieces and put on an oval dish in the shape of the original fillets. Pour the sour cream between the fillets and garnish with finely chopped dill or parsley, or with onion rings or finely chopped spring onion.

To make a spread chop the above ingredients finely and mix well. Use only 1 tablespoon of sour cream to each large herring fillet. Serve on black bread with iced vodka in small glasses, drink the vodka in one gulp.

Salted herring pie

serves 6-8

3 or 4 salted herring fillets	25 g (1 oz) 2 tablespoons butter
600 g (1½ lb) boiled potatoes	breadcrumbs
250 ml (½ pt) 1¼ cups sour cream	

Slice the herrings and potatoes and put them in alternate layers in a greased casserole, ending in a potato layer. Pour in the sour cream. Sprinkle with breadcrumbs and dot with butter. Cook in a moderate oven 180°C (350°F) Mark 4 for about half an hour until brown. Serve hot.

This is a good supper dish or a hot zakuska. Serve with black bread and butter and iced vodka. A great favourite in North Russia.

Slav eggs

To each egg allow:

knob of butter	sprig parsley
salt and pepper to taste	breadcrumbs

Hard boil the eggs. Cut them in half through the shells with a very sharp knife. Remove the yolks and sieve them. Mix the yolks with a little softened butter, salt, pepper and chopped parsley. Return the yolks to the whites. Sprinkle with breadcrumbs, dot with butter and grill for a few minutes until brown. Serve hot.

Another version of this recipe can be made by removing both yolks and whites after hard boiling the eggs. Chop them finely. To four eggs add one ounce softened butter, one tablespoon sour cream and a little chopped parsley or dill. Season and return the mixture to the shells. Finish as above.

This dish is served without any accompaniments. Served with iced vodka if possible.

When hard boiling the eggs do not over cook, ie about 8 minutes when they start to boil and plunge them into cold water at once. Over boiling results in a grey lining to the yolk and the white may be tough.

Katushki *(meatballs)*

serves 6-8

600 g (1½ lb) 3 cups raw minced meat (beef, veal, pork or veal and pork)
1 onion
3 slices stale french bread
salt and pepper to taste
butter for frying

Chop the onion finely and fry it lightly in butter. Remove the crusts and soak the bread in water. Squeeze out the excess liquid. Mix the meat, onion and bread together by hand, adding a little water if the mixture is too dry. Season and form into meatballs. Fry them in butter for about 20 minutes. Serve cold on cocktail sticks with slices of salted cucumber.

This mixture can also be formed into cotletti, coated in breadcrumbs and fried in the same way. These cotletti are softer than those made with egg (page 41). They can be sliced and served cold on rye bread.

These zakuski are useful to serve with drinks for a change. They are great favourites with vodka at all Russian bazaars.

Studen

serves 8

½ pig's head
1 pig's trotter
400 g (1 lb) stewing veal
1 onion
2 carrots
salt to taste
4 peppercorns
1 bayleaf
2 hard boiled eggs
a few cooked green peas (optional)

Clean the pig's head and trotter, making sure that there are no hairs left on them. Put all the above ingredients, except the hard boiled eggs and peas in a large saucepan. Cover with water and simmer with the lid on for about 1½ hours or until the veal is cooked. When it is ready remove it from the saucepan and chop. Leave the pig's head and trotter to simmer for about another hour or until they are very soft. When cooked, lift them out of the stock with the carrots. Strain the stock and skim off any fat. Take a large mould for the studen. Slice the hard boiled eggs and the cooked carrots and put them with the peas at the bottom of the dish for decoration. Chop all the edible parts of the pig's head and trotter and put them in the dish with the cooked veal on top. Pour in the strained stock and leave to set. When ready, turn out on to a large dish and garnish with watercress. Serve with horse-radish cream (page 91).

This is a great favourite for parties in Russia and always on the table at Easter and Christmas when there are many guests. Serve with Russian salad and iced vodka. Rye bread and butter if available.

Stuffed beetroot

serves 4

4 round beetroots (about 600 g (1½ lb))
25 g (1 oz) 2 tablespoons butter
dry breadcrumbs
3 tablespoons sour cream

STUFFING
2 carrots
1 stalk celery
1 small onion
1 sprig parsley
butter or oil for frying
25 g (1 oz) 2 tablespoons rice
salt and pepper to taste

Boil the beetroot (page 67) until tender. Remove from the saucepan and allow to cool slightly. Peel off the skin and cut off the tops. Scoop out the centres with a teaspoon.

STUFFING
Prepare the stuffing while the beetroot is cooking. Peel the carrots and onion and scrape the celery. Chop them into very small pieces and stew them, with the parsley, in oil or butter for 15-20 minutes until tender. Meanwhile, boil the rice in salted water. When the rice is ready, strain and mix with the cooked vegetables and any fat left in the pan. Season and stuff the beetroot with this mixture.

Put the beetroot in a buttered fireproof dish, sprinkle with breadcrumbs, dot with butter and bake in a moderate oven 180°C (350°F) Mark 4 for a further 15-20 minutes. Add the sour cream and serve with meat or game or as a hot zakuska.

This is a lovely hot dish and original. It needs no accompaniments except black bread and butter if you are hungry. It is rather filling.

If no fresh beetroot is available use canned or bottled beets. The flavour will be different but they will be equally tasty. Just heat through. I suggest 10 minutes, although this can be done much quicker in a lidded saucepan.

GLOBE ARTICHOKES

Preparation and cooking: Soak the artichokes for an hour in cold salt water to remove dust and insects. Cut off the stalks and the tough outer leaves. Trim the tops of the other leaves to a neat shape with scissors and remove the choke from the centre. Wash again thoroughly and rub the base with lemon to prevent discoloration during cooking. If they are not to be cooked immediately leave in cold water to which lemon juice has been added.

Cover with boiling salted water in a saucepan and simmer with the lid on for 30-45 minutes, depending on their size and age. When cooked, the leaves will pull out easily. Be careful not to overcook. Drain well and serve with hollandaise sauce (page 90).

Artichoke hearts with ham and cheese sauce

serves 4

4 artichokes
salt to taste
25 g (1 oz) 2 tablespoons butter
50 g (2 oz) ¼ cup lean ham
25 g (1 oz) ¼ cup grated cheddar or gruyère cheese

SAUCE
125 ml (¼ pt) ⅔ cup white sauce (page 89)

Prepare artichokes and boil until half cooked. (See above.) Remove the leaves and fry the hearts in butter for a few minutes

SAUCE
Add the finely chopped lean ham to the white sauce. Put the artichoke hearts into a buttered fireproof dish and cover with the sauce. Sprinkle with the grated cheese and add knobs of butter.

Bake in a fairly hot oven 200°C (400°F) Mark 6 for about 15 minutes until brown. Serve as a separate course or a hot zakuska.

This is rather a rich dish and iced vodka goes very well with it. Globe artichokes are in season from July to October unless imported.

Liver pâté

serves 4

200 g (½ lb) chicken or calf's liver
3 rashers streaky bacon
1 small carrot
1 small onion
1 small stalk celery

GARNISH
1 hard boiled egg
1 salted cucumber

ASPIC
8 g (¼ oz) 1 envelope gelatine
125 ml (¼ pt) ⅔ cup meat stock
15 g (½ oz) 1 tablespoon butter
1 bayleaf
salt and pepper to taste
pinch grated nutmeg
1 dessertspoon Madeira or dry red wine

Remove the skin and membrane from the liver. Wash and chop. Cut off the rind and chop the bacon. Clean and chop the vegetables. Melt the butter in the frying-pan and gently stew the liver, bacon and vegetables with the bayleaf. Remove the bacon when it is ready and continue cooking the liver and vegetables until they are tender. Be careful not to overcook the liver as this will make the pâté dry. Remove the bayleaf and season. Put the bacon, liver and vegetables through a mincer twice. Add the nutmeg and wine. Adjust seasoning, mix thoroughly and form into a loaf shape. Leave to cool and garnish with sliced hard-boiled egg and serve or set in aspic.

If served as a separate dish. Beetroot salad (page 82) or pickled mushroom (page 149) go well with this dish. Serve with chilled vodka.

ASPIC
Skim the stock to remove all fat. Dissolve the gelatine in a little water and add enough stock to make up 125 ml (¼ pt) ⅔ cup of liquid. Leave to cool. When it begins to gell pour it over the pâté, leave to set and garnish with sliced hard boiled egg.

Serve with Russian salad (page 83) or on black bread and butter with slices of salted cucumber.

Veal and liver pâté

serves 6

puff pastry (page 102)
150 g (6 oz) calf's liver
6 rashers streaky bacon
1 small carrot
1 small onion
1 stalk celery
1 bayleaf
butter
300 g (¾ lb) cooked veal
salt and pepper to taste
2 slices stale french bread
pinch of grated nutmeg
1-2 eggs

Prepare the pastry (page 102). Meanwhile remove the skin and membrane and wash the liver. Cut off the rind and chop the bacon. Clean and chop the vegetables. Gently stew the liver, bacon and vegetables in butter with the bayleaf, stirring frequently. Put the bacon aside when it is ready and continue frying the liver and vegetables until they are cooked. Season, then discard the bayleaf. Slice the liver thinly and put aside. Mix the cooked veal with the vegetables and bacon and put them twice through the mincer. Remove the crusts and soak the bread in water. Squeeze out the excess liquid and put through the mincer. Mix the veal, bacon and vegetables with the bread, egg and nutmeg. Moisten with a little gravy made from adding 2-3 tablespoons of water to the pan where the liver and bacon were cooked. Cool.

Divide the pastry in two and roll out. Line a 23 cm (9 in.) cake tin or oval fireproof dish with one half, pressing the pastry well down so that it touches the corners. Put in half the veal mixture. Cover with a layer of sliced liver. Put the rest of the veal on top and cover with the rest of the pastry. Trim and pinch the edges. Cut a small slit in the top to allow the steam to escape. Brush with beaten egg, if you wish, and bake in a hot oven 230-260°C (450-500°F) Mark 8-9 for 35-45 minutes, turning the oven down when it begins to brown.

Serve cold with Russian salad. This can also be eaten as a main course for lunch. Serve it hot. A little dry white wine will improve the flavour if you add it to the mixture.

Salted herring pâté

serves 3-4

1 salted herring or
2 salted herring fillets
1 large eating apple
half an onion
squeeze of lemon
trace of grated nutmeg (optional)
2 tablespoons olive oil

GARNISH
1 red eating apple
4 sprigs parsley

Clean and prepare the herring (page 10) or use two prepared fillets. Peel and core the apple and peel the onion. Chop the fish, onion and apple separately and then together, until they are well mixed. Add the lemon, nutmeg and oil and blend well. Mould into a herring shape on a suitable dish, adding the head and tail for decoration if a whole herring has been used. Chill for 10 minutes. Garnish with parsley and slices of red apple. Serve with black bread and butter and eat at once.

To save washing-up, butter small pieces of black bread and spread the pâté on the bread. Make a few minutes before serving vodka or the canapé will dry.

Fish pâté

serves 6

600 g (1½ lb) fillet of cod, hake, haddock or pike
3 slices stale french bread
½ onion
1 large egg or 2 small
dry breadcrumbs
1 carrot
1 stalk celery
salt to taste
6 peppercorns
1 bayleaf
squeeze of lemon
1 tablespoon gelatine
1 hard boiled egg

This is most successful when made from a mixture of two types of fish. Remove the skin and mince the fish. Remove the crusts and soak the bread in water. Squeeze out the excess liquid and put through the mincer. Peel and chop the onion finely. Mix the fish, bread, onion and egg well by hand, adding a few dry breadcrumbs if the mixture is too wet. Form into a large oval shape and coat in breadcrumbs. Wrap in a napkin or a double piece of muslin. Half fill a large saucepan with water and add the cleaned and chopped carrot and celery, the salt, peppercorns, bayleaf and lemon juice. Bring to the boil and place in it the fish in the napkin. Cover and poach for 25 minutes. When ready, lift out carefully and put on a dish to cool.

Adjust the seasoning in the stock so that it is rather salty. Strain half a pint and dissolve the gelatine in it. Leave it to set.

When the pâté has cooled, transfer it to a clean dish and decorate it with chopped cooked carrot, sliced hard boiled egg and chopped aspic. Serve with horseradish cream (page 91) and beetroot salad (page 82).

This is called *Telnoye* in Russian. Reference to this dish can be found in manuscripts of the sixteenth and seventeenth centuries. A good starter to a meal or can be a main course of a light lunch with salad.

Katushki *(fish balls)*

serves 4

600 g (1½ lb) fresh white fish (cod, whiting, hake, haddock or mixture)
3 slices day-old french bread
1-2 eggs
salt and pepper to taste
breadcrumbs

Remove the skin and bones and put the fish through a mincer. Discard the crusts and soak the bread in water. Squeeze out the excess liquid. Knead the bread, fish and eggs well by hand, to obtain a firm mixture. Salt and pepper to taste. Form into balls about 4 cm (1½ in.) in diameter. Roll in breadcrumbs and steam in a fish-kettle or steamer for about 20 minutes until cooked.

Serve with white wine sauce (page 90). Katushki can also be eaten cold with Russian salad (page 83), beetroot salad (page 82) and horseradish cream (page 91).

This dish is best served with rye bread and butter and chilled vodka. It can also be eaten as a main course for lunch. If hot serve with boiled potatoes and horseradish cream. If cold with Russian salad, potato salad, beetroot salad, etc.

Fish cutlets

Follow the recipe for katushki but form the mixture into rissole shapes instead of balls. Coat in breadcrumbs and fry for about 20 minutes in oil or fat until golden brown. Serve with tomato sauce (page 89) or pickled mushroom sauce (page 89).

This dish can be eaten quite well for lunch. Eat

with boiled potatoes sprinkled with dill. It is a favourite dish for Lent. Serve with chilled vodka if available.

Farshmak *(See also page 43)* *serves 4-6*

100 g (4 oz) meat from the soup (see page 17)
200 g (8 oz) roast veal
½ stale Vienna loaf
250 ml (¼ pt) 1¼ cups milk
1 large cooked potato
3 tablespoons dry bread-crumbs
1 egg
¼ teaspoon pepper
grated nutmeg
3 tablespoons sour cream
25 g (1 oz) 1 tablespoon butter
1 salted herring fillet

Cut the meat and veal into small pieces and put through the mincer. Remove crusts from the bread and soak in milk. Squeeze out excess moisture and put all ingredients through the mincer, ie the salted herring, bread, beef, boiled potato and veal. Mix the ingredients with the egg, sour cream, pepper, and grated nutmeg.

Butter a pie dish and dust with half the bread-crumbs. Add the mixture. Dot with butter and dust with crumbs, Cook for about 30 minutes 180°C (350°F) Mark 4 or till the top browns. Serve in the same dish.

Serve with more sour cream on the table if you wish and beetroot salad (page 82) or make the beetroot salad with sour cream dressing (page 92). Salted cucumbers go well with this. Can be a hot zakuska or supper dish.

Eggs with caviar *serves 2-4*

4 eggs
2 tablespoons caviar red or black (or lump fish roe)
1 tomato
2 spring onions
parsley or dill
mayonnaise (page 91) or 1 lemon

Boil the eggs for about 8 minutes. Rinse under cold water to cool. Remove shells. Cut in half length-wise. Take out the yolk. Fill the white with caviar. Put on to a small plate.

GARNISH:
Cut the tomato in quarters, peel off the outer skin of the spring onions and chop. Chop parsley or dill. Surround the eggs with the tomato, spring onions, parsley and sieved yolk. Serve with mayonnaise, or wedges of lemon.

Chilled vodka goes well with this. This dish is recommended for those who have a prolonged illness or after an operation. You do not, however, have to wait for this to happen. So try them now!

Herring salad *serves 4*

1 salted herring
1 medium sized apple
1 salted cucumber
2-3 boiled potatoes
1 cooked beetroot
2 hard boiled eggs
3 green onions
parsley or dill
3 tablespoons oil
2 tablespoons vinegar
1 teaspoon mustard
salt to taste

Clean and bone the herring. Cut into small pieces. Peel, core and chop the apple. Peel potatoes and cut into 6 mm (¼ in.) strips. Likewise the beetroot. Quarter, then slice cucumber.

Prepare sauce: Blend mustard and salt with the yolks of the hard boiled eggs. Add the oil drop by drop till it thickens stirring all the time. Finally add the vinegar. The sauce should be thick.

Garnish: Remove the outside skin of the onion Take the white of the eggs, parsley and onion and chop finely. Mix. Combine the salad with the sauce. Garnish with the hard boiled white of egg, the parsley and the onion.

This is suitable for a light lunch or as a starter to a meal. Can be eaten only in the winter as salted herring is not sold in the summer months.

Mushroom caviar *serves 0*

200 g (8 oz) mushrooms (fresh)
juice of 2 lemons
salt and pepper to taste
oil for frying
1 onion
1 tablespoon chopped fresh dill or parsley
1 garlic clove (optional)

Peel onion and chop coarsely. Peel large mushroom and slice thickly. Cut small mushrooms in half and remove stalks. Fry lightly in oil with the onion and crushed garlic if you are using it. Put through a mincer. Add lemon juice, salt and pepper to taste and parsley or dill. Combine all ingredients. Chill.

Spread on lightly buttered brown or black bread cut into small pieces and serve with cold drinks.

The secret of a successful caviar is not to over-cook the mushrooms. These can also be boiled if you wish but the onion should be fried to give more flavour. Dried mushrooms can also be used. Soak for a couple of hours beforehand and boil only. The flavour of dried mushrooms is much stronger than fresh ones. Can be made well in advance of a party or before you serve drinks. Chilled vodka is best, as usual, or any dry sherry.

Herring à la Kiev

1 salted herring	pepper to taste
100 g (4 oz) ½ cup butter	1½ teaspoons prepared mustard
50 g (2 oz) ½ cup grated cheddar cheese	1 sprig parsley or dill
1 slice stale wholemeal bread	1 hard boiled egg (optional)
250 ml (½ pt) 1 cup milk	

Clean herring (page 10) and cut into portions. Remove crusts from bread and soak in milk. Squeeze out excess liquid. Mince the bread and herring through the finest blade twice. Add well creamed butter, the grated cheddar, mustard and pepper. Place on a small oval dish in the shape of a fish and add the head and tail. Flatten the head by pulling the gills out, so it rests on the plate. Garnish with chopped parsley or dill and a chopped hard boiled egg if liked.

This dish should be kept in the fridge until the last minute before serving. There is nothing worse than a warm salted herring.

Roe appetizer

200 g (8 oz) fresh roe (pike or cod)	1 tablespoon vinegar
½ small onion	salt and pepper to taste
1½ tablespoons oil	1 tablespoon chopped parsley

Remove the membrane from the roe. Pour boiling water over and allow to stand for 10 minutes. When the roe has turned white, drain. Add salt, vinegar and pepper, finely chopped onion and oil. Blend all ingredients thoroughly. Put into fridge for at least one hour before serving.

Serve on a dish garnished with parsley. Eat with rye bread and butter and chilled vodka.

Vinaigrette with herring and beetroot

serves 6

DRESSING

2½ teaspoons powdered mustard	165 ml ($\frac{1}{3}$ pt) ¾ cup sour cream
2 tablespoons warm water	1 teaspoon sugar

The Razumovsky salad that follows this recipe combines with the dressing to make a good zakuska.

Put the dry mustard with ¼ teaspoon of the sugar into a small bowl, stir in 1-2 tablespoons warm water to make a thick paste. Set aside for 15 minutes and mix in the sour cream and the remaining sugar.

Razumovsky salad

2 hard boiled eggs	2 sour dill pickles (cucumbers)
2 large or 4 small boiled beetroot	1 fillet of pickled herring
4 medium boiled potatoes	400 g (1 lb) cooked meat (ham, beef, etc.)
	1 large cooking apple

Peel the boiled potatoes and cut into oblongs. Slice the cucumbers and cut in strips. Peel the beetroot and dice. Drain the pickled herring, and cut into small squares. Peel eggs and chop. Remove all fat from meat and dice. Peel and core apple and dice. Mix all ingredients well together in a large mixing bowl. Add the sour cream dressing and combine thoroughly.

In the Razumovsky household in Russia this was often used as a light lunch during the summer.

Ukrainian rice pilaf with dried fruit and nuts

serves 4

50 g (2 oz) ½ cup currants	25 g (1 oz) ¼ cup almonds
4 medium sized prunes	2½ teaspoons honey
40 g (1½ oz) ¼ cup chopped dried apricots	150 g (6 oz) ¾ cup long grain rice
50 g (2 oz) ¼ cup butter	

Soak the currants, apricots and prunes in a bowl of hot water for 20 minutes. Drain. Remove the stones from the prunes and chop the prunes and apricots. Blanch and chop the almonds. Melt butter in a large frying pan over high heat and add the apricots, currants, prunes and almonds. Reduce heat to low and cook uncovered for 4 minutes until the nuts are slightly brown. Mix in honey and rice, cover with 375 ml (¾ pt) 2 cups of water and bring quickly to the boil. Then lower the heat. Cover the pan and simmer for about 25 minutes or till the rice has absorbed the water. Serve hot as a main course.

Suggested as a main course on a very hot day. Try green salad with this. This is a very light lunch.

Curd cheese cotletti

300 g (12 oz) 1½ cups curd cheese	125 ml (¼ pt) $\frac{2}{3}$ cup sour cream
3 medium-small potatoes	15 g (¾ oz) 1½ tablespoons butter
3 eggs	salt to taste
3 tablespoons plain flour	

Boil the potatoes in salted water in their jackets for 20 minutes with lid on. Drain and mash. Mix with the curd cheese, eggs, salt and flour. Blend thoroughly so that there are no lumps. Dust a pastry board with flour and make the cotletti on it. Cover both sides with flour and fry in butter till golden brown. Serve with sour cream.

This can be a starter to a light meal or a supper dish in Lent with various salads.

Soups

Beef bouillon or stock

400 g (1 lb) beef (topside, silverside or chuck steak)
400 g (1 lb) beef bones
2.50 l (4 pt) 10 cups water
1 carrot
1 onion
1 stalk celery
1 sprig parsley
salt and pepper to taste

Wash the beef and bones and put them in a saucepan with the cold water. Bring to the boil and remove any scum. Reduce heat, cover and simmer gently. Meanwhile, peel and wash the vegetables. Cut the carrot and onion in half and scorch them gently on a hotplate or in a frying-pan without fat for a few minutes. This gives colour to the soup. Add the vegetables and parsley to the saucepan, bring to the boil, cover and simmer for at least two hours. When ready, strain and remove any fat.

There are various ways of using the meat from the soup. The most popular is to make it into a pirog (page 103), in which case the meat should be removed from the stock after an hour, leaving the bones to simmer for a further hour. The stock will then be rather weak and better used as a basis for other soups than drunk on its own.

For a stronger bouillon the meat should be left to simmer with the bones for about two hours or until the meat is tender. The meat can then be used to make blinchati piroshki (page 109) or farshmak (page 14). It can also be cut up and put back into the soup or can be eaten as a separate course.

This stock can be used wherever beef stock is indicated. You can add a handful of vermicelli or pasta made into letters for children. We used to love reading the letters when small. Do not waste the beef. Eat with boiled potatoes and carrots and horseradish sauce (page 91) or as indicated opposite.

Beef bouillon makes a good stock for frikadelki (page 18), pelmeni (page 105) or semolina klyotski (page 18).

Bone stock

1 kg (2 lb) beef or ham bones
2.50 l(4 pt) 10 cups water
2 carrots
1 leek or onion
2 sprigs parsley
salt and pepper to taste

This is a light stock. Wash the bones and put them in a saucepan with the cold water. Cover and boil for a few minutes. Reduce heat and simmer for 1-2 hours. Skim off any fat formed during cooking. Peel and wash the vegetables and cut them into coarse strips. Add them with the parsley and salt and pepper to the stock and simmer for a further hour. When ready, strain. Use as a basis for other soups.

This stock can be used when you do not wish to use meat. It is not suitable on its own. If you want to enrich it add a bouillon cube. Use it for gravy, sauces etc. Remember to simmer and not to boil or the results will be cloudy.

Chicken bouillon or stock

1.2-1.4 kg (3-3½ lb) boiling chicken including giblets
3-3.75 l (5-6 pt) 13 cups water
1 carrot
1 onion
2 stalks celery
1 sprig parsley
salt and pepper

Wash and truss the chicken and put it in a saucepan with the cold water. Add the giblets, the cleaned and chopped vegetables, and seasoning. Bring to the boil, reduce heat, cover and simmer for 1-1½ hours until the chicken is cooked. Remove any fat formed during cooking. Before serving: strain, adjust seasoning and garnish with parsley.

Chicken bouillon can be served by itself or used as stock for frikadelki, pelmeni or klyotski (see this page).

The boiled chicken can be eaten hot with rice and hollandaise sauce (page 90).

This stock is also good for borshch, or you can add vermicelli if you wish.

Soup with pelmeni *serves 6*

Use 1.50 l (2½ pt) 6 cups beef, bone or chicken stock (page 17)
Pelmeni using 300 g (12 oz) 1½ cups good quality minced beef (page 105)
Pastry using 225 g (8 oz) 1¾ cups flour (page 105)

Drop the pelmeni into boiling salted water and simmer for a few minutes. Lift out with a perforated spoon and transfer them to the boiling stock. Simmer for 10-15 minutes, depending on size. Serve the pelmeni in the stock.

As this soup takes some time, make an extra quantity of pelmeni and freeze them if you have a freezer so that they can be served as a separate course later.

Klyotski soup
(Semolina dumplings) *serves 5*

1.50 l (2½ pt) 6 cups beef, bone or chicken stock (page 17 and above)
100 g (¼ lb) ¾ cup semolina
knob of butter
salt and pepper to taste
2 small eggs
sprig of parsley or dill

Bring 125 ml (¼ pt) of the prepared stock to the boil. Add the semolina and a little salt and butter. Simmer, stirring all the time, for about five minutes, until the semolina is cooked. It should be very thick. Remove from the heat, add the beaten eggs and stir well. Cool slightly and form into little balls. Bring the remainder of the stock to the boil, add the dumplings and simmer for 5-7 minutes. Add the salt and pepper to taste. Garnish each plate with a little chopped parsley or dill.

Remember to be very careful when adding the eggs so as not to curdle them. Allow plenty of time for the semolina to cool. This is a good soup if you have been boiling a chicken and have plenty of stock.

Soup with frikadelki *serves 6*

1.75 l (3 pt) 7½ cups beef, bone or chicken stock (page 17 and opposite)
200 g (8 oz) 1 cup fresh minced beef or veal
salt and pepper to taste
sprig of parsley

Put the meat twice through the mincer so that it is very finely minced. Add salt and pepper and 1-2 tablespoons of water to form a smooth consistency. Make into small balls of about 25mm (1 in.) diameter and drop into the boiling stock. Simmer for 10-15 minutes. Be careful not to let the stock boil too quickly as the meat balls may disintegrate. Serve the frikadelki in the stock. Garnish each plate with a little chopped parsley.

This is a very quick and easy soup. If you do not have time use a stock cube and add 1 carrot and 1 onion to give it a fresh flavour. The frikadelki can also be made from veal, pork or chicken.

If making chicken frikadelki choose a large bird or you will find that it is all skin and bone. The breast can be used for chicken à la Kiev. For chicken frikadelki whip up 1 egg white and fold into the minced chicken adding 1 stale slice of bread with the crusts removed which has been soaked in milk and squeezed out. Salt and pepper and put again through the mincer. Mix well, form into balls and boil in chicken stock.

If you wish, the soup can be served as a separate course with black bread and the frikadelki as the main dish. You can add either vermicelli to the clear soup or a tablespoon of tomato purée. The frikadelki can be eaten hot with rice or vegetables or cold with Russian salad if served separately.

BORSHCH

Borshch is a soup known all over the world and there are many varieties. It is especially popular in South Russia. The characteristic basis is, of course, beetroot. Served with either pirog or kasha as a side-dish it forms a fairly substantial meal and many Russians dispense with a second course.

Although it is not difficult to make, it takes quite a long time to prepare and is usually made in fairly large quantities to last several days. In fact it tastes better on the second day.

When preparing the borshch it is important to cut all the vegetables finely. The root vegetables should be sliced fairly thinly and cut into strips of 25-50 mm x 3 mm (1-2 in. by 1/8 in.) and the cabbage should be shredded, once the outer leaves and thick veins have been removed. Lemon juice or vinegar is added to the borshch to give it flavour and preserve the colour. A small quantity of raw grated beetroot cooked for a few minutes in a little water will restore colour to the borshch if by any chance it has been cooked too long.

SHCHI
This is cabbage soup which originated in North Russia. The vegetables should be prepared in the same way as for borshch and it can be served with the same accompaniments.

For a change add a few black olives or chopped mushrooms towards the end of cooking. You can also add small frankfurter sausages (the cocktail size) or diced ham. Heat through and serve the soup with black bread. It is not advisable to reheat the soup if you add these extra ingredients. You can also add a knob of lard halfway through cooking. Flavour it with a crushed clove of garlic. Some cooks thicken the borshch. To thicken, fry the root vegetables for a few minutes in 1 tablespoon of butter and then add 1 tablespoon of flour.

The meat from the stock can be served as a separate dish with boiled potatoes which can be cooked whole in the soup or eaten with cold potato salad. Horseradish cream and Russian mustard go well with boiled beef.

To make Russian mustard take 1 teaspoon of oil and 1 of vinegar, add a pinch of sugar and salt and mix with the dried mustard to a smooth paste. This gives it a shiny effect and it prevents it from drying too quickly.

The meat from the stock can also be cut into small pieces and a portion put into each plate. Accompaniments to borshch: black bread, kasha or pirog or piroshki (any type).

Ukrainian borshch *serves 10*

3 l (5 pts) 12 cups beef, chicken or bone stock
600 g (1½ lb) white Dutch cabbage
2 medium carrots
1 large potato
400 g (1 lb) raw beetroot
1 leek
1 onion
½ medium turnip
½ medium parsnip
½ medium swede
1 stalk celery
1 sprig parsley
200 g (8 oz) fresh tomatoes or 2 tablespoons tomato purée
salt
6 peppercorns
1 bayleaf (optional)
juice of ½ lemon
2 teaspoons sugar
250 ml (½ pt) 1¼ cups sour cream

Wash the vegetables and peel them, leaving the tomatoes on one side. Chop the onion and parsley finely and cut the other vegetables into fine strips. Put the stock in a large saucepan and add the vegetables, keeping back a small amount of beetroot for colouring. Bring to the boil, cover and simmer for 30 minutes, stirring occasionally. Add the quartered fresh tomatoes or purée, the salt, bayleaf, peppercorns, sugar and lemon juice. Simmer for a further 30 minutes or until the vegetables are soft. Grate the rest of the beetroot and add it to the soup 10 minutes before serving. This will give the borshch a deep red colour. Serve with one dessertspoonful of sour cream per plate.

Clear beetroot borshch *serves 5*

1.50 l (2½ pt) 6 cups beef or bone stock or water
200 g (8 oz) mixed root vegetables (carrot, turnip, parsnip, etc.)
300 g (12 oz) raw beetroot
1 onion
2 dried mushrooms (optional)
2 peppercorns
1 clove garlic (optional)
1 bayleaf
juice of ½ lemon
1 teaspoon sugar
salt
165 ml ($\frac{1}{3}$ pt) ¾ cup sour cream

If dried mushrooms are used they should be soaked in a little water for several hours before making the soup. The water they have been soaked in can be added to the stock.

Peel and wash the vegetables and cut them into fine strips. Put all the vegetables, except for the beetroot and dried mushrooms, into a saucepan with the stock or water. Add the peppercorns, garlic and bayleaf. Cover and boil for 10-15 minutes. Add the beetroot and dried mushrooms and simmer for a further 20-30 minutes. Salt to taste. Add sugar and lemon juice. Strain and serve with one tablespoon of sour cream per plate.

This is a good party soup. Serve in cups with either pirog or piroshki. Rusks are also a good accompaniment to this type of borshch. To make rusks cut french bread thinly and dry in the oven for about 10-15 minutes at 200°C (400°F) Mark 6. You can also add a little wine to this soup. Sauterne is recommended (a sweet white wine).

Cold borshch

serves 4

1.25 l (2 pt) 5 cups water
400 g (1 lb) young raw beetroot
salt
1 teaspoon sugar
juice of ½ lemon
2 spring onions
2 hard boiled eggs
½ fresh cucumber
4 dessertspoons sour cream

Peel and wash the beetroot and cut into fine strips. Put in a saucepan with the cold water and bring to the boil. Reduce heat, cover and simmer for about 30 minutes until the beetroot is cooked. Strain and add salt, sugar and lemon juice. Cool.

Chop the spring onions and hard boiled eggs finely and peel and slice the cucumber. Add these just before serving together with one dessertspoonful of sour cream per plate. Serve with an ice cube to each plate or chill for 15 minutes before adding the sour cream.

This is a very exotic borshch and easy to prepare. Needs no accompaniments. Very welcome on a hot day. If you have any kvass available you can use half kvass half water for this soup. If you like onions use 4 (1 each) instead of 2. It gives a stronger flavour. (See page 144 for Kvass)

Green borshch

serves 6

1.75 l (3 pt) 7½ cups beef stock
600 g (1½ lb) spinach
2 carrots
½ small turnip
1 medium potato
1 onion
2 sticks celery
salt and pepper
juice of ½ lemon
1 teaspoon sugar
3 hard boiled eggs
6 dessertspoons sour cream

Remove the hard stems from the spinach and wash it thoroughly. Put it in a saucepan with a little salted water. Cover and boil for 15 minutes or until cooked. Sieve and transfer it to the stock together with the water it has cooked in. Peel and wash the rest of the vegetables and cut them into fine strips. Add them to the stock. Bring to the boil and season. Cover and simmer for about 20 minutes. Add the lemon juice and a little sugar and serve with one dessertspoon of sour cream and a little chopped hard boiled egg to each plate.

This is best when the spinach is young in the spring. Serve with rye bread. You can, of course, use frozen spinach if fresh is not available.

Moscow borshch

serves 6

600 g (1½ lb) raw beetroot
1 onion
200 g (8 oz) potatoes
1 stalk celery
50 g (2 oz) 4 tablespoons butter
200 g (8 oz) tomatoes
1 tablespoon tomato purée
salt and pepper
1.75 l (3 pt) 7½ cups water (boiling)
juice of ½ lemon
1 teaspoon sugar
6 tablespoons sour cream

Peel and wash the vegetables. Chop the onion finely and cut the beetroot, potato and celery into thin strips. Melt the butter in a large saucepan. Add the onion and beetroot, cover and cook slowly for 20 minutes, stirring frequently. Pour in the boiling water and add the potatoes, celery, quartered tomatoes and tomato purée. Salt and pepper to taste and add the lemon juice and sugar. Bring to the boil, cover and simmer for 30-40 minutes until the vegetables are ready. Serve with one tablespoon of sour cream to each plate.

This is a quick and easy borshch to prepare. It is a smaller quantity than the Ukrainian borshch. Accompaniments, rye bread or pirog or piroshki (any type). Kasha can also be served either on a side plate or 1 tablespoon put into the soup. This thickens the soup and makes it very filling. In fact it is a meal in itself.

Shchi

serves 8

2.50 l (4 pt) 10 cups beef or bone stock
600 g (1½ lb) white Dutch cabbage
2 medium carrots
1 large potato
1 leek
1 onion
½ medium turnip
½ medium parsnip
½ small swede
1 stick celery
1 sprig parsley
4 peppercorns
1 bayleaf (optional)
salt

Peel and wash the vegetables and cut them into fine strips. Chop the sprig of parsley finely. Add the vegetables to the stock together with the peppercorns and bayleaf. Bring to the boil, cover and simmer for about an hour until the vegetables are cooked. Stir occasionally. Ten minutes before serving add the salt. This soup should be eaten very hot. Serve with one or two tablespoons of hot kasha (page 66) in the middle of each plate.

This is one of the most popular soups in Russia and is eaten every day. In fact there is a saying *Shchi Da Kasha pishtia nasha*. Translated this means that *Shchi and Kasha are our food*. The peasants lived on a diet of this and black bread and were very strong on it.

If you wish to vary this soup add 1 tablespoon of tomato purée or 200g (8 oz) of fresh tomatoes.

Accompaniments: Kasha, either 1 tablespoon in the plate of soup or on a side plate, also pirog or piroshki or, alternatively, rye bread. The meat can be cut up and put into the soup, or, as with borshch, eaten as a separate dish with vegetables.

Roscolnick *(Kidney soup with salted cucumbers)*

serves 6

1.75 l (3 pt) 7½ cups beef, chicken or bone stock
300 g (12 oz) kidney
1 tablespoon pearl barley (optional)
200 g (8 oz) potatoes
1 large onion
1 carrot
1-2 salted cucumbers
1 bayleaf
salt and pepper
125 ml (¼ pt) ⅔ cup sour cream
parsley to garnish

Remove the fat and membranes from the kidneys. Put them in a saucepan of cold water and bring to the boil. Remove the kidneys and rinse them under the cold tap. Cut them into small pieces and put them into the prepared stock with the pearl barley. Bring to the boil, cover and simmer for 30 minutes. Meanwhile, peel and wash the vegetables. Chop the onion finely, slice the cucumber and cut the potatoes and carrot into thin strips. Add the vegetables and bayleaf to the stock and simmer for a further 40 minutes. Ten minutes before serving, add salt and pepper to taste. Serve with one tablespoon of sour cream per plate and garnish with chopped parsley.

This is a most original soup and easy to prepare. It can be made from bone or game stock. If you have any game bones left this is a good way to use them.

Game stock *(See also page 25)*

Bones of game bird (1 large or two small)
Giblets
salt
cold water to cover
1 onion
white peppercorns

Simmer for 2 hours. Strain the stock through a metal sieve and use for roscolnick. You can also use giblets from chicken, turkey, goose or duck instead of the kidneys. At Christmas time when there may be several birds in the fridge save the giblets of each and use them for this soup.

Giblets go off very quickly so use them as quickly as possible.

Cream of carrot soup

serves 5

1.35 l (2¼ pt) 5½ cups beef stock or water
400 g (1 lb) carrots
1 lump of sugar
salt and pepper
1 egg yolk
4 tablespoons fresh cream
knob of butter

Clean the carrots and chop them finely. Add them to the stock or water. Bring to the boil, cover and simmer for 30 minutes or until they are tender. Lift the carrots out of the stock with a perforated spoon and sieve. Return them to the stock and bring it back to the boil. Add the sugar, salt and pepper. Mix the egg yolk with the cream in a cup. Take the soup off the heat and stir in the egg and cream mixture and a knob of butter. Return to the heat for a few minutes, being careful not to allow the soup to boil. This soup may be made with swedes instead of carrots. If so, they should be peeled and chopped finely.

Best eaten in the spring when carrots are young. Specially if you grow them in your garden. If you use the egg yolk this soup cannot be reheated and should be eaten at once. It is rather rich so really needs no accompaniment except rusks if you are hungry. To make rusks see page 113.

CREAM OF SWEDE SOUP
Follow instructions as above for *Cream of carrot soup*.

CREAM OF SQUASH
Follow instructions as above for *Cream of carrot soup*.

Ukha *(Fish soup)*

serves 4

4 herrings or 600 g (1½ lb) white fish or sturgeon
1.25 l (2 pt) 5 cups water
1 teaspoon salt
4 peppercorns
1 bayleaf (optional)
2 medium potatoes
1 small onion or leek
1 sherry glass of dry white wine or juice of ½ lemon

If herrings are used, remove heads and gut. Clean fish and cut into large portions. Put the fish in a saucepan with the cold water, salt, peppercorns and the bayleaf. Peel and wash the vegetables. Cut the potatoes into strips and chop the onion or slice the leek. Cover and simmer for 20 minutes. Add more salt to taste and the wine or lemon juice. Simmer for another 10 minutes. Remove fish and serve as separate course. The soup should not be strained; the vegetables are served with it.

Extra potatoes to serve with the fish can be put to cook in the soup about 20 minutes before serving.

This is a famous Russian fish soup. In fact a poem was written about it: A guest was pressed to eat too much soup and in the end he jumped out of the window!

It is, however, an acquired taste. Recommended fish for this soup are perch and bass for their flavour, ling and allied fish for sweetness and delicacy. You can also use pike, cod, turbot, halibut, salmon, bream or sterlet.

For a richer soup use fish stock, ie cook cod's head and tails or some cheap fish you do not fancy eating by itself. Cover the fish or cod's head with water adding 1 onion, carrot, 2 peppercorns and salt and cook slowly for about 30 minutes. Strain and use for soup. Before serving add 1 cup champagne instead of the wine.

If you decide to eat the fish separately try mushroom sauce with white fish if hot (page 90) or white wine sauce (page 90). If eaten cold fish is good with beetroot salad or Russian salad and horseradish cream (pages 83 and 91).

Okroshka
(Cold summer soup)

serves 4

1.25 l (2 pt) 5 cups semi-sweet cider or kvass (page 144)
½ fresh cucumber
2 medium cold cooked potatoes
4 spring onions
2 hard boiled eggs
dill or parsley
salt to taste
4 tablespoons sour cream

Peel and slice the cucumber. Cut the potatoes into strips and chop the spring onions, hard boiled eggs and dill or parsley. Salt to taste. Left-over cooked meat can also be chopped into small pieces and added to the okroshka. Mix all the ingredients together and gradually add the cider. Garnish with a little chopped dill or parsley. Chill by putting into the refrigerator for 10 minutes before serving or by adding one ice cube to each plate. Serve with one tablespoon of sour cream per plate.

You can also use slightly salted cucumbers instead of fresh, in which case, prepare the cucumbers 1 week in advance of making the soup. This is the time it takes for them to reach maturity. If kept longer they will be too salt (page 149). If you use these do not salt the egg and onion. If you use the fresh cucumber you can add salt and pepper to the eggs, onions and cucumber if you like.

Alternative method. Scoop out the yolks and mix with a little salt and ½ teaspoon made mustard. Blend with the sour cream. Add to the kvass or cider. Prepare the rest of the ingredients and add to the soup. This, however, gives a cloudy appearance and does not look as good as the recipe above. If you feel extravagant use semi-sweet champagne or sparkling wine. Serve chilled in the garden on a hot spring or summer's day (1 bottle champagne is enough for 4 plates).

Lapsha *(Milk soup)*

serves 4

1.25 l (2 pt) 5 cups milk
50 g (2 oz) $\frac{1}{3}$ cup vermicelli
1 teaspoon sugar
pinch of salt
knob of butter

Bring the milk to the boil and add the salt, sugar and vermicelli. Simmer with the lid off for 15 minutes or until cooked, stirring frequently. Before serving add a knob of butter and stir until it melts. Serve with more sugar if you wish.

This is a great favourite with children. Can be given to them as a pudding if you wish. Also suitable for those on a milk diet, or invalids.

Cherry soup

serves 4

375 ml (¾ pt) 2 cups water
400 g (1 lb) morello cherries
75 g (3 oz) 6 tablespoons sugar
½ teaspoon cinnamon
125 ml (¼ pt) $\frac{2}{3}$ cup red wine
4 tablespoons fresh or sour cream

Remove the stalks and stones from the cherries. Put the cherries in a saucepan with the sugar and cold water and bring to the boil. Simmer for about 5 minutes until they are soft. Sieve and return to the saucepan. Add the wine, cinnamon and sour cream and simmer gently for one minute, stirring all the time. Serve with vanilla rusks (page 113).

This is a beautiful soup best made when you

can get fresh cherries. You can, however, use canned dessert cherries or frozen ones out of season. If you do this, however, add a little lemon juice to the liquid or the soup will be too sweet.

Kholodetz *(made with berries)*

serves 6

600 g (1½ lb) fruit (raspberries, strawberries or redcurrants)
500 ml (1 pt) 2½ cups water
150 g (6 oz) ⅔ cup sugar
165 ml (⅓ pt) ¾ cup dry red wine
squeeze of lemon
1 little grated lemon rind
125 ml (¼ pt) ⅔ cup sour cream

Remove the stems and wash and sieve the berries. Boil the water and sugar for a few minutes to make a syrup. Cool and then add the sieved fruit, the wine, lemon juice and grated lemon rind. Stir well and serve chilled with sour cream and vanilla rusks (page 113).

This is best eaten on a hot July day when the berries are in season. You can of course eat it out of season using frozen fruit. You may need a little more cream for this soup as Russians use cream rather sparingly.

Kholodetz *(made with chocolate or vanilla)*

serves 6

3 egg yolks
100 g (4 oz) ½ cup castor sugar
250 ml (½ pt) 1¼ cups milk
½ vanilla pod
200 g (8 oz) strawberries or raspberries or 100 g (4 oz) bitter chocolate
500 ml (1 pt) 2½ cups single cream
2 sponge fingers per head
1 meringue or 1 tablespoon ice cream per head

Beat the egg yolks with the sugar in a bowl till white. Put the milk and vanilla in a saucepan and bring to the boil. Remove from the heat and pour over the eggs and sugar, stirring all the time. Transfer the mixture back to the saucepan. If you are making chocolate kholodetz add the broken chocolate now. Cook very slowly over a low heat until the custard thickens. Stir all the time and on no account allow it to boil or it will curdle. Cool the custard and add the cream.

To make vanilla kholodetz, thicken the custard and add both cream and fruit.

Serve with suitably flavoured ice cream, sponge fingers or one meringue as decoration in the middle of each plate.

As this is rather an expensive and delicious soup be very careful not to curdle the eggs. They are safer cooked in a double boiler.

Cream of cucumber soup

serves 6

1.50 l (2½ pt) 6 cups vegetable stock
1 leaf tarragon
1 sprig rosemary
1 blackcurrant leaf
1 sprig chervil
800 g (2 lb) fresh cucumbers
sprig of dill
small teaspoon salt
2 onions
2-3 cloves
2 tablespoons butter
1 tablespoon flour
2 tablespoons pearl barley
2 yolks
4 tablespoons fresh cream
pepper to taste

Prepare stock adding the rosemary, blackcurrent leaf and chervil. Peel 400 g (1 lb) of cucumbers and add the peel to the stock. When the vegetables are done, strain.

Cut each peeled cucumber in four, lengthwise, remove seeds, place in saucepan with two peeled and sliced onions and two or three cloves. Melt one tablespoonful of butter, add a tablespoon of flour, fry lightly, slowly adding 250 ml (½ pt) 1¼ cups of stock. Pour over the cucumbers, simmer for 5 minutes and rub through a sieve. Pour into a large saucepan and add the rest of the strained stock. Blend in the pearl barley purée (see recipe for yoghurt and barley soup page 28). Mix the yolks with the cream and a tablespoon of butter, pour the mixture into the soup which should be hot but not boiling. Season to taste.

Peel the remaining 400 g (1 lb) of cucumbers, scoop out the seeds, put into boiling salted water, cook for 3-4 minutes, drain, rinse with cold water and allow to dry. Slice in strips and add to the soup. Reheat soup but do not allow to boil or the eggs will curdle. Serve with chopped dill or parsley.

Bozbash *(Armenian mutton soup)*

serves 6

400 g (1 lb) lamb (scrag end of neck)
1.50 l (2½ pt) 6 cups water
150 g (6 oz) 1 cup split peas
400 g (1 lb) potatoes
2 apples
2 onions
2 tablespoons tomato purée
2 tablespoons butter
salt and pepper to taste
1 sprig parsley

Wash and cut the lamb into pieces. Cover with water and add salt. Simmer under a lid for 1 hour.

Rinse the peas and add 400-600 ml (¾-1¼ pt)

2-3 cupfuls of cold water and bring to the boil. Cook over a low heat for 1 to 1½ hours. Remove lamb from the soup and bone. Add the peas to the meat. Strain the stock and make up to 1.50 1 (2½ pt) 6 cups. Peel the onion, chop and fry lightly in butter. Peel the potatoes and cut in strips, peel and core apples and slice in strips. Add all the ingredients to the soup. Salt and pepper and cook slowly for a further 20 minutes. Serve sprinkled with chopped parsley.

This is rather a filling soup and can take the place of the main course.

Pickled cabbage shchi

serves 8

1.75 l (3 pt) 7½ cups beef stock (page 17)
400 g (1 lb) sauerkraut
1 leek
1 stick celery
1 small turnip
1 onion
1 large carrot
butter
2 tablespoons tomato purée
1 bayleaf
salt and pepper to taste
125 ml (¼ pt) ⅔ cup thick cream

Prepare beef stock as indicated on page 17. Test sauerkraut. If it is too sour press out excess liquid and reserve. Put the sauerkraut in a saucepan and cover with water. Simmer for 1 hour. Meanwhile wash and peel the vegetables. Chop the onion. Slice the turnip and carrot and cut into strips. Slice the celery.

Fry the vegetables lightly in butter, add the tomato purée and combine with the sauerkraut when ready. Cover with stock and cook gently for a further 30 minutes. Ten minutes before serving season and add the bayleaf. If the flavour is too mild add the reserved sauerkraut juice. Serve with a tablespoon of cream in the middle of the plate.

Shurpa

serves 6

400 g (1 lb) beef
750 ml (1½ pt) 3½ cups stock
2 onions
2 carrots
2 tablespoons tomato purée
2 tablespoons butter
600 g (1½ lb) potatoes
1 teaspoon salt
½ teaspoon pepper
sprig of parsley or dill

Prepare stock (page 17). Peel the onions, carrots and potatoes. Slice the onion and fry in butter. Cut the meat in 25mm (1 in.) squares. Fry the meat till well browned then add the fried onion, the carrot cut in cubes and the tomato puree. Cook for a further 5 minutes. Combine the meat and vegetables with the stock and bring to the boil. Then add the potatoes cut into oblong strips, salt, pepper and cook for a further 20 minutes.

This is quite a filling soup for a cold day and could be in place of the main course followed by a sweet.

Hunter's Yushka
(Ukrainian giblet soup)

serves 6

400 g (1 lb) chicken giblets or 1 set of turkey giblets
4 medium potatoes
1 carrot
2 sprigs parsley
2 bayleaves
1 onion
1 small leek
75 g (3 oz) ½ cup millet
3 rashers streaky bacon
4 peppercorns
1.50 l (2½ pt) 6 cups water
salt to taste

Wash and clean giblets. Put into a large saucepan with the water. Bring to the boil. Reduce heat to simmering point and cook under a lid for 1 hour. Strain.

Meanwhile wash the millet, peel the carrot, potatoes and onion. Dice the carrot and potatoes and chop the onion and 1 sprig parsley.

Fry the bacon then fry the vegetables lightly in the bacon fat. Return giblets to stock and add the fried vegetables, millet and pepper and salt. Cook for a further 20-30 minutes. Ten minutes before serving add the bayleaves. Chop parsley and peel off outer leaves of leek. Slice finely. Garnish each plate with the chopped parsley and sliced leek.

The giblets can be eaten with the soup, in which case remove them before serving and chop. Return to the soup and re-heat.

Asparagus soup

serves 6

800 g (2 lb) asparagus (thin)
4 tablespoons butter
2 tablespoons flour
1.25 l (2 pt) 5 cups vegetable stock
salt and pepper to taste

Cut the thick end off the asparagus and reserve the tips for garnish. Cook these separately for 15 minutes in 500 ml (1 pt) 2½ cups of water with a little salt added.

Cut the remainder of the stalks in small pieces and cook for about 30 minutes in the stock till tender. Put the asparagus through a sieve.

FIRST METHOD:

Melt 2 tablespoons of butter in a saucepan and add the flour. Mix ingredients to a thick paste and dilute gradually with the vegetable stock. Add the asparagus purée to the thickened soup. Season with salt and pepper. Add 2 tablespoons of butter to the soup and garnish with small pieces of the asparagus tips cooked previously. Cook through.

SECOND METHOD:
Cook asparagus in 500 ml (1 pt) 2½ cups water then add 1.25 l (2 pt) 5 cups milk instead of the vegetable stock. Thicken as above.

THIRD METHOD:
Make a roux with the flour and butter and thicken soup. Finally add 2 egg yolks mixed with 125 ml (¼ pt) ⅔ cup thick cream. Bring to boiling point only. The soup should not boil after you add the eggs.

Game stock *(see also page 21)*

carcase of game bird (pheasant or 2 partridges)	1 onion
giblets	4 white peppercorns
cleaned feet of bird	1 sprig parsley or dill
salt to taste	1 carrot
	1 stick celery

Put the carcase, giblets, feet and salt into a large saucepan and cover with water. Bring to the boil. Reduce heat to simmering point, cover with lid and cook for 1 hour. Clean vegetables and add whole, also salt, peppercorns, and parsley or dill and cook slowly for a further 2 hours.

Strain stock and cool. Use for borshch or roscolnik.

Game purée soup

serves 6

1.50 l (2½ pt) 6 cups meat stock see page 17	6 mushrooms
1 partridge	salt to taste
½ small french loaf	125 ml (¼ pt) ⅔ cup thick cream
50 g (2 oz) 4 tablespoons butter	a little grated nutmeg
	1 glass of red wine (optional)

Roast the partridge first, ie clean and wash the bird and insert a piece of butter into the body. Cover breast with streaky bacon and roast at 200°C (400°F) Mark 6 for about 30 minutes. Baste when necessary. Cool and remove meat from carcase. Put the carcase into the stock to improve the flavour of the soup. Bring the stock to boiling point, reduce heat and simmer under a lid for a further hour.

Meanwhile cut up the meat into small pieces. Remove crusts from half a stale french loaf. Cut into slices and soak in hot stock. Mix with the pieces of meat and put through a mincer 2-3 times or through a wire sieve.

Cook the mushrooms separately. Peel if large and chop. Cover with water to which has been added a little salt and boil for about 20 minutes or till ready.

When the stock is ready, strain. Add the purée, mushrooms, butter, cream and a little grated nutmeg. A glass of wine may be added to the soup before serving if liked. Bring to the boil and serve.

This can of course be made from left-over game.

White stock

800 g (2 lb) knuckle of veal	1 stick celery
2.50 l (4 pt) 10 cups cold water	4 white peppercorns
1 teaspoon salt	small strip of lemon rind
1 dessertspoon lemon juice	1 bayleaf if liked
1 onion	1 sprig parsley

Wash the knuckle in hot water. Put into a pan and add cold water and salt. Soak for 30 minutes. Bring to the boil, reduce heat to simmering point and cook under a lid for 1 hour. Clean vegetables and add whole also the pepper, parsley, small strip of rind and juice. Bayleaf may be added later if liked.

Cook for a further 2 hours with lid on. Strain stock and use. This makes about 1.75 l (3 pt) 7½ cups of stock. Cooking time 3 hours.

Pokhylopka

serves 6

100 g (4 oz) dried or 200 g (8 oz) fresh mushrooms	2 tablespoons butter
2 tablespoons pearl barley	2 tablespoons sour cream
2 onions	½ tablespoon flour
2 leeks	4 peppercorns
2 carrots	2 bayleaves
2 large potatoes	1.75 l (3 pt) 7½ cups water
	1 teaspoon salt
	2 sprigs dill or parsley

Soak the mushrooms, if they are dried, for at least 2 hours in 500 ml (1 pt) 2½ cups of water. Cook the pearl barley in the mushroom water for 30 minutes, meanwhile prepare the rest of the ingredients. Peel and chop the onions and fry lightly in butter. Peel and slice the leeks and carrots, add to the fried onion and cook for a further few minutes.

Slice the mushrooms, dice the peeled potatoes and put into the saucepan together with the bay-leaves, peppercorns, pearl barley, salt and the fried onions, leeks and carrots. Add 1.25 l (2 pt) 5 cups water and cook slowly under a lid with the salt for a further 20 minutes or till the potatoes and pearl barley are tender. Five minutes before serving mix the cream and flour and stir into the soup.

Serve sprinkled with chopped dill or parsley. This is a cheap country soup without stock.

Ukrainian kulish with salt pork

serves 8

2.50 l (4 pt) 10 cups water
100 g (4 oz) ⅔ cup millet
6 medium potatoes
2 onions
9 rashers salt streaky bacon
1 tablespoon chopped parsley
salt and pepper to taste

Pick over and wash millet. Pour into simmering water and cook for 30 minutes slowly with lid on. Peel potatoes and dice. Add to the soup. Cook for a further 20 minutes.

Chop bacon into small pieces and fry together with the finely chopped onion till lightly brown. Add to the soup. Check seasoning. Cook slowly for a further 5 minutes.

Serve with chopped parsley in the middle of each plate.

Borsch à la Poltava

serves 6-8

1.75 l (3 pt) 7½ cups chicken or goose stock
1 small hard white cabbage
3 medium potatoes
2 medium beetroots
100 g (4 oz) buckwheat
2 rashers salted fat bacon
150 g (6 oz) 1½ cups flour
25 g (1 oz) 2 tablespoons butter
125 g (5 oz) ⅔ cup tomato purée
125 ml (¼ pt) ⅔ cup sour cream
1 carrot
1 sprig parsley
1 onion
1 egg
salt and pepper to taste

Prepare stock (see page 18 for chicken, substitute goose if you wish). Strain. Peel and slice beetroot, cut into thin strips and sprinkle with vinegar. Fry separately in butter till half cooked. Peel carrot, onion and chop. Fry all vegetables lightly in butter including the chopped parsley. Add to the stock. Also the tomato purée. Stir and bring to the boil. Reduce heat and simmer for another 30 minutes under a lid.

Meanwhile peel the potatoes and dice. Remove outer leaves of cabbage and shred. Put into the soup together with the bacon and cooked beetroot. Add salt and cook for a further 15 minutes. Allow to stand for 15-20 minutes. Meanwhile make the Galushki (dumplings).

Take 1/3 of the flour and combine with a little boiling water. After cooling add the beaten egg gradually stirring the dough all the time to take out any lumps. Add more flour to make a dough suitable for dumplings, ie fairly stiff so that they do not disintegrate during boiling.

Boil water separately in a saucepan with a little salt and drop teaspoons of the mixture into the boiling water. When they rise to the surface they are ready and can be transferred to a warm dish. Keep warm.

Re-heat soup and serve with little pieces of chicken or goose from the stock plus the galushki and cream in the middle of each plate.

This is a very filling soup and a meal in itself. Follow with a pudding only.

Caucasian kharcho

serves 6

400 g (1 lb) beef or lamb
2 onions
2-3 cloves of garlic
4 tablespoons rice
100 g (4 oz) sour plums or damsons
1 teaspoon salt
2 tablespoons tomato purée or 200 g (8 oz) fresh tomatoes
1 tablespoon butter
½ teaspoon pepper
1.50 l (2½ pt) 6 cups water

The best beef for this is ribs of beef but can be substituted by breast of lamb. Wash the meat, cut into small pieces. About 3-4 pieces per portion. Put into a saucepan and cover with water and bring to the boil. Remove any scum formed. Reduce heat to simmering point. Cook for 1½-2 hours then add finely chopped onion, crushed cloves of garlic, rice, plums, salt and pepper and cook for a further 30 minutes with lid on.

Slice the tomatoes and fry slightly in butter and add to the soup 5-10 minutes before serving. When serving sprinkle with finely chopped parsley or dill.

This is a filling soup and can be substituted for the main course.

Armenian soup
serves 6

400 g (1 lb) beef
100 g (4 oz) $\frac{2}{3}$ cup rice
1 tablespoon butter
1 onion
2 egg yolks
1.50 l (2½ pt) 6 cups water
sprig of thyme
1 bayleaf
salt and pepper to taste
1 sprig parsley or dill

Wash the meat and cut into small pieces. Put into a saucepan with cold water and a teaspoon of salt and bring to the boil. Cover and simmer for 1 hour removing any scum formed. Strain the soup then return the pieces of meat to it, together with the rice, previously well rinsed in cold water. Peel the onion and chop finely. Fry lightly in butter and also add to the soup together with the sprig of thyme, bayleaf, salt and pepper.

Cook gently for 30 minutes, occasionally stirring the soup. Beat two egg yolks. Remove the soup from the stove and add the yolks mixed in a little hot water. Mix well. Do not allow to reboil. This soup should be very thick.

Serve with pieces of meat and garnish with chopped parsley or dill.

This soup is rather filling and could take the place of the meat course.

Cream of cauliflower soup
serves 6

1.50 l (2½ pt) 6 cups water
1 medium cauliflower
125 ml (¼ pt) $\frac{2}{3}$ cup thick cream
1 tablespoon flour
1 tablespoon butter
2 egg yolks
salt and pepper to taste
400 g (1 lb) potatoes
1 leek
1 stick of celery
bunch of parsley

Prepare vegetable stock.

Wash the cauliflower and cut into flowerets. Retain stem. Put the cauliflower together with the stem into the vegetable stock to cook for 15 minutes or till tender. Remove cauliflower and discard stem. Put the cauliflower through a sieve.

Mix the butter with the flour in a frying pan and fry lightly without letting it get brown, slowly add one cup of strained stock and bring to the boil. Combine with the remainder of the stock and the cauliflower purée. Bring to the boil.

Mix the yolks with the cream and stir into the soup. Do not boil. Serve.

Re-heat the vegetables used for the stock and eat with the main course.

Hot plum soup
serves 3-4

600 g (1½ lb) plums
100 g (4 oz) ½ cup sugar
125 ml (¼ pt) $\frac{2}{3}$ cup red wine or
165 ml ($\frac{1}{3}$ pt) ¾ cup sour cream
2 cloves
pinch of cinnamon
1 small french loaf

To make rusks slice the french loaf fairly thinly and put into a cool oven for 1-2 hours to dry. Cook till lightly brown at 100°C (200°F) Mark ¼.

To make the soup wash and remove stalks from plums. Put into a saucepan and cover with water. Cook till soft for about 5 minutes, stirring from time to time to prevent the pan burning. Put through a sieve. Add cinnamon, sugar, 2 crushed cloves and 125 ml (¼ pt) $\frac{2}{3}$ cup red wine or the sour cream. Heat through. Prepare soup plates. Put 1 rusk on each plate and pour the hot soup over it.

Make the rusks well in advance. It is as well to keep some in stock as they appear frequently in Russian recipes and are very popular.

Beer soup with sour cream
serves 6

1.25 l (2 pt) 5 cups light ale
250 ml (½ pt) 1¼ cups sour cream
1 tablespoon butter
1 teaspoon salt
2 egg yolks
3 teaspoons sugar
6 rusks (page 119)

In a bowl blend the cream, sugar, yolks, butter and salt together. Dilute with beer. Transfer to a saucepan and bring to the boil. Do not boil. Pour at once on to 1 rusk per plate.

Serve curd cheese separately.

Beer soup (second method)
serves 4-5

1.25 l (2 pt) 5 cups beer (light ale)
1/2 teaspoon caraway seeds
½ tablespoon sugar
3 egg yolks

Bring the beer to the boil with the caraway seeds. Blend the sugar with the yolks till white and add the hot not boiling beer gradually. Stir well, serve at once with rusks (page 119) and curd cheese.

Yoghurt and barley soup *serves 6*

55 g (2¼ oz) ¼ cup pearl barley
375 ml (¾ pt) 2 cups plain yoghurt
4 eggs
1 dessertspoon plain flour
1½ tablespoons finely chopped onion
25 g (1 oz) 2 tablespoons butter
1½ teaspoons salt
1 tablespoon finely chopped fresh mint

Bring 750 ml (1½ pt) 3¾ cups of water to the boil in a medium sized pan. Put in barley. Reduce heat and simmer uncovered stirring occasionally for 45 minutes. Drain barley through a fine sieve and set aside. Mix yoghurt with 750 ml (1½ pt) 3¾ cups cold water in a large mixing bowl until well blended. Break eggs into large saucepan and beat in the flour a teaspoon at a time. Slowly whisk in the yoghurt and water mixture and place on a high heat. Bring almost to the boil, stirring constantly. Lower heat and simmer for 2-3 minutes until it thickens slightly. Do not allow to boil. Add the barley, chopped onion, butter and salt and cook through for another minute. Pour into a tureen and sprinkle with the chopped mint leaves.

This is a summer recipe. Given to me by Count Razumovsky.

GALUSHKI

Galushki are Ukrainian dumplings, and are very popular in South Russia. They can be made from flour, cereals or potatoes, etc. Roll the dough 15 mm (½ in.) thick and cut into small squares. Drop in boiling salted water and cook till they rise to the surface. After draining serve with melted butter, small pieces of streaky bacon fried with the fat in the pan, or onions chopped finely and cooked in sunflower oil. Pour straight from the pan together with the oil. Here are a few recipes.

Galushki made with flour *serves 6*

300 g (12 oz) 3 cups plain flour
2 eggs
60 ml ($\frac{1}{8}$ pt) $\frac{1}{3}$ cup water
2 tablespoons butter
1 teaspoon salt

Make a well in the centre of the sifted flour. Pour in the water and melted butter. Add salt, beaten eggs and stir till you get a very stiff dough. Knead till smooth. Leave for 1 hour. Roll out and cut the galushki into small squares. Cook in salted boiling water for 10 minutes, drain. Put into a hot greased frying pan and fry lightly. Serve coated with melted butter or with the sour cream.

You can substitute salt pork for the butter. Cut the pork into tiny cubes, fry till crisp and pour straight from the pan on to the galushki.

This can be served as a starter to a meal.

Galushki with bacon *serves 4*

200 g (8 oz) 2 cups plain flour
1 egg
60 ml ($\frac{1}{8}$ pt) $\frac{1}{3}$ cup water
75 g (3 oz) 6 tablespoons butter
6 rashers streaky bacon sliced

Make the galushki as above. After draining them rinse with cold water in a sieve or they will stick. Grease a fireproof dish. Put the galushki in it. Melt the remaining butter and pour over. Remove rind from bacon and cut in half. Mix with the galushki. Cook in an oven for 20 minutes at 180°C (350°F) Mark 4.

This can be a starter to a meal.

Fish

COOKING METHODS

Boiled fish: Do not remove the skin till the fish is cooked. Put the fish in boiling water, cover and simmer for 7-10 minutes to the 400 g/1 lb and 10 minutes over. When cooking white fish add a teaspoon of salt to 500 ml/1 pt/2½ cups water and a little lemon juice or vinegar. This preserves the colour and prevents the fish from breaking. Boiled (white) fish can be served with tomato sauce, horseradish cream, caper sauce, mushroom sauce, hollandaise sauce, mushroom sauce with wine, or pickled mushroom sauce (see Sauces pages 89-95).

Cold boiled fish can be served with horseradish cream, mustard dressing, mayonnaise, or egg and caper dressing (see Sauces pages 89-95).

Baked fish: Rub fish with salt. Brush with melted butter or oil, dust with breadcrumbs and place in greased baking-dish. Bake at approximately 200°C (400°F) Mark 6, 10-12 minutes per 400 g/1 lb, basting frequently.

Fried fish: Dry fish very thoroughly. Dip in seasoned flour. Fish can be coated in egg and breadcrumbs and can be shallow-fried in oil or butter or deep-fried in oil or fat.

Steamed fish: Allow about 10-15 minutes to 400 g/1 lb and 10 minutes over. For small pieces of fish use a deep plate over a pan of boiling water. Salt the fish, add knob of butter and cover with another plate. Steam for 10-20 minutes. Use the same sauces as for hot and cold boiled fish.

Solanka (1)

serves 4

600 g (1½ lb) fresh white fish (cod, haddock)
2 small onions
40 g (1½ oz) 3 tablespoons butter
200 g (8 oz) tomatoes or 2 tablespoons tomato purée
2 salted cucumbers
1 tablespoon capers
1 bayleaf
salt and pepper to taste

GARNISH
parsley or dill
slices of lemon
1 tablespoon olives (optional)

Remove the bones, wash the fish and cut into serving portions. Fry the chopped onions lightly in butter. Add the chopped tomatoes or tomato purée and cook gently for five minutes, stirring all the time. Add the fish, chopped salted cucumbers, capers, bayleaf and salt and pepper. Very little salt is needed as the cucumbers make it slightly salt. Cover with boiling water and simmer for a further 15 minutes. Before serving garnish with chopped parsley or dill, slices of lemon and olives.

This is a good dish if made with freshwater fish which has a more delicate flavour than salt water fish. It was a great favourite with my grandmother who used to ask the boys to catch some fish for dinner and a very tasty Solanka was the result.

Solanka (2)

serves 4

600-800 g (1½-2 lb) fresh white fish
salt to taste
breadcrumbs
oil for frying
1 onion
50 g (2 oz) ¼ cup butter
400 g (1 lb) sauerkraut
2 medium cooking apples
1 tablespoon sugar
1 tablespoon flour

Wash the fish and cut into serving portions. Salt and coat in breadcrumbs. Fry in oil for about 20 minutes until cooked. Meanwhile, peel and chop the onion and fry it lightly in butter in a saucepan. Pour cold water over the sauerkraut, if it is very sour, and squeeze out the excess liquid. Add the sauerkraut, the sugar and the peeled and chopped apples. Cover and cook slowly, stirring from time to time. If the sauerkraut gets too dry add one tablespoon of water. When the fish is cooked, stir the flour into the sauerkraut. Put layers of sauerkraut and layers of fish in a buttered pie-dish, ending with a sauerkraut layer. Sprinkle with dry breadcrumbs and knobs of butter and cook in a moderate oven 180°C (350°F) Mark 4 for about half an hour or until brown.

This is also good if made with freshwater fish. It brings out the flavour. You can equally well make this dish from left-over fried fish. Serve with boiled or mashed potatoes.

Fried fish *(with sour cream and cheese)*

serves 4

600 g (1½ lb) cod or haddock fillet
salt and pepper to taste
flour
butter or oil for frying
100 g (4 oz) 1 cup chopped mushrooms
2 hard boiled eggs
25 g (1 oz) ¼ cup grated cheese

SAUCE
1 teaspoon melted butter
½ teaspoon flour
250 ml (½ pt) 1¼ cups sour cream

Wash the fish and cut it into slices. Coat in seasoned flour and fry in butter or oil. Clean and chop the mushrooms and fry them separately. When the fish is cooked, put it in a deep casserole and cover with the mushrooms and sliced hard-boiled eggs.

SAUCE
Make a roux from the butter and flour. Heat the sour cream and add it gradually to the roux. Simmer for a few minutes.

Pour the sauce over the fish, sprinkle with grated cheese and put under a hot grill to brown for five minutes.

This is rather a delicious dish and simple to make. Try carp, bass, bream or halibut for this dish. Serve with boiled new potatoes and green peas, or a plain green salad with french dressing.

Fish and potato pie

serves 4

600 g (1½ lb) cod or haddock fillet
8 large cooked potatoes
165 ml ($\frac{1}{3}$ pt) ¾ cup milk
2 eggs
salt and pepper to taste
dry breadcrumbs
butter

Remove the skin and cut the fish into fairly small pieces. Grease a pie-dish and fill with alternate layers of sliced cooked potatoes and fish, ending with a layer of potatoes. Mix the eggs with the milk and add salt and pepper. Pour over the fish and potatoes. Sprinkle with breadcrumbs and dot with butter. Bake in a moderate oven 180°C (350°F) Mark 4, for about half an hour until brown.

This is quick and easy to prepare and a great favourite for Lent when you have to think up ways of avoiding meat. Try bass for a change. Serve with boiled carrots, spinach or a green salad.

Cod pie *(with sour cream)*

serves 4

600 g (1½ lb) cod or haddock fillet
salt to taste
1 egg yolk
165 ml ($\frac{1}{3}$ pt) ¾ cup sour cream
1 tablespoon butter
3 slices day-old french bread

Cook the cod in salted water for 20 minutes. Mix the sour cream with the egg yolk and pour half the mixture into a buttered pie-dish. Remove the crusts and fry the bread lightly in butter. Remove the skin from the cod and fill the dish with alternate layers of bread and fish, ending with a layer of bread. Pour in the rest of the sour cream mixture and brown in a moderate oven 180°C (350°F) Mark 4 for about 40 minutes.

Archangel cod

serves 4

600 g (1½ lb) cod
8 medium potatoes
75 g (3 oz) 6 tablespoons melted butter
1 sprig parsley

SAUCE
2 hard boiled eggs

Boil the potatoes in salted water. They should be ready at the same time as the cod. Clean the cod, cut into serving portions and cook it in salted water (page 29). When cooked, strain and remove the skin.

SAUCE
Melt the butter and stir in the chopped hard boiled eggs and chopped parsley. If the butter is unsalted, add a little salt.

Serve the sauce with the cod and potatoes. This dish is Polish in origin but very popular in North Russia.

In Archangel where I was born, in the old days where fresh fish was not obtainable all the year round this dish was often made with salted, dried cod. It was a great favourite with the peasants not only in Lent but every day. My mother used to tell me that her maid had it for breakfast every morning. However, this type of cod has gone out of favour and is difficult to get. Harrods of London stock it in the fish department and the better fish shops have it on Good Fridays. If you manage to get hold of some remember to soak it overnight. Do not be put off by the appearance. It has a distinctive flavour and is well worth trying.

Dublin bay prawns *(with cream)*

serves 4

200 g (8 oz) frozen Dublin Bay prawns
salt to taste

SAUCE
1 egg yolk
1 sprig parsley
250 ml (½ pt) 1¼ cups cream
pinch of grated nutmeg
1 lemon

Allow the prawns to defrost and boil for a few minutes to heat through. Beat the egg and chop the parsley. Bring the cream to the boil and remove it from the heat. Add the egg, salt, grated nutmeg and parsley. Return to a low heat for about a minute, stirring all the time. Do not let it boil.

Put the prawns in a dish. Pour the sauce over them and serve with wedges of lemon.

If you can get only thin cream and thick cream but nothing between the two, it is best to mix the cream, ie half thick and half thin. If you wish to use only thin cream, however, add 1 teaspoon dried breadcrumbs to the sauce to thicken. Sour cream can also be used for this recipe and is more digestible. If the sauce is too thick dilute with dry white wine.

Try adding thyme to the sauce instead of parsley or dill, in which case omit nutmeg. Only a small quantity will do or it will ruin the flavour.

You can eat this as a main course with boiled potatoes and green peas and follow by a light pudding as it is rather rich, say lemon ice (see page 131) or have it as a hot zakuska with chilled vodka and rye bread.

Carp in wine

serves 6

1.20 kg (3 lb) carp
2 sticks celery
4 salted cucumbers
4 sprigs parsley
10 peppercorns
2 bayleaves
pinch of grated nutmeg
500 ml (1 pt) 2½ cups dry white wine
500 ml (1 pt) 2½ cups water
2 tablespoons butter
1 tablespoon flour

Fillet the carp and cut it into serving portions. Put the fish in a large saucepan with the chopped celery, salted cucumbers, parsley, peppercorns, bayleaves and nutmeg. Add the wine and water or salt water from the cucumbers. The fish should just be covered. Cook slowly for about 20 minutes until tender.

Make a roux with the butter and flour. Strain the liquid from the fish and stir it gradually into the roux. Stir until the sauce thickens. Put the fish on a serving dish and pour the sauce over it.

This dish is equally good if made with bass. Try adding a little grated nutmeg to the water. Serve with mashed or boiled potatoes and green peas or green salad with french dressing.

Kamchatka crabs in wine

serves 4

2 large cooked crabs about 400 g (1 lb) each
165 ml ($\frac{1}{3}$ pt) ¾ cup dry white wine
salt and pepper to taste

GARNISH
1 salted cucumber
1 hard boiled egg
1 sprig parsley

Remove the meat from the shells and cut into

pieces. Put into a saucepan with the wine. The liquid should cover the crab meat so add a little water if necessary. Season and cook gently for about 10 minutes with the lid on. When ready, remove from the saucepan with a perforated spoon. Put on to a serving-dish and pour the liquid over. Garnish with sliced salted cucumber, chopped parsley and chopped or sieved hard boiled egg.

Fresh crabs take from 30-45 minutes to cook, depending on the size.

You can make a sauce of the liquid if you wish. Add 1 teaspoon flour mixed with 1 teaspoon softened butter to the boiling liquid after you have lifted the bits of crab out. Boil through, stirring all the time. Pour the sauce over the crab meat and serve with potatoes (pages 65-79) and green salad or without the sauce you can eat it cold with beetroot salad (page 82), or rice salad (page 83). Crab meat makes a good filling for sandwiches. Any leftover bits can be mashed up. Add a little french dressing made with wine vinegar if you find the mixture too insipid.

Bream in wine *(with sultanas)* *serves 4*

1 bream 800 g-1 kg (2-2½ lb)
375 ml (¾ pt) 2 cups water
1 carrot
1 stick celery
1 leek
1 onion
40 g (1½ oz) 4 tablespoons cleaned sultanas
10 peppercorns
1 bayleaf
1 sprig parsley
¼ lemon
125 ml (¼ pt) ⅔ cup dry white wine
2 tablespoons vinegar

SAUCE
25 g (1 oz) 2 tablespoons butter
1 tablespoon flour
1 teaspoon sugar

Ask the fishmonger to fillet the fish. Scrape off the scales with a sharp knife.

Peel, wash and chop the vegetables and put them in a fish-kettle or large saucepan with the water. Bring to the boil, cover and simmer for 15-20 minutes. Add most of the sultanas, the peppercorns, bayleaf, parsley, lemon without pips, wine and vinegar. Put in the fish. It should just be covered by the liquid so add more water, if necessary. Replace the lid and simmer for a further 15-20 minutes. Remove the fish and keep it warm.

SAUCE
Make a roux from the butter and flour. Gradually add 250 ml (½ pt) 1¼ cups strained fish stock, stirring all the time. Add the sugar. A little lemon juice may be necessary if it is not very sharp. Cook the sauce for a few minutes.

Pour the sauce over the fish and decorate with the rest of the sultanas.

Freshwater bream can be of poor flavour and it is better to use sea-bream which has more flavour. It is in season all the year round but best from July to October.

Serve with boiled potatoes and turnips in cream or tomato salad (page 81) or beetroot salad (page 82).

Trout in wine *serves 4*

4 trout (about 200 g- 8 oz each)
200 g (8 oz) turnip or parsnip
1 small onion
1 small leek
1 stick celery
375 ml (¾ pt) 2 cups water
salt to taste
10 peppercorns
1 bayleaf
1 sprig parsley
125 ml (¼ pt) ⅔ cups dry red wine
2 tablespoons wine vinegar
1 tablespoon rum (optional)

SAUCE
25 g (1 oz) 2 tablespoons butter
1 tablespoon flour
250 ml (½ pt) 1¼ cups fish stock

Remove the gills from the trout and gut. Wash thoroughly. The trout can be cooked whole or the heads removed. If the heads are cut off they should be cooked with the fish as they improve the flavour of the stock.

Peel, wash and chop the vegetables and put them with the water in a large saucepan or fish-kettle. Bring to the boil, cover and simmer for 15-20 minutes. Add the salt, peppercorns, bayleaf, parsley, wine, wine vinegar and rum if used. Put in the fish head-to-tail. They should just be covered by the liquid so add more water, if necessary. Replace the lid and simmer for a further 10-15 minutes. When they are ready, remove the fish and skin. Keep them warm while making the sauce.

SAUCE
Make a roux from the butter and flour. Gradually add the strained fish stock, stirring all the time until it thickens. Simmer for a few minutes.

Pour the sauce over the fish. Garnish with parsley and serve with new potatoes.

Beetroot in sour cream (page 68) is a good accompaniment as a second vegetable to the above. Try cucumbers in sour cream if you want to eat the trout with a salad.

Trout stuffed with kasha

serves 4

4 trout
salt to taste
butter
dry breadcrumbs
4 tablespoons sour cream

STUFFING
1 large onion
3 sprigs parsley
8 tablespoons cooked kasha (page 66)
butter

Cut the heads off the fish and gut. Wash the fish under a cold tap and salt thoroughly. Coat in breadcrumbs.

STUFFING
Peel and chop the onion fairly finely and fry it slowly in plenty of butter for about five minutes until transparent. Add the kasha and half the chopped parsley and cook very gently for a further five minutes, breaking up the kasha grains until they are quite separate.

Stuff the fish with this mixture. If it is done carefully there will be no need to sew the fish up. Place the fish head-to-tail in a buttered fireproof dish adding just enough butter to prevent them drying out while cooking. Cook in a fairly hot oven 200°C (400°F) Mark 6 for 20 minutes. Add the sour cream and the rest of the chopped parsley. Cook for a few minutes longer and serve with the sour cream sauce.

Double quantities of the stuffing can be made and cooked round the fish and served with it.

This dish can also be made with fresh herrings.

This can be done with bass or plaice as an alternative. If using plaice, allow 1 fillet per head and put the stuffing at the wide end of the fish and roll up. Tie with cotton. Serve with potatoes and turnips in cream (pages 65, 68) or swedes in white sauce (page 68). Garnish with fresh watercress.

Stuffed haddock

serves 6

1 whole haddock (about 1 kg-2½ lb)
salt
dry breadcrumbs
butter

STUFFING
100 g (4 oz) ⅔ cup rice
salt
1 onion
25 g (1 oz) 2 tablespoons butter

Ask the fishmonger to remove the bones from the fish leaving the back skin intact. Wash the fish.

STUFFING
Boil the rice in salted water. Peel and chop the onion and fry it in butter. When the rice is cooked, strain and pour cold water through it. Mix the rice with the onion adding a little melted butter, if necessary, to obtain a smooth mixture.

Stuff the fish with this mixture and sew up with a strong thread. Rub salt well over the fish and coat with breadcrumbs. Dot with butter and put on a greased baking sheet in a fairly hot oven 200°C (400°F) Mark 6 for about half an hour.

This dish can be equally well done with sea bass or filleted plaice. Allow one large fillet per head and put the stuffing at the broad end of the fish and roll up. Tie with thread and bake. Serve with boiled potatoes and beetroot with sour cream (page 68) or green peas or green salad with french dressing.

Stuffed herrings

serves 4

4 medium-to-large herrings
1 onion
8 tablespoons stale breadcrumbs
1-2 eggs

extra dry breadcrumbs
oil for frying
salt and pepper to taste
1 lemon
1 sprig parsley

Clean and gut the fish. Dry them and sprinkle with salt. Keep any soft roe for the stuffing.

STUFFING
You may use either white or brown breadcrumbs. Put them in a bowl with the finely chopped roe and onion. Add salt and plenty of pepper and bind the mixture with an egg. It may be necessary to use two if they are small.

Stuff the herring with this mixture. Any leftover stuffing can be fried with the fish and then kept warm until the fish is ready.

Dip the fish in beaten egg and then in dry breadcrumbs and fry in oil or butter for about 20 minutes. Turn once, taking care not to let the stuffing fall out. The heat should not be too high otherwise the fish will burn and not cook through.

Garnish with parsley and wedges of lemon.

As an alternative use 2 small sea bass about 400 g (1 lb) each or 1 large one about 800 g (2 lb) instead of herring. Or 1 large fillet of plaice per head. Place the stuffing at the broad end of the fillet and roll up and tie with string. Serve with boiled potatoes and green salad, or celery in sour cream (page 69) or with Ukrainian stewed vegetables (page 69).

Ukrainian fried fish *serves 4*

600 g (1½ lb) cod or haddock fillets
flour for coating
salt to taste
oil for frying
parsley

SAUCE
2 onions
2 carrots
oil for frying
2 tablespoons tomato purée
125 ml (¼ pt) ⅔ cup wine vinegar
2 peppercorns
1 clove
1 bayleaf

Wash the fish and cut it in slices. Coat in seasoned flour and fry in oil until cooked. Cool and put into a serving-dish.

SAUCE
Clean and chop the onions and carrots finely and fry them gently for about 20 minutes until tender. Add the tomato purée, wine vinegar, peppercorns, clove, bayleaf and a little water. Stir and cook through.

Pour the sauce over the fish and allow to stand for a few hours before serving. Garnish with chopped parsley.

This dish can be done with any white fish or sea bass. Serve with boiled young potatoes and a green salad or rice salad, potato salad or Russian salad (see Salads 81-87).

Jellied sturgeon or halibut *serves 6-8*

1 kg (2½ lb) sturgeon or halibut
200-300 g (8-12 oz) hake or pike
salt to taste
4 peppercorns
1 bayleaf
1 slice lemon rind
1 onion
1 carrot
1 calf's foot or gelatine
1 hard boiled egg

Wash the fish and put all the ingredients, except the egg and the gelatine (if you are using this to make the jelly) into a saucepan and cover with boiling water. Cook for about 20 minutes or until tender. Take out the fish and remove the skin and bones. If a calf's foot has been used it should be left to simmer for at least another hour. If gelatine is used mix it in a little cold water and add it to the liquid. (Use 15 g (½ oz) 2 envelopes gelatine to each 500 ml (1 pt) 2½ cups of liquid.) Strain and cool. Put sliced hard boiled egg and sliced cooked carrot at the bottom of a large dish. Cooked green peas may also be added. Divide the fish into small pieces and put them in the dish. Pour the stock over. Serve when set with Russian salad (page 83), horseradish cream or mustard sauce (page 91).

Potato salad and beetroot salad go well with all cold fish (pages 83 and 82). To do justice to this luxury dish serve ice-cold in the garden on a hot day with chilled dry white wine. You can of course serve this as a zakuska in which case it will go further. In Russia this was often served on Christmas Eve since it is the end of the religious fast which precedes Christmas.

Tasty scampi *serves 4-6*

375 ml (¾ pt) 2 cups sour cream
125 ml (¼ pt) ⅔ cup dry white wine
1 tablespoon butter
a little caraway seed
30 cooked scampi
salt and pepper to taste
1 sprig parsley
1 lemon

Clean the scampi. Put the sour cream, wine, butter and a few caraway seeds in a saucepan. Allow to boil. Add the shelled scampi and reduce heat to simmering point. Cook for 10 minutes. Check for seasoning. Add a little salt and ground pepper as necessary.

Divide the lemon into quarters. Chop the parsley and serve in a dish garnished with parsley and wedges of lemon.

This is a hot zakuska but could be the main meal with boiled potatoes if you wish.

Prawns in batter *serves 4*

1.25 l (2 pt) 5 cups large prawns
1 salted cucumber
oil or fat for deep frying
salt to taste
batter
1 lemon

Shell prawns. Make the batter.

Heat the fat or oil in a deep pan till it sizzles. Dip the prawns in batter and fry in the hot oil till they are golden brown. Remove with a slotted spoon on to kitchen paper to drain and then on to a warm plate to keep hot. Cut the salted cucumber in quarters and the lemon. Garnish with lemon and cucumber.

This can be a hot zakuska or a main course.

Bream with horseradish and apples

serves 4-6

800 g (2 lb) bream
200 g (8 oz) cooking apples
100 g (4 oz) horseradish
125 ml (¼ pt) $\frac{2}{3}$ cup vinegar
1 tablespoon sugar
1 sprig parsley
1 carrot
1 onion
8 medium potatoes

Clean and wash the bream. Cut into serving portions. Cover with water and a little vinegar and leave for 5 minutes. Transfer fish to another pan. Clean the carrot and onion. Add together with the salt, peppercorns, bayleaf and parsley. Cover with water and cook under a lid for 20 minutes. Peel the potatoes and cook in salted water (with the lid on the saucepan) for 20 minutes. Try and arrange for the potatoes and fish to be ready at the same time. Lift out the fish and place on a large oval dish. Remove the potatoes with a perforated spoon and put round the bream. Grate the horseradish and peel, core and grate the apple on a coarse grater. Add the sugar and a little vinegar to make a sauce. Serve with green peas, carrots, etc.

This can be adapted to blue fish, bass, cod or haddock.

Stuffed sole

serves 2

2 soles
1 tablespoon chopped parsley
salt, pepper and nutmeg to taste
½ lemon
3 tablespoons stale breadcrumbs
4 tablespoons butter
100 g (4 oz) crayfish tails or crabmeat
1 egg

Remove the head and clean the fish. Slit with a sharp knife from the middle to make an opening for the stuffing. (As if you were going to fillet the fish)

STUFFING
Remove the meat from the cooked crayfish, or use cooked crabmeat. Mix 2 tablespoons butter with the breadcrumbs, parsley, crayfish or crab and slightly beaten egg. Reserve a little egg to brush the fish with later. Add a little grated nutmeg, salt and pepper. Combine all ingredients and stuff the fish, leaving the side open. Melt 1 tablespoon butter and put into an ovenproof dish and add the fish. Brush with the egg which is left over and sprinkle with dry breadcrumbs and dot with the remaining butter. Bake at 180°C (350°F) Mark 4 for 7-10 minutes.

Garnish with lemon wedges and eat with fried potatoes and your favourite vegetables. This can be done when you have crab left over after a meal. It can also be adapted to plaice or mullet.

Plaice in wine with sour cream sauce

serves 4

Either 4 dabs or 2 plaice (about 400 g (1 lb) each)
salt and pepper to taste
1 teaspoon flour
1 teaspoon butter
1 sprig parsley
1 lemon
1 cup cream
250 ml (½ pt) 1¼ cups dry white wine
2 egg yolks

Clean the fish, remove the skin and fillet. Wash and dry. Rub with lemon. Peel the onion. Chop the onion and parsley and fry together in a large frying pan. Add salt and ground pepper to taste.

When the onion is light brown add the fish and squeeze the lemon juice over it. Cover with the wine. Cover with lid and cook slowly for 15-20 minutes. When ready remove the fish and put on to a warm plate and keep hot. Make the sauce.

SAUCE
Mix 1 teaspoon flour with 1 teaspoon of melted butter. When well mixed add the cream gradually and the two yolks. Mix well and heat till boiling point. Add more salt and lemon juice to taste. Stir and pour over the fish. Eat with boiled potatoes and another vegetable.

If you have not got a fish-kettle a large saucepan will do, with a lid.

Pike babka

serves 6

800 g (2 lb) pike
100 g (4 oz) ½ cup butter
1 onion
1 tablespoon chopped parsley
grated nutmeg
½ vienna loaf
1 tablespoon dry breadcrumbs
4 eggs
milk

Fillet the pike and remove the skin. Put through a mincer and blend with half the butter. Peel the onion and chop the parsley and onion. Fry together in butter. Add to the fish. Season with salt and pepper and a little grated nutmeg. Cut the crust off the bread and soak in milk. Squeeze out any excess liquid leaving about two-thirds of the milk as the mixture should not be too solid. Put all ingredients again through the mincer.

Separate eggs. Add the yolks to the mixture and blend thoroughly. Whip the whites till they stand in peaks and fold into the mixture.

Grease a bowl and dust with breadcrumbs. Pour the Babka into it. Cover with greaseproof paper, and steam for 1 hour in a large saucepan or steamer.

Eat with mashed potatoes, carrots, peas and any fish sauce in the book. This can also be made from any white fish.

Plaice with tomato and green pepper

serves 4

600 g (1½ lb) filleted plaice
1 onion
1 green pepper
oil for frying
3 large tomatoes
3 tablespoons water or fish stock
1 clove garlic
1 tablespoon flour
salt and pepper to taste
1 lemon

Season the fillets with salt and pepper. Cover with flour and fry in hot oil for 2 minutes each side. Set aside. Peel and chop the onion and fry lightly in oil. Top the pepper, remove the seeds and slice in thin strips. Add to the onion and fry for a further 5 minutes.

Put the tomatoes in a bowl and pour boiling water to cover. Leave for 5 minutes. Remove skin and discard seeds. Chop finely and add to the onion. Crush the garlic and also add. Season. Add the fried fish and stock. Cover and simmer gently for 10 minutes in the sauce.

Serve the fish together with the tomato and green pepper sauce and boiled potatoes. Garnish with lemon wedges. This can be adapted to any flat fish or red snapper.

Fish cotletti

serves 4-6

600 g (1½ lb) filleted fish (cod, blue fish, bass, haddock, etc)
2 slices stale white bread
125 ml (¼ pt) ⅔ cup milk
4 tablespoons dry breadcrumbs
1 tablespoon butter
oil for frying
1 teaspoon salt
pepper to taste
mushroom sauce (page 90)

Skin the fillets and put the flesh through the mincer. Remove the crusts from the bread and soak in milk. Squeeze out so that the bread is very dry or the mixture will be too wet and difficult to handle. Cream the butter and mix with the rest of the ingredients except the breadcrumbs and oil. Season and mix. Sprinkle a pastry board with dry breadcrumbs. Take tablespoons of the mixture and with the aid of a blunt knife make cutlets coating both sides with the breadcrumbs. Heat a frying pan, put in enough oil to cover. Wait till it gets very hot and put in the cutlets. Fry till golden brown.

Serve with pickled mushroom sauce, caper sauce (page 89) or mushroom sauce (page 90). This can be a starter to a meal or the main course. Usually eaten during Lent.

Stuffed cotletti *(for the above)*

STUFFING
100 g (4 oz) fresh mushrooms
1 onion
1 tablespoon stale white breadcrumbs
sprig of parsley
oil for frying
salt and pepper to taste

Wash mushrooms and peel if large. Peel the onion. Chop the mushrooms, parsley and the onion finely and fry lightly in oil. Add the breadcrumbs, salt and pepper. Take a wet tea towel and spread on the table. Divide the fish mixture into 8 rounds about 15mm (½ in.) thick. Put a teaspoon of the stuffing in the middle and bring the ends together to form a little pie. Pinch the edges. Roll in dry breadcrumbs and flatten to form a cutlet. Fry as above.

These stuffed cotletti can be served with white wine sauce (page 90) or with any sauce recommended for fish except mushroom. Mashed potatoes and green peas or carrots go well with this dish. Usually eaten during Lent.

Cod swiss roll

serves 6

800 g (2 lb) cod
2 medium potatoes boiled and mashed
1 onion
1 egg
2 tablespoons butter
2 eggs for omelette
50 g (2 oz) 1 cup grated breadcrumbs
1 teaspoon salt
½ teaspoon pepper
pinch of nutmeg

Simmer the fish under a lid in salted water for

15 minutes. Skin, bone and put through mincer. Add the mashed potato, peeled and chopped onion, egg, salt, pepper and nutmeg.

Sprinkle a pastry board with flour and spread the mixture on it about 15 mm (½ in.) thick. Melt a little butter in a frying pan about 20 cm (8 in.) in diameter (the omelette must be smaller in diameter than the fish pancake.) Beat the eggs, season with salt and pepper and fry in a hot pan with butter as an omelette (see page 98 for instructions). When the underside is done turn it out on to the fish mixture, cooked side up and form a swiss roll of even appearance. Roll slowly or you will split it. Sprinkle with breadcrumbs. Put in a greased baking dish, add dabs of butter and bake in a hot oven at 200°C (400°F) Mark 7 till brown, about 15 minutes.

Serve this with any fish sauce in the book. Mashed or boiled potatoes or rice go with this. Can be adapted to bass, blue fish or haddock.

Cod with cabbage and tomato

serves 4

600 g (1½ lb) cod fillet
2 tablespoons flour
2 tablespoons butter
oil for frying
1 medium hard white cabbage
250 ml (½ pt) 1¼ cups tomato sauce (page 89)
salt and pepper to taste
sprig parsley
1 medium onion

Cut the cod into portions. Salt and sprinkle with pepper. Dredge with flour and fry in oil both sides till light brown then set aside. Shred the cabbage, peel and chop the onion. Heat the frying pan. Add a little oil and the cabbage and onion. Cook through. Add the tomato sauce and cook for a further 5 minutes. Transfer to another saucepan. Put a layer of cabbage on the bottom then a layer of fried fish till all the ingredients are used up ending with a cabbage layer. Cover with a lid and simmer gently for 30 minutes or till the cabbage is ready.

Transfer to serving dish and sprinkle with chopped parsley. Eat with boiled or mashed potatoes.

Crab soufflé

serves 4

25 g (1 oz) 2 tablespoons butter
300 g (12 oz) crab meat (preferably white)
fresh ground pepper
125 ml (¼ pt) ⅔ cup white sauce (page 89)
1 tablespoon double cream
3 eggs
1 tablespoon dry breadcrumbs
1 lemon
25 g (1 oz) 2 tablespoons butter for top

Melt the first quantity of butter in a saucepan, add the crab meat and season well. Add the white sauce and cream and heat through. Draw aside. Separate eggs. Add the yolks, season with lemon juice, whip whites till they stand in peaks and fold in.

Butter a soufflé dish. Pour in the mixture and sprinkle with breadcrumbs and dot with butter. Put into the oven for 20 to 25 minutes at 200°C (400°F) Mark 6.

This can also be done with cooked left-over salmon. If you prefer, steam the soufflé for 30 minutes covering it with greaseproof paper first. Serve in the same dish.

Meat

Fillet steak with wine

serves 4

800 g (2 lb) fillet steak
1 tablespoon butter
1 tablespoon wine vinegar
1-2 pieces of lump sugar
1 teaspoon flour
125 ml (¼ pt) $\frac{2}{3}$ cup red wine
salt
bouillon or water

Cut the steak into serving portions and grill or cook on a spit for about 5 minutes. Baste meat with a mixture of melted butter and wine vinegar. Burn the sugar in a saucepan and add the flour, wine and enough water or bouillon to make a sauce. Simmer for a few minutes. Put the steak, which should not be completely cooked, into the sauce pan, season and stew gently in the sauce for about 20 minutes until tender.

Serve with new potatoes in sour cream (page 65), sprouts or tomato salad (page 81).

Cossack steaks

serves 4

400 g (1 lb) rump steak
2 slices day-old french bread
1 tablespoon grated onion
25 g (1 oz) $\frac{1}{3}$ cup grated suet (optional)
1 egg yolk
salt and pepper to taste
dry breadcrumbs
oil or butter for frying
1-2 tablespoons sour cream
1 sprig dill

Chop the meat up finely. Discard the crusts and soak the bread in water. Squeeze out the excess liquid and mix the bread with the meat, onion, suet and egg yolk. Add a little water if necessary. Season and make into four patties. Coat in breadcrumbs and fry on both sides for about 20 minutes. Remove the steaks and keep warm. Stir a little water and the sour cream into the fat to make the gravy. Warm through and pour over the steaks. Garnish with dill. Serve with kasha (page 66) and a quarter of salted cucumber per person.

This is very similar to cotletti but made from beef. Serve with potatoes and swedes in white sauce (page 68) or beetroot with sour cream (page 68). Tomato salad or cucumber salad also go well with this dish (page 81).

Beef stroganoff

serves 4

600 g (1½ lb) fillet steak
1 large onion
200 g (8 oz) mushrooms
butter for frying
salt and pepper to taste
1 dessertspoon flour
125 ml (¼ pt) $\frac{2}{3}$ cup stock or water
4 tablespoons sour cream

Cut the steak into thin strips of about 50mm x 6 mm (2 in. by ¼ in.). Peel the onion and chop. Wash the mushrooms and slice them finely. Fry the onion lightly in a little butter for a few minutes. Add the mushrooms and fry for a further 5 minutes, stirring all the time. Add the steak and season. Continue stirring and cook the steak for about 6-10 minutes until it is tender. Mix the flour with 125 ml (¼ pt) ⅔ cup stock or water; add to the beef stroganoff. Bring to the boil, stirring all the time. Cook for a few minutes, then reduce the heat and add the sour cream. Heat through and serve with potatoes or kasha (page 66).

This is now an international dish and was named after a Count Stroganoff who lived from 1794-1882. He owned 95,000 serfs.

The classic accompaniment to this dish is purée of potatoes and green peas. Or you can have a green salad instead of vegetables if you prefer. Although expensive this dish goes a long way as there is no waste when you are cooking it. The beef should not be overcooked if it is fillet steak. Most Russians use topside or rump steak as it is cheaper. It requires longer cooking however.

Beef stroganoff *(with tomato and mustard)*

serves 4-6

1 kg (2 lb) fillet or rump steak
salt and pepper to taste
1 large onion
butter for frying
1 dessertspoon flour

1 tablespoon tomato purée
1 teaspoon made mustard
250 ml (½ pt) 1¼ cups stock or water
2 tablespoons sour cream

Cut the steak into thin strips of about 50 mm x 6 mm (2 in. x ¼ in.). Peel and chop the onion and fry it lightly in butter. Add the meat, season and cook for about 6-10 minutes until it is tender, stirring all the time. Sprinkle with flour and add the tomato purée, mustard and the stock or water. Bring to the boil, still stirring. Reduce heat and add the sour cream. Simmer for a few minutes and serve with fried potatoes and green salad.

This can be served with kasha (page 66) and some green vegetable as an alternative, or potato purée and green peas or green salad as above.

Zraza *(meat roll with mushroom sauce)*

serves 6

6 slices thin top rump or topside about 15 cm x 10 cm (6 in. x 4 in.)
butter for frying
salt and pepper to taste
375 ml (¾ pt) 2 cups mushroom sauce (page 91)

STUFFING
1 onion
12 tablespoons breadcrumbs
1 egg yolk

Season the meat and fry it lightly in butter.

STUFFING
Mince or chop the onion finely and mix it with the breadcrumbs, egg yolk and a little water to form a fairly stiff paste.

Put some of the stuffing on to each slice of meat and roll up. Pack the rolls tightly in a greased baking-dish and cover with mushroom sauce. Bake in a moderate oven 180°C (350°F) Mark 4 for about half an hour.

Accompaniment: purée of potato, and some green vegetable but hot beetroot (page 68) goes very well with this dish. If you prefer a salad to hot vegetables try green salad with french dressing or tomato salad (page 81).

Chilav

Per head:

rice (according to appetite)
salt and pepper to taste
150-200 g (6-8 oz) fillet steak

25 g (1 oz) 2 tablespoons butter
1 egg yolk
parsley

The method of cooking the rice is Caucasian and rather unusual. Soak the required amount of rice overnight in water. Next morning strain the rice in a sieve and pour cold water through. Add a little salt. Put the sieve over a saucepan of boiling water, cover with a lid and allow it to steam slowly until the rice is cooked. Each grain will be separate.

Season the steak, cut it into small cubes, brush with butter and thread on to a skewer. When the rice is ready grill the steak quickly. Serve the rice topped with a large lump of butter, one raw egg yolk and the skewer of steak. Garnish with parsley.

Serve green salad on a side plate or tomato salad (page 81). A Caucasian gourmet gave me this recipe.

Steak tartare

Per head:

100-150 g (4-6 oz) best fillet
or porterhouse steak
1 egg yolk
1 anchovy fillet
1-2 teaspoons french
dressing (page 92)

Cut away any fat and put the steak through a coarse mincer. Add the french dressing. This softens the steak. Mix well and form into a mound with a slight hollow on top. Chill. Before serving garnish with a raw egg yolk and 1 anchovy fillet.

This has now become an international dish. It was originally invented by the Tartar warriors who put a steak under their saddles when they went on campaigns. It has now, however, achieved a transformation no doubt for the best!

Hussar's steak

serves 6-8

1.2 kg (3 lb) joint of
roasting beef
½ teaspoon salt
100 g (4 oz) ½ cup butter
or 6 tablespoons oil
1 onion
2 carrots

STUFFING
½ salted herring fillet
75 g (3 oz) ¾ cup grated
stale black bread
1 egg
50 g (2 oz) ¼ cup melted
butter
2 spring onions

Sprinkle salt on the meat. Peel and wash the onion and carrots and slice them. Put them in a saucepan with the butter and fry lightly. Add the meat and fry till it is brown on all sides. Take out the meat and cut into 8 or 9 slices, almost to the end, but leave the slices joined together at the base of the joint.

STUFFING
Chop the herring and spring onions and mix them with the bread, egg and melted butter.

Put the stuffing between the slices and tie the joint with a piece of string. Return the joint to the saucepan adding a little water or stock as necessary. Simmer for about 1½ hours until tender, basting from time to time. Serve with roast potatoes or kasha (page 66) and a green vegetable.

This may sound very strange but you do not taste the fish in the stuffing and it is well worth trying. As an alternative try boiled or mashed potatoes with this and tomato salad (page 81).

Russian stew

serves 4

400 g (1 lb) stewing steak
flour or breadcrumbs
butter or oil for frying
2 onions
bayleaf
6 peppercorns
200 g (½ lb) carrots
1 thick slice stale black
bread
stock or water
salt to taste
3 tablespoons sour cream

Trim off the fat and cut the meat into small pieces. Coat in flour or breadcrumbs and fry till brown on all sides. Put one of the peeled and chopped onions, the bayleaf, and the peppercorns on the bottom of a saucepan. Cover with the meat, half the peeled and chopped carrots and the black bread, which should be cut into small cubes. Put the rest of the chopped onion and carrot on top and add enough stock or water to cover. Cook slowly with the lid on for about 1½ hours until the meat is tender. Add salt during the last 10 minutes of cooking. Just before serving add the sour cream and heat through.

This is best served with kasha (page 66) or with mashed potato and some green vegetable, or green salad if you prefer, with french dressing.

Cotletti

serves 6

600 g (1½ lb) raw minced
meat (ground beef, veal,
pork or veal and pork)
3 thick slices day-old french
bread
1-2 eggs
salt and pepper to taste
fat for frying
dry breadcrumbs
1 tablespoon sour cream

Discard the crusts and soak the bread in water. Squeeze out the excess liquid. Add the meat and beaten eggs and mix well by hand. A little water may be necessary if the mixture is too dry. Season and make into cutlet shapes. Coat in dry breadcrumbs and fry for about 20 minutes. To make the gravy, remove the cutlets and keep warm. Add a little water to the fat and stir in the sour cream. Heat through.

Serve with kasha (page 66) and a mushroom sauce (page 90).

This is one of the Russian national dishes and eaten very frequently in Russian households. Use the best mince which should not be fat. Top rump is a good cut if you mince the beef yourself. The mince should be coarse and not fine for good results. Some cooks add a small knob of butter or ice inside the cotletti to make them moist.

My father who went to the Forest Institute in Ekaterinburg had cotletti with macaroni every day for dinner there yet it remained his favourite dish to the day of his death. This shows that simple food never tires.

ROULETTE

Using the same ingredients as for cotletti, form into a large meat loaf, coat in breadcrumbs and bake in a hot oven 230°C (450°F) Mark 8 in a little fat for 1-1¼ hours.

Katushki with tomatoes

serves 6

600 g (1½ lb) raw minced /ground beef
3 thick slices day-old french bread
1-2 eggs
salt and pepper to taste
dry breadcrumbs
butter for frying
1 large onion
200 g (½ lb) tomatoes or 2 tablespoons tomato purée
½ teaspoon sugar
lemon juice
250 ml (½ pt) 1¼ cups water
2-3 tablespoons fresh or sour cream
parsley to garnish

Remove the crusts and soak the bread in water. Squeeze out the excess liquid. Mix the bread, meat and beaten eggs well by hand, adding a little water if necessary. Season, form into meatballs and coat in breadcrumbs. Fry in butter for about 20 minutes until brown. Strain the meatballs and transfer them to a large saucepan. Fry the chopped onion and add to the meatballs together with the peeled and chopped tomatoes or tomato purée, salt, sugar and lemon juice to taste. Pour in enough water to cover the meatballs (about 250 ml (½ pt) 1¼ cups). Simmer with the lid on for 15 minutes. Before serving, add the cream and warm through. Garnish with parsley.

The flavour of these katushki is of course determined by the type of meat you use. Try to get a good coarse mince for best results. It should not be fat. The cheaper cuts of meat will need a little longer cooking time than indicated.

You can vary this dish by adding some mushrooms. Amount for this quantity 200 g (8 oz). Fry the chopped mushrooms with the chopped onion in oil for a few minutes and add to the browned meatballs.

The best accompaniment to this dish is potatoes. You can of course have some green vegetable if you wish or green salad.

Katushki with prunes

serves 6

600 g (1½ lb) raw minced/ ground beef
3 thick slices day-old french bread
1-2 eggs
dry breadcrumbs
300 g (¾ lb) prunes
sugar
juice of ½ lemon
salt to taste
2 peppercorns
1 clove
bayleaf
2-3 tablespoons fresh or sour cream

Make meatballs as in the previous recipe. Meanwhile, simmer the prunes in water with a little sugar for about half an hour until soft. Allow one prune to each meatball. Put the prunes and meatballs in a large saucepan and cover with water. Simmer gently with the lid on for 15 minutes. The juice is the best part of this dish. It can be thickened with a little flour before serving. Add the fresh or sour cream and warm through.

Although this recipe comes from the Ukraine its origins are Greek. It is well worth trying. Eat boiled potatoes with it or rice.

Zraza
(with vegetable stuffing)

serves 6

600 g (1½ lb) raw minced meat (ground beef, pork, veal or veal and pork)
3 thick slices french bread
1-2 eggs
salt and pepper to taste
butter or oil for frying
dry breadcrumbs

STUFFING
2 carrots
1 onion
2 sticks celery
1 leek
a little swede, turnip or parsnip or a mixture of these
a little chopped parsley

Prepare the mince as for cotletti (page 41). Sprinkle a board with breadcrumbs and roll out the meat.

STUFFING

Clean and chop the vegetables finely and cook them in butter or oil very slowly for 5 to 10 minutes. Do not allow them to brown.

Spread the stuffing on the meat and roll it up. Put into a greased dish, dot with butter and bake in a hot oven 230°C (450°F) Mark 8 for about an hour, basting frequently. Slice and serve hot or cold.

Alternative stuffings are rice and onion, rice and egg, rice and mushroom or buckwheat and chopped hard boiled egg or if eaten cold two hard boiled eggs.

Get the best mince which should be coarse but not too fat. Add 1 or 2 tablespoons sour cream to the gravy when ready or 1 dessertspoon tomato purée and 1 tablespoon sour cream in a little water. If you want a thicker sauce add 1 heaped teaspoon flour to the fat in the pan then add the rest of the ingredients. Best accompaniment to this dish is roast potatoes which can be done round the Zraza.

Left-over Zraza is good on rye or brown bread and butter if sliced with a piece of salted or pickled cucumber on top as an appetiser or snack.

Farshmak *(See also page 14)* *serves 4*

300 g (12 oz) cooked beef
1-2 eggs
1 fillet salted herring
1 onion
1 tablespoon butter
1 large slice stale bread
4 tablespoons sour cream
dry breadcrumbs
pepper to taste
milk

Peel and chop the onion and fry lightly in butter. Remove any skin and bones from herring. Mince the meat, salted herring and fried onion. Discard the crusts and soak the bread in milk. Squeeze out the excess liquid. Mix bread well with meat, herring, onion and eggs. Add pepper and more milk if necessary. The mixture should be soft and not dry. Form into a loaf, coat in breadcrumbs and put into a fireproof dish. Dot with butter and cook in a moderate oven 180°C (350°F) Mark 4 for about 30 minutes. When ready pour the sour cream over the farshmak and serve.

This can be served as a main course when it will be enough for 3-4 people or as a zakuska hot or cold in which case it is enough for 6. Boiled meat from the stock is usually used for this but you can also use left-over cooked veal, game, chicken or turkey. If the meat is very dry add 1 tablespoon melted butter to the mixture. The mixture should be soft but not too wet or it will fall apart. If too stiff it will crack when cooking. A good idea is to use a pâté dish without the lid.

Be careful not to overcook this dish. It should be just heated through as the meat is already cooked. Do not be put off by the ingredients, it is very tasty. Suggested vegetables: potatoes, hot beetroot (page 68) or turnips in cream (page 68).

This is a good way to use any left-over boiled beef after making stock or soup.

Galuptsi
(stuffed cabbage leaves) *serves 4*

1 large white Dutch cabbage
butter or oil for frying

STUFFING
1 onion
400 g (1 lb) raw minced/ground beef
salt and pepper to taste
1 tablespoon rice

SAUCE
200 g (8 oz) ripe tomatoes or 2 tablespoons tomato purée
125-250 ml (¼-½ pt) ⅔-1¼ cups water or stock
flour
salt to taste
2 tablespoons sour cream

The leaves of the cabbage should be softened before use. The quickest way is to cook the whole cabbage in boiling salted water for about 5 minutes or until the leaves are soft enough not to break when bent.

STUFFING
Peel and chop the onion finely and fry for a few minutes in oil or butter. Add the meat, season and cook for a further 10-15 minutes until the meat is lightly browned. Meanwhile, boil the rice for about 10 minutes in salted water. Strain and mix with the meat and onion.

Separate the leaves of the cabbage, removing any thick stalks. Place 1-2 tablespoons of the stuffing in the middle of each leaf. Fold in the sides of the leaf and roll up. The leaves can be tied with cotton thread if it seems necessary. Fry them on both sides until brown. Remove from the saucepan and pack tightly into a large saucepan or casserole.

SAUCE
In a frying-pan put either the peeled, quartered tomatoes with the smaller amount of liquid or the purée with the larger amount. Cook for a few minutes. Sprinkle in a little flour and add salt to taste. Stir. When the sauce has thickened pour it over the stuffed cabbage leaves. Cover and cook slowly for 30 minutes on top of the oven or for 40 minutes in a casserole in the oven. (Put in at 200°C (400°F) Mark 6 turning down to 170°C (325°F) Mark 3 after 10 minutes.) Before serving add the sour cream and warm through.

This is a great favourite in all parts of Russia since the ingredients are easily available. It does take a bit of time however. You can save time by adding the minced beef uncooked to the rice. This gives a very good flavour. In fact some prefer it. The only accompaniment to this dish should be boiled potatoes or just rye bread and butter.

Dolma *(stuffed vine leaves)* *serves 4*

200 g (8 oz) young vine leaves	400 g (1 lb) 2 cups raw minced mutton or lamb fillet
mutton stock or water	salt and pepper to taste
250 ml (½ pt) 1¼ cups fresh or sour cream or yoghurt	2 cloves crushed garlic (optional)
STUFFING	2-3 tablespoons cooked rice (optional)
1 onion	

Wash the vine leaves in water and cut off the stems. Pour boiling water over the leaves and leave them to soften for about 10 minutes.

STUFFING
Peel and chop the onion finely. Add the meat, garlic and seasoning. Mix in the cooked rice.

Put a teaspoonful of the mixture on to each vine leaf. Fold the leaves over to form small 'parcels' and pack them tightly into a saucepan, adding a little water or mutton stock to prevent them catching. Cover and cook slowly for about three-quarters of an hour. Add the cream or yoghurt and heat through before serving. Some people prefer fresh cream as the vine leaves have a slightly sour taste.

This dish comes from the south. It is very popular in Uzbek and the Caucasus. The vine leaves are best when young or they will be tough and need longer cooking. So there is a limited season for this dish unless you can buy them in a tin in a delicatessen shop. You can if you wish serve the yoghurt separately. In which case add the grated garlic to the yoghurt, salt and caster sugar mixed with cinnamon in separate little dishes (one for each person).

Kidneys with sour cream *serves 4*

400 g (1 lb) beef kidneys	salt and black pepper to taste
1 tablespoon flour or dry breadcrumbs	1 bayleaf
50 g (2 oz) ¼ cup butter	125 ml (¼ pt) ⅔ cup sour cream
1-2 small onions	parsley or dill

Skin the kidneys and remove the membranes. Soak in cold water in a saucepan for about two hours. Bring the water to the boil. Remove the kidneys and rinse them in cold water. Cut in slices and coat in flour or breadcrumbs. Do not salt. Fry lightly for a few minutes in a saucepan with the peeled and chopped onion. Add a little water, pepper and a bayleaf. Simmer for about an hour, stirring from time to time. Test with a fork to find out when the kidneys are ready. Add salt to taste and the sour cream. Bring to the boil. Garnish with parsley or dill before serving.

You can do this with lamb's kidneys. If so, cook for about 20 minutes. Overcooking will make them tough. Serve with boiled potatoes, sprouts, green beans or peas, etc.

Lamb with wine sauce *serves 4*

600 g (1½ lb) leg of lamb (boned) or 4 lamb chops	SAUCE
1 carrot	15 g (½ oz) 1 tablespoon butter
1 onion	1 lump sugar
salt to taste	juice of ½ lemon
5 peppercorns	125 ml (¼ pt) ⅔ cup dry red wine
1 bayleaf	1 egg yolk
	1 dessertspoon flour
	250 ml (½ pt) 1¼ cups stock

Take 4 lamb chops or thick slices from a leg of lamb and put them in a saucepan. Cover with water and bring to the boil. Strain the liquid and return it to the saucepan. Add the peeled onion and carrot. Cover and simmer for about 40 minutes until tender. Add the salt, peppercorns and the bayleaf and simmer for a further few minutes.

SAUCE
Make a roux from the butter and flour in a separate saucepan. Slowly add 250 ml (½ pt) 1¼ cups stock from the meat, or stock and water, to make a smooth sauce. Add the sugar, lemon juice and wine. Bring to the boil. Remove from the heat and stir in the egg yolk. Heat through but do not boil.

Put the lamb on a serving-dish and pour over the sauce. Serve with kasha (page 66).

Shashlik *serves 4*

600 g (1½ lb) lamb or mutton off the leg	1 lemon (optional)
1 large onion	1 clove garlic (optional)
1 spring onion (optional)	wine vinegar
	salt and pepper to taste

Cut the meat into small pieces suitable for putting on skewers. Put in a cool place with half the peeled and finely chopped onion and garlic if used. Cover with a mixture of wine vinegar and water in equal parts. Marinate for 2-3 hours. Drain the meat, season and thread on skewers interspersed with the remainder of onion cut into rings. Grill or cook on a spit for 10-15 minutes. If you grill the shashlik they should be turned frequently. Serve on the skewer in the middle of a bed of hot rice. If desired pour over a little melted butter before serving.

The shashlik can be garnished with slices of lemon or chopped spring onion if you wish.

This is a Caucasian dish.

When cutting the meat make small incisions so that the meat does not gather. There are many variations of this dish in the South. For Shashlik à la Karski add lamb's kidneys. These should be skinned first, cut in half and marinated with the meat and then put on skewers as above.

You can use lemon juice in place of the vinegar and water if you wish.

Try with a tart plum sauce, ie tkemaly (page 94) and garnish with tomato quarters.

Ukrainian lamb chops *serves 4*

4 lamb chops
150 g (6 oz) prunes
1 onion
1 teaspoon tomato purée
stock or water
salt and pepper to taste
2 teaspoons sugar
2 teaspoons vinegar
1 clove
pinch of cinnamon
1 teaspoon flour

Dried prunes should be soaked in water overnight. Californian prunes, however, can be cooked immediately.

Fry the chops in a little lamb fat or grill for a few minutes until brown. Put them in a suitable saucepan and add the peeled and chopped onion and the tomato purée. Cover with stock or water and simmer gently with the lid on for about ten minutes. Add the remaining ingredients except the flour. Simmer for a further 30 minutes or until both the chops and prunes are tender. Remove the chops and prunes and keep these warm. Thicken the liquid in the saucepan with a teaspoon of flour mixed with a little water. Simmer for a few minutes stirring all the time. Serve with the chops and prunes.

This is a very unusual combination and extremely good. Serve with boiled rice only.

Uzbeck Plov *(lamb and rice)* *serves 4*

400 g (1 lb) lamb
oil or butter for frying
1 large onion
400 g (1 lb) carrots
300 g (12 oz) 2 cups rice
750 ml (1½ pt) 3¾ cups water
salt to taste
4 peppercorns
chopped parsley

Heat the butter or oil in a fairly large saucepan. Add the peeled and chopped onion and fry till golden brown. Cut the meat into small pieces and add to the onion and brown lightly. Add the peeled and finely chopped carrots and stew for about 30 minutes until tender, stirring frequently. Wash the rice several times in cold water. Add to the meat together with 750 ml (1½ pt) 3¾ cups water, the salt and peppercorns. Cover and cook slowly for about 15 minutes until the rice has absorbed all the water. Garnish with chopped parsley.

Plov is mainly eaten in South Russia where there is a great deal of lamb and it is more popular than beef. There are many recipes, some made with fowl, eggs or with dried fruit, nuts or vegetables. This dish really requires no accompaniment unless you would like green salad on a side plate. Do *not* put it on the same dish as the plov: the lamb will go cold and greasy and you will wonder what you are eating!

Turkmenian pilaf *serves 4*

600 g (1½ lb) leg of lamb (or chicken or veal)
100 g (4 oz) prunes
1 tablespoon sultanas
½ lemon
200 g (8 oz) 1⅓ cups rice
500 ml (1 pt) 2½ cups stock or water
1 onion
50 g (2 oz) 4 tablespoons butter
4 peppercorns

Cover the dried fruit with boiling water. Add the lemon and leave to stand while the lamb is cooking. Wash the rice several times in cold water, cover with boiling water and leave to stand. Salt the lamb and cut it into small pieces. Peel and chop the onion and fry it lightly in butter. Add the lamb and brown lightly. Cover with stock or water, add the peppercorns and simmer with the lid on for 20 minutes. Strain the rice and pour cold water through. Add to the meat together with the strained prunes and sultanas. Pour in enough stock or water to cover and adjust seasoning. Cook slowly with the lid on until the rice has absorbed all the stock. It should take about 20 minutes in a saucepan or 30 minutes in a casserole 180°C (350°F) Mark 4.

This dish requires no accompaniment. It is good for a dinner party since you can put it in the oven and forget about it whilst you are dressing. You can also make it from left-over bits of lamb, chicken or veal.

Braised shoulder of veal *serves 4-5*

1 kg (2 lb) shoulder of veal
salt to taste
1 clove garlic
sprig rosemary
oil for cooking
1 onion
125 ml (¼ pt) ⅔ cup dry white wine
125 ml (¼ pt) ⅔ cup water

Ask the butcher to bone half a shoulder of veal. Salt and rub with garlic. Sprinkle with a little rosemary. Roll and tie with string. Peel the onion but do not slice. Put the veal and onion in a saucepan with the oil and brown meat all over. After half an hour pour off the excess fat and add the wine and water. Cover and simmer for a further hour or until ready, basting frequently. This may be eaten hot or cold. If it is to be served cold, put the meat into a serving-dish, pour the gravy over and leave to set into a jelly.

This is a good dish if you cannot afford a leg of veal or want a change. Excellent with salad. Try chicory and fruit salad with this or celery and pineapple. Remember when choosing veal that milk fed veal is best. It is a pale pink colour almost white. Do not choose the darker veal which is almost red. This comes from older animals fed on grain. Veal that looks blown up is the result of excessive bleeding to lighten the colour.

Solanka
(sauerkraut and meat) *serves 4-5*

1 onion
400-600 g (1-1½ lb) sauerkraut
50 g (2 oz) 4 tablespoons butter
2 peppercorns
1 bayleaf
salt to taste
½ teaspoon sugar (optional)
400 g (1 lb) cooked ham or cooked pork
100 g (4 oz) 6 slices garlic sausage

If the sauerkraut is very sour run cold water through and squeeze out the excess liquid. Chop the onion and fry it lightly in butter. Add the sauerkraut, cover and cook over a very low heat for about half an hour or until tender. Stir frequently, adding a little bouillon or water if it gets too dry. When the sauerkraut is cooked add the peppercorns, bayleaf, salt and sugar. Chop the cooked meats into small pieces and add to the saucepan. Simmer for a further 10 minutes and serve.

This is a good dish to make with left-overs. You can add old bits of tongue if you have any or chicken. Serve with boiled potatoes only.

Stuffed belly of pork *serves 6*

1.2 kg (3 lb) belly of pork
salt to taste
1 onion
3 tablespoons water

STUFFING
400 g (1 lb) sauerkraut
1 large cooking apple
25 g (1 oz) 2 tablespoons butter

Ask the butcher to remove the bones from the pork. Salt it.

STUFFING
Pour cold water over the sauerkraut and squeeze out the excess liquid. Peel and chop the apples finely. Mix the sauerkraut and apples with 25 g (1 oz) 2 tablespoons melted butter.

Stuff the pork with this mixture and sew up with thread. Put into a meat-tin with the chopped onion. Brown in a hot oven 250°C (500°F) Mark 10 and add three tablespoons of water for basting. Reduce heat and cook for another hour and a half at 180°C (350°F) Mark 4 or until tender.

This is a very economical dish and extremely tasty. Serve with roast potatoes. Put the potatoes in soon after the meat. Skim off the fat during cooking if you feel that there is too much, otherwise the potatoes will become soggy.

Ham with prunes or cherries *serves 8*

1.2 kg (3 lb) leg of ham
125 ml (¼ pt) ⅔ cup wine
125 ml (¼ pt) ⅔ cup wine vinegar
375 ml (¾ pt) 2 cups water
4 bayleaves
black pepper

SAUCE
200 g (8 oz) prunes or morello cherries
4-5 lumps sugar
¼ teaspoon cinnamon
¼ french loaf
knob of butter

Remove the skin from the ham. If the ham is too salty, soak it for a few hours in water. Put it in a saucepan and add the wine, wine vinegar, water, bayleaves and pepper. Cover and simmer till cooked, 20 minutes to each pound and 20 minutes over.

SAUCE
Meanwhile, cover the prunes or cherries with water and cook with the sugar and cinnamon till tender. Grate the french loaf, having removed the crusts, and fry in butter. Sieve the prunes or cherries, add the fried breadcrumbs and dilute with juice from the ham.

Pour the sauce over the ham and serve.

This can equally well be made from slices of gammon which are sold loose. Allow one thick slice per head. If you use the joint, however, any left-overs can of course be eaten cold with salad. There are many recipes in this book. My choice is potato salad (page 83) pineapple and celery (page 84) or chicory and fruit salad (page 84).

Small pieces left-over can be minced and made into sandwiches. If you have not less than 200 g (8 oz) left over make it into a ham pâté. Mince the ham including the fat. This is important because it gives flavour to the pâté. Add 1 tablespoon flour or breadcrumbs, 1 minced onion, 2 pepper-corns, 1 juniper berry, 1 raw egg, and a little water. Mix all the ingredients thoroughly and put into a pâté dish, cover and cook for about 30 minutes at 180°C (350°F) Mark 4. A pâté dish is a fireproof dish with a little hole in the lid to let the steam out. Ham pâté can be eaten hot or cold with salad or on open sandwiches. Good with drinks.

Deep fried lamb dumplings *serves 4-6*

To make 40 dumplings

40 g (1½ oz) 3 tablespoons butter
300 g (¾ lb) finely minced lean lamb (from leg)
3 tablespoons finely chopped parsley
1 egg
1 tablespoon finely chopped fresh coriander
1½ teaspoons salt
2½ tablespoons cold boiled rice
vegetable oil for deep frying

DOUGH
3 eggs
225 g (8 oz) 1¾ cups plain flour
180 ml ($\frac{3}{8}$ pt) 1 cup water
1 teaspoon salt

Melt the butter in 1 tablespoon of vegetable oil in a large frying pan. When it begins to brown add the meat. Cook 6 minutes, stirring all the time with a fork till it is light brown. Put in mixing bowl and add chopped parsley, coriander, salt and rice. Mix well. Leave to cool. Roll out pelmeni dough on a lightly floured board until 3 mm (1/8 in.) thick. Spread it out until almost paper thin. Use 65 mm (2½ in.) pastry cutter to cut out 80 rounds. Top half of the rounds with 1½ teaspoons of filling and flatten slightly. Moisten edges with beaten egg, using a pastry brush to make sure they stick. Seal edges well. Heat vegetable oil to boiling point, add the dumplings 6 at a time for 3 minutes until evenly browned. Do the same to the remainder only putting in 6 at a time into the pan. Drain on kitchen paper and serve as a separate course.

Only use lean lamb. This can be the basis of a main meal or as a hot zakuska for more people.

Ox kidney with cucumbers *serves 4*

400 g (1 lb) ox kidney
4 medium potatoes
1 onion
3 salted cucumbers
1 tablespoon flour
50 g (2 oz) 4 tablespoons butter
1 bayleaf
5 peppercorns
1 sprig of parsley

Soak the kidney in tepid salt water for 15 minutes. Wash well, skin if necessary. Remove the core and any fat. Put into a saucepan. Cover with water and simmer with salt and pepper for about 1 hour with lid on.

Melt the butter and combine with the flour. Add 1½ cups of the kidney stock slowly to form a smooth sauce, stirring all the time. Cook through.

Peel the onion and slice. Peel the potatoes and cut into cubes. Slice the kidney and fry together with the onion and potatoes till lightly brown. Slice the cucumbers.

Combine all ingredients in a saucepan, pour over the sauce and cook for a further hour with the lid on or till the kidneys are done. Add bayleaf towards the end of cooking. Transfer to dish and garnish with chopped parsley.

This can also be done with pigs kidneys but do not boil before frying.

Stewed lamb Steppe style *serves 4*

600 g (1½ lb) loin neck or breast of lamb
2 tablespoons rye flour
1½ tablespoons butter
2 onions
3 carrots
1 stalk parsley
pinch of ginger
1 stick celery
1 parsnip
½ teaspoon caraway seeds
2 peppercorns
1 bayleaf
6 cloves
salt to taste

Cut the lamb into portions suitable for serving.

Heat the butter in a frying pan and fry the lamb dredged in flour till light brown. Salt. Peel the onion, carrots, and parsnip. Slice. Clean the celery and cut into small pieces. Mix all the vegetables with the pepper, bayleaf, cloves, pinch of ginger and caraway seeds.

Put a layer of vegetables at the bottom of a casserole dish, cover with the lamb then a layer of vegetables and so on till the lamb and vegetables are used up.

Add stock to cover the meat. Cover with lid. Cook in an oven for 1½-2 hours at 180°C (350°F) Mark 4.

This can also be done in a saucepan on top of the stove. Serve with fried potatoes. Use 4 medium potatoes for this quantity. Dill pickle also goes well with this dish.

Boiled pork with beer

serves 4

600 g (1½ lb) pork from the leg
2½ tablespoons oil
1 carrot
1 sprig parsley
1 onion
4 peppercorns
1 bay leaf
1 tablespoon butter
375 ml (¾ pt) 2 cups ale or light ale
1 sprig of mint
salt to taste

Brown the pork in a frying pan, salt and put into a saucepan with the beer. Peel the carrot and onion and add to the pork together with the parsley. Also the peppercorns, bayleaf and 1 sprig of mint. Cook slowly under a lid for about 30 minutes.

Remove the pork from the saucepan and cut into serving pieces. Strain the stock and bring to boiling point adding 1 tablespoon butter.

Serve with boiled potatoes and chestnut purée and the sauce from the pork.

Braised pork chops with garlic

serves 4

4 pork chops
6 rashers salted streaky bacon
2 onions
salt and pepper to taste
1 tablespoon chopped parsley
2 cloves of garlic
375 ml (¾ pt) 2 cups stock
4 salted cucumbers
4 slices bread

Sprinkle the chops with salt and pepper and brown in a frying pan in oil. Remove the rind from the bacon and put at the bottom of a casserole dish. Place the browned chops on top. Peel the onions and slice. Fry in oil till lightly brown. Put on top of the chops. Pour in the stock and simmer under a lid for 30 minutes at 180°C (350°F) Mark 4. Peel the garlic and chop finely. Combine with the parsley.

Remove crusts from bread and toast for a few minutes before serving. Place the chops on the toast together with any juices in the pan. Garnish with the chopped garlic and parsley. Serve with potatoes and cucumbers.

The cucumbers can be sliced and put on separate little dishes or on the same plate as the chops.

Macaroni and beef pie

serves 3

200 g (8 oz) macaroni
200 g (8 oz) 1 cup minced/ground beef
2 tablespoons dry breadcrumbs
1 tablespoon butter
1 onion
pepper

Cook the macaroni in boiling salted water till just done, about 15-20 minutes. Strain. Peel and chop the onion and fry in butter. Add the minced meat, salt and pepper and cook together slowly for 15 minutes. Add a little of the water from the macaroni if it gets dry.

Butter a baking dish. Remove the mince from the stove and add to the macaroni together with the egg. Put into the dish, sprinkle with breadcrumbs and dot with butter. Bake in the oven at 180°C (350°F) Mark 4 for 20-30 minutes or till it browns on top.

This is usually made from left-over meat either boiled meat from the soup or the left-over joint. It is a good supper dish. Serve with a green salad or some vegetables such as sprouts.

Stuffed veal

serves 6

1 kg (2½ lb) shoulder of veal
2 tablespoons fat
4 hard boiled eggs
3 rashers salted streaky bacon
50 g (2 oz) 3 slices ham
4 cloves of garlic
1 tablespoon flour
salt and pepper to taste
1 tablespoon chopped parsley

Ask the butcher to bone the veal. Wash and flatten

with a rolling pin. Salt and pepper. Cut rind off streaky bacon and cut ham into strips. Peel the eggs and quarter. Place strips of bacon, ham and quartered hard boiled eggs in shoulder cavity.

Roll the meat up. Tie with string. Rub with garlic and dust with flour. Brown the roll on all sides in a large saucepan or frying pan and put into a large casserole. Add a little water to cover. Cook at 180°C (350°F) Mark 4 for 1½-2 hours. When serving remove the string and slice.

Serve with sprouts and mashed potatoes garnished with parsley.

Stew with tomato purée or sour cream

serves 4

600 g (1½ lb) stewing steak
25 g (1 oz) 2 tablespoons fat
4 medium potatoes
3 medium carrots
1 small turnip or swede
1 onion
1 tablespoon tomato purée or sour cream
1 tablespoon flour
1 bayleaf
salt and pepper
2 cloves
cinnamon
4 mint leaves

Cut the meat into portions and beat a little with a rolling pin. Peel the onion, carrots, turnip and potatoes. Slice the onion and carrots. Cut the turnips into cubes and cut the potatoes in half.

Fry the meat together with the onion till slightly brown. Put into a saucepan. Add a little water to the frying pan and stir. Transfer the gravy to the saucepan. Add the salt, pepper, 2 cloves, a pinch of cinnamon, 4 mint leaves, the tomato and the vegetables. Cover with lid and cook slowly for 2½ hours or till the meat is tender. Add a little stock towards the end of cooking if necessary and 1 bayleaf. Transfer to dish and serve.

Dried mint can be used for this recipe when fresh is not available.

Spiced meat casserole

serves 4

600 g (1½ lb) chuck steak
6 peppercorns
6 cloves
salt to taste
4 tablespoons dry breadcrumbs
25 g (1 oz) 2 tablespoons oil or butter
4 medium potatoes (optional)
½ small french loaf (stale)
milk
2 small eggs or 1 large
1 large onion

Oil or butter a casserole and sprinkle with dry breadcrumbs. Beat the meat with a rolling pin on a board. Cut into small pieces. Peel and chop onion. Crush peppercorns and cloves with rolling pin.

Put half the onion at the bottom of the dish. Cover with half the beef. Sprinkle with half the cloves, salt and pepper. Peel, wash and slice the potatoes and cover the meat. Add another layer of meat and sprinkle with the remainder of the cloves, pepper and salt. Cover with lid and put into the oven for 2 hours at 180°C (350°) Mark 4. Meanwhile cut crusts off bread and grate on coarse grater. Beat the egg and add a little milk. Blend ingredients with the addition of salt and set aside. The bread mixture should be moist but not too wet. An hour before serving remove lid and spread the bread and milk mixture over the meat. Sprinkle with dry crumbs, dot with butter and leave for a further hour to brown.

Serve with sprouts, carrots, etc, or with a green salad if you are slimming.

The amount of topping for this will depend on the size of the dish. You have to use your judgement for this. The bread mixture should be about 15 mm (½ in.) thick. Add a little more breadcrumbs and milk if you think it is not enough. It will rise in the oven. You can of course use a cheaper cut of meat. Allow an extra half an hour for cooking if you do this.

Chanakhi *(Caucasian lamb stew)*

serves 3-4

600 g (1½ lb) stewing lamb
6 medium potatoes
salt and pepper to taste
1 aubergine (egg plant)
3 medium tomatoes
200 g (8 oz) string beans
parsley
1 onion

Cut the lamb into pieces allowing 2-3 pieces per head. Put into fireproof dish or saucepan. Add the peeled and chopped onion. Skin the tomatoes, quarter, cut the ends of the aubergine and cut into cubes. Cut ends off string beans and break in half, peel and wash the potatoes, chop parsley and add all these to the stew. Salt and pepper and cover with water. Put lid on and cook for 1½-2 hours at 180°C (350°) Mark 4.

Serve in the casserole if you are using one.

If you do not like the bitter taste of the aubergine, slice the aubergine and salt. Leave for half an hour and then drain off the liquid.

This is best eaten in the summer when both aubergines and beans are in season, ie September.

Pork with prunes

serves 3-4

600 g (1½ lb) hand of pork or spare ribs
25 g (1 oz) ½ cup stale breadcrumbs
1½ tablespoons sugar
1 dessertspoon vinegar
1 bayleaf
oil for frying
100 g (4 oz) prunes
pinch of cinnamon
3 juniper berries
5 peppercorns
1 wineglass white wine
1 teaspoon salt
165 ml ($\frac{1}{3}$ pt) ¾ cup water to boil prunes
lemon juice

Soak the prunes overnight. Cut pork into portions and fry on both sides till golden. Add water to cover with the wine, bayleaf, peppercorns, juniper berries and a pinch of cinnamon and salt. Cover with lid and cook slowly for 1 hour or till ready.

Meanwhile cook the prunes till tender in sugar and a little water. Adding a little lemon juice during cooking. This improves the flavour. When quite tender put through a sieve. Add a little salt. Grate the breadcrumbs and combine the prunes and crumbs. Test for flavour. It should be sweet-sour. When the pork is ready strain the liquid and add the gravy gradually to the prunes to form a thick sauce. Serve the pork with the prune sauce poured over with boiled or mashed potatoes only.

Other types of pork may be used for this dish but this will of course alter the cooking time. It is best however, to use the cheaper cuts as this improves the flavour and you have a cheap and economical meal.

Sucking pig *(not more than 3 weeks old)*

serves 9-10

1 sucking pig
Butter or oil for cooking
salt to taste
125 ml (¼ pt) $\frac{2}{3}$ cup sour cream
1 onion
1 pig's liver

GARNISH
1 small orange
1 bunch watercress

STUFFING
400 g (1 lb) 2 cups cooked kasha (buckwheat)

Wash the sucking pig in cold water. Put it into boiling water for two or three minutes. Take out and with a knife shave off the bristles being careful not to damage the skin. Slit with a sharp knife down the belly and remove entrails. Wash and dry thoroughly with dry towel. Salt the inside.

STUFFING

Take two cooked cups of kasha (buckwheat see page 66) which should be prepared in advance. Peel and chop onion finely. Wash the liver and soak in water. Lightly fry the onion and the liver. Chop the liver finely. Mix all the ingredients and stuff the pig with this. Sew up with thick thread.

Put pig on a sheet with the belly downwards. Brush with sour cream and pour over a little oil or melted butter. Pour 125 ml (¼ pt) $\frac{2}{3}$cup water into the tin where the pig is cooking for gravy as there is plenty of fat. Cook for about 1 hour, ie 25 minutes per 400 g (1 lb) and 25 minutes over at 180°C (350°F) Mark 4. Baste frequently during cooking. Wash and trim the watercress.

Before serving cut off the head and split pig down centre back on a wooden board. Lay the two halves on a warm plate with head at one end. Put a small orange in the mouth. Decorate the dish with the prepared watercress.

Serve with apple sauce (page 95), horseradish sauce (page 91), roast or boiled potatoes and any vegetable you fancy for pork. Serve sauce separately.

Sucking pig is a delicate and tender flavour. Have on festive occasions such as anniversaries. Often eaten at Christmas in Russia. Follow with a fruit compôte.

Hunter's steak

serves 4-6

800-1 kg (2-2½ lb) rump steak
3 eggs
100 g (4 oz) boiled ham
salt and pepper to taste
bacon fat or streaky bacon
oil or butter for frying
1 tablespoon milk
2 spring onions

Break the eggs into a bowl. Add salt and pepper and the milk. Whisk. Heat a large frying pan. Add oil and the ham cut into small pieces. Heat through. Pour the omelette mixture into the pan when it is quite hot and sizzling. Reduce heat till the omelette sets. Set aside. Put the steak on a wooden board and beat with a rolling pin to flatten. Sprinkle with salt and pepper. Carefully remove the omelette and cover the steak. Roll up as for swiss roll. Tie with string. Wrap with bacon fat and put into a hot oven for approximately 20 minutes at 230°C (450°F) Mark 8. If you decide the steak is ready earlier take out immediately or the meat will be overcooked. Carve into slices and garnish with chopped spring onion. Serve with horseradish sauce.

This is not easy to do. If the meat is too thin it will be hard and if overcooked the same thing will happen. Can also be eaten cold on buttered bread like an open sandwich. Excellent for a super picnic lunch. Hence the name Hunter's steak. Serve with potatoes and green peas if hot.

Tongue with raisins

serves 6-8

1 ox tongue 800g-2kg (4½ lb)	1 sprig parsley
1 carrot	1 bayleaf
1 small turnip	1 tablespoon flour
1 onion	½ lemon
2 tablespoons butter	salt and pepper to taste
250 ml (½ pt) 1¼ cups stock	2 tomatoes
100 g (4 oz) ⅔ cup raisins	

Wash the tongue thoroughly. Soak for 2 hours in cold water. If the tongue is hard and dry soak for a further 10 hours. If pickled soak for 3 to 4 hours.

When ready put the tongue in a large saucepan, add the cleaned and washed vegetables which should be cut into fairly large pieces. Add salt and pepper, bayleaf and parsley. Cover the tongue with hot water so the level of the water is 25 mm (1 in.) above the level of the ingredients. Boil through and skim off any scum which forms. Cover with lid and cook slowly for 30 minutes per 400 g (1 lb) and 30 minutes over.

When ready plunge into cold water and remove the skin. Place the tongue on warmed dish and keep warm. Meanwhile make the sauce thus:– Melt 1 tablespoon butter and mix with 1 tablespoon flour gradually dilute with all of the tongue stock. Bring to the boil stirring all the time. Add the washed raisins and simmer for a further 5-10 minutes. Remove from heat, add lemon juice, 1 tablespoon butter and additional salt and pepper if necessary.

Do not re-heat but stir to blend the ingredients. Pour the sauce over the tongue and garnish with halved tomatoes and green peas. Serve with mashed potatoes and green peas.

This can also be done with pig's tongue. Allow 1 per head. The stock is a good foundation for a nourishing soup. If too salty add a few whole potatoes 20 minutes before the end of cooking and serve with the tongues. Any left-over tongue can of course be eaten cold with potato salad or green salad, beetroot salad or tomato salad (see Salads pages 81-87).

If you decide to have just potatoes either as a salad or hot when eating the cold tongue, try the salad dressing (page 92) called egg and caper dressing. This is quite original if poured over the cold tongue and eaten, as in French family restaurants. Any left-over scraps can be put into an okroshka (page 22), cold soup or solanka (page 29).

Poultry and game

Kiev cutlets

serves 2

1 roasting chicken (about 1.4 kg (3¾ lb) drawn)
100 g (4 oz) ½ cup butter
dry breadcrumbs
salt to taste
butter or oil for frying
1 egg
½ lemon

Wash and dry the prepared chicken. Using a very sharp knife, cut away each breast and remove the skin. Make a slit in the middle of each breast and stuff it with the butter, which should be very hard, otherwise it will trickle out during cooking. Fold the flesh over the butter to resemble a tube. Coat in seasoned breadcrumbs, dip in beaten egg and coat in breadcrumbs again. Fry in plenty of hot butter or oil for a few minutes on each side. Garnish with slices of lemon.

This can be prepared in advance and put in the fridge to enable the butter to harden before cooking. The rest of the chicken can be minced and used for porjarski cutlets.

This has now become an international dish and served in the best restaurants all over the world. However, it is not nearly as popular in Russia owing to the expense and difficulty in filleting the breast of the chicken. It is a luxury dish which you have when you eat out.

I have tried to simplify this so that the average housewife can still try it. You can, of course, use a larger bird, then you will have a larger breast.

Serve with baked roast potatoes and some green vegetables, or with green salad on a side plate made with a french dressing or oil and wine vinegar or lemon juice.

Porjarski cutlets

serves 4

1 chicken (about 1 kg (2½ lb) drawn)
100 g (4 oz) six slices day-old french bread
milk or cream
salt and pepper to taste
dry breadcrumbs
butter for frying

Wash and dry the prepared bird. Remove the meat from the bones and put it through a mincer. Remove the crusts and soak the bread in milk or cream. Squeeze out the excess liquid. Put the chicken through the mincer a second time with the bread. Add the salt and pepper and mix well by hand. Form into cutlets, coat in breadcrumbs and fry in butter on both sides until cooked (about 15-20 minutes).

Chicken with prunes

serves 4

1 roasting chicken (about 2 kg (5 lb) drawn)
salt and pepper to taste
50 g (2 oz) 4 tablespoons butter
1 carrot
1 stalk celery
1 onion
1 sprig parsley
1 bayleaf
200 g (8 oz) prunes
1 tablespoon lemon juice
1-2 lumps sugar
1 tablespoon flour

Wash and dry the prepared chicken. Joint, season and fry the pieces lightly in butter till brown. Put them in a saucepan with the prepared vegetables, parsley and bayleaf. Add a little water, cover and stew for 45 minutes till cooked. Meanwhile, cook the prunes separately with the lemon juice and sugar in a little water for 30-40 minutes till tender. Make a roux from 2 tablespoons butter and a tablespoon of flour. Gradually stir in the prune juice and enough strained chicken bouillon to make up 250 ml (½ pt) 1¼ cups. Pour the sauce over the chicken and prunes and serve.

This is best eaten with roast or boiled potatoes and needs no other vegetable. Some prunes are moist and require hardly any cooking whilst others need soaking in boiling water till they swell. Make sure that the prunes will be ready at the same time as the chicken.

Stuffed glazed chicken

serves 4-5

1 chicken or capon (about 2 kg (5 lb) drawn)

STUFFING
100 g (4 oz) ½ cup fresh minced veal
2 slices stale french bread
25 g (1 oz) 2 tablespoons butter
black pepper
salt to taste
¼ teaspoon grated nutmeg
1 egg

chicken giblets
2 carrots
1 or 2 sticks celery
1 onion or leek
1 sprig parsley
1 bayleaf
salt to taste
5 peppercorns
1 pig's trotter or gelatine
2 lumps sugar
1 tablespoon wine vinegar or 1 sherry glass dry sherry

GLAZING
1.25 l (2 pt) 5 cups water

Wash and dry the prepared chicken or capon. Cut through the breast bone and remove all the bones. Put the flesh back into the skin of the chicken. Sew up where the skin has been cut. (If you are unable to do this, the chicken can be stuffed and glazed without removing the bones but it must not then, or course, be put under a press when cooked.)

STUFFING
Remove the crusts and soak the bread in water. Squeeze out the excess liquid and mix the bread with the minced veal, melted butter, grated nutmeg, salt and pepper. Put these ingredients through a mincer or coarse sieve. Add the beaten egg and mix well. Stuff the bird with this mixture and sew up.

GLAZING
Wrap the bird in a napkin and put it in a large saucepan in about 1.25 l (2 pt) 5 cups of water. Add the bones, if you have removed them, the giblets, the cleaned vegetables, the salt, peppercorns, bayleaf and parsley and the pig's trotter, if you use one. Cover and simmer for about two hours until tender.

Remove the bird when it is cooked and put it on a plate. If the bones have been removed, cover it with another plate and a 800 g (2 lb) weight and leave for about two hours. Cut the chicken in slices, or joint it if the bones have been left in, and put it in a deep serving dish.

To make the jelly, strain the stock. If a pig's trotter has been used, brown two lumps of sugar and add them to the strained stock. Stir quickly and leave it to cool. If gelatine is used, it should be dissolved in a little water and added to the hot strained liquid. Use 25 g (1 oz) 2 pkts of powdered gelatine per 500 ml (1 pt) 2½ cups of stock. Stir and cool. When the stock has cooled, add the vinegar or sherry. When it starts to gell, pour it over the bird and leave it to set. Any remaining jelly can be chopped and used as garnish.

Serve with mayonnaise (page 91) or mustard sauce (page 91) and Russian salad (page 83).

This is a very complicated recipe and should not be attempted by the amateur cook. I had an aunt in Russia who was an expert at making this dish and was famed in her district as a result.

Try sauerkraut and cranberry salad (page 83) or fruit salad with mayonnaise for a change (page 85).

Chicken livers with Madeira sauce

serves 4

400 g (1 lb) chicken livers
250 ml (½ pt) 1¼ cups milk
flour
butter
2 onions
25 g (1 oz) $\frac{1}{3}$ cup chopped mushrooms
salt and pepper to taste

SAUCE
1 tablespoon flour
25 g (1 oz) 2 tablespoons butter
250 ml (½ pt) 1¼ cups water or stock
1 wineglass madeira

Soak the livers in milk for several hours. This whitens

and distends them. Drain and coat in flour. Peel and chop the onions and mushrooms and fry them lightly in butter. Add the livers and cook slowly for 10 minutes or quickly for 5 minutes. When they are ready, put aside and keep warm.

SAUCE
Make a roux from the butter and flour and gradually add 250 ml (½ pt) 1¼ cups water or stock, stirring to form a smooth sauce. Boil for several minutes, then add the madeira and simmer for 2-3 minutes, stirring continuously.

Salt and pepper the livers and put them in a deep dish with the onions and mushrooms. Pour the sauce over them and serve with rice.

Liver should not be overcooked as it makes it hard, so test by cutting a small piece off. It should remain pink inside.

This dish can also be eaten with mashed potatoes and some other vegetable. Try turnips in cream (page 68) or cauliflower with butter and bread-crumbs (page 67).

Turkey with apples and cherry sauce

serves 8-10

1 turkey 3 kg (8 lb)
(trussed and drawn)
salt to taste
butter
6 medium cooking apples
cherry sauce using 400 g
(1 lb) morello cherries
(page 92)

Wash and dry the prepared turkey. Rub it with salt and brush with melted butter. Put it into a greased baking-tin with a little water in a hot oven 230°C (450°F) Mark 8, turning the oven down to 180°C (350°F) Mark 4 after 15 minutes when the bird starts to brown. Cook for approximately 15 minutes per 400 g (1 lb) and 15 minutes over, basting frequently. Potatoes can be put round the turkey to roast 1¼ hours before it is ready. A little extra butter should be added with the potatoes. Peel and core the apples and place them either inside or round the bird about 45 minutes before serving. Make the cherry sauce while the turkey is cooking. Serve with the apples, roast potatoes and cherry sauce.

Since cherries are only fresh for a short season, canned or frozen cherries can be used for this recipe.

Turkey with liver stuffing

serves 8-10

1 turkey 3 kg (8 lb)
(trussed and drawn)
salt to taste
butter
4 slices streaky bacon

STUFFING
400 g (1 lb) calf's liver
1 turkey liver
½ small day-old french loaf
50 g (2 oz) 4 tablespoons
melted butter
salt, black pepper
125 ml (¼ pt) ⅔ cup milk
2 eggs

STUFFING
Mince the livers. Remove the crusts and grate bread. Mix the breadcrumbs with the livers and add the melted butter, milk, salt, pepper and enough beaten egg to bind.

Wash and dry the prepared turkey and rub it with salt. Stuff it with the above mixture and sew up. Put it into a greased baking-tin, brush with melted butter and cook as in the previous recipe. Serve with roast potatoes and hot red cabbage (page 66).

Cover breast with streaky bacon at the beginning of cooking as it may become dry. Remove when the bacon has dried up to allow the breast to brown. Left-over turkey can be made into a pie. Fry 200 g (8 oz) 2⅔ cups chopped and washed mushrooms with 1 chopped onion. Add 250 ml (½ pt) 1¼ cups white sauce. Mix with the cut up small pieces of turkey. If the sauce is too thick, add some cream. Put into a fireproof dish and cover with short or puff pastry. This makes a filling and delicious way of using left-overs.

Roast goose with sauerkraut and apple sauce

serves 6

1 goose 2.5 kg (6 lb)
(trussed and drawn)
salt to taste
125 ml (¼ pt) ⅔ cup water
apple sauce using 600 g
6 medium apples (page 95)

STUFFING
400 g (1 lb) sauerkraut
1 onion
25 g (1 oz) 2 tablespoons
butter
3 peppercorns (optional)

STUFFING
Pour cold water over the sauerkraut and strain well. Fry the peeled and chopped onion lightly in butter and add with the peppercorns to the sauerkraut. Cover and cook slowly for about half an hour, stirring frequently. Add a little water, if necessary, to prevent it burning.

Wash and dry the prepared goose and rub it with salt. Stuff it with sauerkraut and put it in a large baking-tin. Goose does not usually need any extra fat for cooking but add 125 ml (¼ pt) ⅔ cup of water for basting. Roast as for turkey. Peeled potatoes can be put round the goose to cook 1¼ hours before serving. Serve with roast potatoes and the apple sauce.

Save any goose fat left over. You will find that when making the gravy excess fat has to be skimmed off. This is excellent if used to roast potatoes if you are doing a chicken.

Goose *(stuffed with kasha)*

serves 6

1 goose (trussed and drawn)
1 tablespoon flour
salt to taste
6 medium cooking apples

STUFFING
giblets
500 ml (1 pt) 2½ cups water
1 onion
butter for frying
250 ml (½ pt) 1¼ cups cooked kasha (page 66)
salt and pepper to taste
1 sprig parsley

STUFFING
Simmer giblets for half an hour in 500 ml (1 pt) 2½ cups salted water. Strain and reserve the liquid. Put the giblets through a mincer. Fry the peeled and chopped onion lightly in butter and mix with the giblets, kasha, salt, pepper and chopped parsley. If the stuffing is too dry add a little stock from the giblets.

Wash and dry the prepared goose and rub it with salt. Stuff it with the above mixture and sew up. Put the goose in a baking-tin and add 125 ml (¼ pt) ⅔ cup of stock from the giblets for basting. Put into hot oven 230°C (450°F) Mark 8 and reduce the heat to 180°C (350°F) Mark 4, after 15 minutes when it is fairly brown and crisp. Baste frequently with the stock and cook for approximately 15 minutes per 400 g (1 lb) and 15 minutes over. Peeled potatoes can be put in the tin to roast 1¼ hours before the goose is ready. Core the apples but do not peel them. Arrange them round the bird 45 minutes before serving. Lift out the goose, potatoes and apples when cooked. Pour off the excess fat and thicken the stock with a little flour. Serve the goose with this gravy, the apples, roast potatoes and red cabbage (page 66) and stuffing.

The stuffing makes the goose go further and is quite filling. Geese shrink since they are so fat. You can serve this with kasha since it absorbs the fat from the goose. Roast goose is a great favourite at Christmas.

Roast duck with Madeira sauce

serves 4-5

1 duck about 2 kg (5 lb) drawn and trussed)
salt to taste
2 bayleaves
6 peppercorns
1 sprig parsley
1 stick celery
1 carrot
1 small onion
8 medium potatoes (optional)

SAUCE
1 tablespoon flour
juice of ½ lemon or 1 tablespoon wine vinegar
1 wineglass madeira
250 ml (½ pt) 1¼ cups stock or water

Wash and dry the prepared bird and rub it with salt. Put it into a greased baking-tin together with the bayleaves, peppercorns, chopped parsley and cleaned and chopped celery, carrot and onion. Most ducks are fat and do not need any extra fat. However, if you cook the potatoes round the duck, add some extra butter or lard. Add two tablespoons water for basting. Put into a hot oven 230°C (450°F) Mark 8 and turn down to 180°C (350°F) Mark 4, after 10-15 minutes. Allow 15 minutes per 400 g (1 lb) and 15 minutes over. Baste frequently. When the bird is cooked remove it from the pan and place on a dish to keep warm.

Duck is very good with kasha (page 66). The carcase of the duck with the giblets can be used for stock. Mushroom soup (page 25) and roscolnick are good if made with duck stock (page 21).

SAUCE
Pour off any excess fat and add the flour to the pan. Stir until it thickens, gradually adding 250 ml (½ pt) 1¼ cups stock or water. Bring to the boil and add the lemon juice or wine vinegar. Simmer for a few minutes and add the madeira. Cover and simmer for a few more minutes. Strain and pour over the carved duck.

This duck can be cooked in a large saucepan with a lid. Take some fat bacon and slice thinly. Put at the bottom of the saucepan and the duck on top. Add the vegetables and herbs. Cook slowly under a lid. When the vegetables start to fry add a little stock or water and cook slowly, turning the duck from time to time for 1½ hours.

Veal stuffing for duck

400 g (1 lb) minced veal
1½ tablespoons butter
180 ml ($\frac{3}{8}$ pt) 1 cup milk
salt to taste
1 onion
3 eggs
a little grated nutmeg
10 peppercorns
½ stale vienna loaf

Make an omelette from 2 eggs (page 98). Peel onion, chop and fry lightly in butter. Slice the bread and remove crusts. Soak in milk. Wring out any excess moisture. Put the bread, minced veal, omelette, fried onion and the rest of the butter through the mincer.

Grind the pepper and add together with the grated nutmeg and the salt. Combine all ingredients thoroughly including the remaining raw egg. Stuff the bird. Sew up.

This is recommended as a stuffing for the duck opposite. It will make the bird go further since ducks are not very economical. Eat with roast potatoes and green peas.

Wild duck with mushrooms

serves 4-6

2 wild ducks 800 g - 2 kg (2-5 lb; drawn and trussed)
salt to taste
25-50 g (1-2 oz) 2-4 tablespoons butter (optional)

SAUCE
1 onion
200 g (8 oz) 2$\frac{2}{3}$ cups chopped mushrooms
butter for frying
1 tablespoon flour
salt and pepper to taste

Wash and dry the prepared birds and rub them with salt. Put them in a roasting-tin with a little water and 25-50 g (1-2 oz) 2-4 tablespoons butter, if necessary. Put into a hot oven 230°C (450°F) Mark 8 and turn down to 180°C (350°F) Mark 4, when the ducks are fairly brown and crisp. Baste frequently. Allow 15 minutes per 400 g (1 lb) and 15 minutes over. Prepare the sauce 20 minutes before serving.

SAUCE
Clean and chop the onion and mushrooms and fry them in a little butter until tender. Remove the ducks from the roasting-tin when cooked and put on a dish to keep warm. Thicken the juice in the tin by stirring in a tablespoon of flour. Add the onion, mushrooms, salt and pepper and more water, if required. Simmer for a few minutes.

Pour the sauce over the ducks or serve separately.

Stuffed partridges

serves 6

6 partridges (drawn and trussed)
butter for frying
salt to taste

STUFFING
1 dessertspoon chopped onion
1 small french loaf
milk
400 g (1 lb) minced veal
4 egg yolks
25 g (1 oz) 2 tablespoons butter
salt and pepper to taste
½ teaspoon nutmeg

SAUCE
2 tablespoons flour
juice of lemon

Wash and dry the prepared birds. Rub them with salt and fry for a few minutes in butter in a saucepan, turning them so that they brown on all sides. Remove from the pan.

STUFFING
Fry the chopped onion lightly in butter. Remove the crusts and soak the bread in milk. Squeeze out the excess liquid. Mix the onion and bread with the minced veal, egg yolks, butter, salt, pepper and grated nutmeg. Stuff the birds with this mixture.

Put them back in the saucepan with a little water, cover and cook on a low heat for about 35 minutes or until tender. Joint the birds and keep them warm while you make the sauce.

Serve with kasha (page 66) cucumber in sour cream (page 69), pumpkin in sour cream (page 69). Garnish with pickled grapes or plums (page 149). Choose partridge if you dislike strongly flavoured game. A young partridge will have paler plucked flesh than any other bird and pale yellow-brown feet. They also have long wing feathers which are pointed and not rounded as in older birds. Season: 1 September to 1 February in Britain; about 1 November to 14 February in the US.

SAUCE
Thicken the liquid in the saucepan with 2 tablespoons flour, adding a little more water if necessary. Stir quickly till it boils. Add the lemon juice and pour over the partridges.

Soufflé of game left-overs

serves 4-6

200 g (8 oz) 2 cups boned game left-overs
4 tablespoons grated stale breadcrumbs
3 hard boiled eggs
100 g (4 oz) ½ cup butter
5 eggs (raw)
1 tablespoon dry breadcrumbs
1 tablespoon finely chopped parsley
1 teaspoon salt
1 teaspoon grated lemon rind
¼ teaspoon nutmeg

Remove any sinews and put the meat through the mincer. Add three tablespoons of breadcrumbs. Chop the hard boiled eggs. Rub through a sieve or put through the mincer. Whip the butter till white and add to the meat. Separate the eggs. Blend in the yolks one by one, season with salt and pepper. Add lemon rind and nutmeg. Mix well.

Butter a warmed soufflé dish, sprinkle with dry breadcrumbs mixed with chopped parsley. Whip the whites till they stand in peaks. Fold into the game mixture. Pour into the dish and bake for about 35 minutes at 200°C (400°F) Mark 6.

This is a good supper dish. Eat with mashed potatoes and a second vegetable or a green salad or beetroot salad (page 82).

Woodcock

serves 4

4 woodcocks (drawn and trussed)
salt to taste
125 g (5 oz) ⅔ cup butter
8 slices streaky bacon

STUFFING
100 g (4 oz) 1 cup white breadcrumbs
75 g (3 oz) 6 tablespoons melted butter
salt and pepper to taste
juice of lemon

Take 4 prepared woodcocks. Wash and dry them and rub with salt. Melt 125 g (5 oz) ⅔ cup butter in a saucepan and brown the birds on all sides.

STUFFING
Mix the breadcrumbs with the lemon juice, melted butter and a little salt and pepper. Stuff the birds with this mixture.

Tie two pieces of streaky bacon round the breast of each bird. Put the birds in a baking-tin. Reheat the butter left in the saucepan and pour it over the birds. Put in a hot oven 230°C (450°F) Mark 8, reducing heat to 180°C (350°F) Mark 4 after 10 minutes. Baste frequently and cook for about 30 minutes or until tender. Serve with cherry sauce (page 92) or hot red cabbage (page 66). The birds can also be cooked on a spit.

Roast or boiled potatoes go well with this dish. Garnish with marinated plums or grapes.

Other suggested accompaniments: green salad with sour cream dressing, cucumbers in sour cream on a side plate or pumpkin in sour cream.

Chicken in aspic

serves 4

4 portions of boiling chicken
3 hard boiled eggs
1 onion
1 carrot
250 ml (½ pt) 1¼ cups stock
15 g (½ oz) 2 tablespoons gelatine
1 bayleaf
salt and 3 peppercorns

Wash chicken portions and put into a saucepan. Cover with water. Add salt and peppercorns. Peel the onion and carrot and add to the chicken.

Cover with a lid and allow to simmer for 1½ hours, adding the bay leaf towards the end of cooking. When ready remove from pan. Strain the stock and measure 250 ml (½ pt) 1¼ cups. If not enough add a little water. Check for seasoning. The aspic should be saltier than soup or it has no flavour. Using 15 g (½ oz) gelatine dissolved in a little hot water. Combine with the stock and mix thoroughly.

Shell the eggs. Slice the eggs and carrot. Place at the bottom of a mould to form a pattern. Remove the skin from the chicken pieces and slice. Place on top. Cool the aspic and pour over. Put into a fridge to set.

When serving put the mould into hot water for a few seconds and remove from aspic. Arrange on a bed of dressed salad. Decorate with cucumber and any aspic jelly if left over.

Serve with cold potato salad (page 83), beetroot salad (page 82), cucumber salad (page 81), or fruit salad (page 87).

Chicken soufflé

serves 4

2 chicken breasts (from roasting bird)
25 g (1 oz) 2 tablespoons butter
250 ml (½ pt) 1¼ cups milk
½ vienna loaf
4 eggs
50 g (2 oz) ½ cup cooked shelled prawns
1 teaspoon salt
¼ teaspoon pepper
¼ teaspoon nutmeg
1 tablespoon dry breadcrumbs

Remove the skin from the chicken. Fry lightly in two tablespoons of butter and pass through a mincer. Remove the crusts from the bread and soak in milk, squeeze out lightly. Add the chicken and put through a mincer. Season with salt and pepper. Separate eggs. Add the nutmeg, the prawns and the yolks. Combine well.

Butter a soufflé dish and dust with breadcrumbs.

Whip the whites of the eggs till they stand in

peaks and fold into the mixture. Pour in the chicken mixture and cook in a steamer covered with grease-proof paper for 40-45 minutes. Serve at once with white or tomato sauce (page 90).

Chicken breasts can be bought separately in supermarkets. If you cannot find any cut off the breasts of a 2 kg (5 lb) roasting bird and use the rest another time. Eat with any vegetable. Green peas or carrots in white sauce (page 90) go well with this dish.

Chicken in sour cream

serves 4

1.6 kg (3½ lb) chicken
375 ml (¾ pt) 2 cups sour cream
1 tablespoon dry breadcrumbs
3 tablespoons butter
salt to taste

Cut chicken into 4 portions or buy 4 portions. Brush with melted butter, salt and put into a greased tin to cook in the oven at 200°C (400°F), Mark 6, till almost done, 15-20 minutes. Drain off most of the fat. Sprinkle with breadcrumbs. Pour over the sour cream. Cook covered till done – a further 10 minutes or so. Prick with fork. If no blood is in the juices, it is ready.

Serve with lettuce salad (page 82) and boiled potatoes or mashed and another vegetable.

Chicken stuffed with sardine or salted herring

serves 6

2 kg (5 lb) chicken
5 sardines or 2 salted herring fillets
250 ml (½ pt) 1¼ cups milk
1 teaspoon chopped parsley
2 tablespoons oil for frying
1 tablespoon butter
½ vienna loaf (stale)
1 egg
1 tablespoon grated cheddar cheese
salt to taste

Wash a prepared chicken and dry with towel.

STUFFING WITH SARDINES
Remove tail and bones from sardines and pound in a mortar or crush well with a wooden spoon. Blend with butter. Remove the crusts from the bread and soak in milk. Squeeze out any excess liquid and put through a mincer. Combine the bread, sardines, egg, butter, a little salt, grated cheese and 1 teaspoon chopped parsley

STUFFING WITH SALTED HERRING
Use two herring fillets instead of the sardines and put through a mincer then proceed as above.

Stuff the bird. Season. Brush with oil. Grease a tin and cook for 1½-2 hours or till ready at 200°C (400°F) Mark 6. Baste frequently.

It is usual with a roasting chicken to cook potatoes with it. Peel 8 medium potatoes for the above quantity and add more oil. Eat with a second vegetable. Chestnut purée, sprouts, carrots in white sauce etc. You can also omit the fish in this recipe and use the cheese for flavouring only, but it is more fun with the fish.

Chicken Pie (Koornik)

serves 4

1 kg (2 lb) chicken pieces
4 peppercorns
1 onion
1 sprig parsley
1 carrot
250 ml (½ pt) 1¼ cups sour cream
short pastry using 150 g (6 oz) fat (page 102)
grated nutmeg
150 g (4 oz) ⅔ cup rice
2 hard boiled eggs
100 g (4 oz) 1 cup mushrooms
50 g (2 oz) 4 tablespoons butter
salt and pepper to taste

RICE
Put the rice into cold salted water and cook for 20 minutes or till just tender. Do not overcook. Strain. Pour cold water through to get rid of the starch. Allow to drain thoroughly. Peel and chop the hard boiled eggs. Put the rice back on the stove together with the eggs and a knob of butter to heat through so that the butter melts and the rice does not stick. Add more salt and pepper if necessary. Cool.

Wash the mushrooms and cut into pieces. Fry lightly in butter and add 1 tablespoon sour cream. Cool.

CHICKEN
Put pieces of chicken into a saucepan together with the salt, peppercorns, parsley and the peeled onion and carrot. Cover with water and cook with lid on for 25-30 minutes or till the chicken is tender. Cool. Remove skin and bones from chicken and chop into pieces. Mix with the sour cream and add a little grated nutmeg. Make the pastry (page 102) and put into fridge till needed.

When all the ingredients are ready, ie cold, take a pie dish and roll out three-quarters of the pastry. Line the base and sides of the dish. Put a layer of rice and eggs on the bottom, cover with the chicken and then the mushrooms and finally the remainder of the rice. This will prevent the pastry from getting soggy. Roll out the rest of the pastry and cover the pie. Pinch the edges and make slits in the pastry with a sharp knife to allow the steam to come out. Bake at 220°C (425°F) Mark 7 for 20 minutes or till well browned.

Use the stock from the chicken to make a soup and serve with the pie. Any left-overs can be eaten cold with a green salad for lunch. This can be made from chicken left-overs or boiled meat.

METHOD 2

Use puff pastry and cook the rice in the chicken stock. This will, however, leave you with little stock for soup. Best made from boiled spring chickens and puff pastry.

Poussin with gooseberry sauce

serves 3

3 poussin 400 g (1 lb) each
1 carrot
5 lumps sugar
1 tablespoon flour
1 stick celery
2 tablespoons butter
salt to taste
1 wineglass of white wine (optional)
3 peppercorns
200 g (8 oz) gooseberries

Peel the carrot and put into a saucepan together with the parsley and the prepared chickens. Cover with water. Add salt and peppercorns. Cook slowly under a lid for 45 minutes or till done. Keep warm. Meanwhile pour 2 or 3 cups of the chicken stock (use 2 cups if you are using wine) over the gooseberries which should not be too ripe. Add the sugar, simmer gently for about 5 minutes so that the gooseberries are cooked but do not boil. Melt the butter in a saucepan, blend with the flour and add the hot stock gradually stirring all the time to avoid lumps. Boil through. Mix the gooseberries with the sauce, adding the stock/wine, and then add the chickens. Check seasoning. Simmer for 2-3 minutes more with lid on and serve.

Serve with boiled or mashed potatoes or rice.

Boiled rabbit in white sauce

serves 4

1 young rabbit about 600-800 g (1½-2 lb)
1 carrot
1 onion
bunch of parsley
1 teaspoon salt
1 bayleaf
5-8 peppercorns
milk if neccessary
1 tablespoon butter
1 tablespoon flour

Soak the rabbit for 12 hours in cold salted water. Cut into joints and blanch, ie put into a saucepan with water and bring to the boil. Throw away the liquid. Put back into the saucepan and just cover with water. When the water boils remove scum, lower the temperature so that the water simmers. Add the salt, peppercorns, bayleaf, cleaned carrot and onion. Cover with lid and cook for about 60 minutes or till done.

Add a little milk if the water evaporates too much. When ready lift the rabbit pieces out and put on a dish and keep warm. Chop the parsley finely and strain the liquid in which the rabbit has been boiled. Measure 250 ml (½ pt) 1¼ cups of liquid and make a sauce by melting 1 tablespoon butter and adding 1 tablespoon of flour to make a roux. Then add the hot liquid gradually stirring all the time so that the sauce does not go lumpy. Cook through.

Pour the sauce over the rabbit and garnish with chopped parsley. Serve with boiled potatoes, green peas, carrots or green salad.

The season for rabbit is from September to March. The soaking and blanching of the rabbit removes the strong flavour and whitens the flesh.

Game pâté

serves 6-8

1 wild duck about 600 g (1½ lb) or 2 pigeons
400 g (1 lb) minced belly of pork or sausage meat
grated nutmeg
1 egg
juice of ½ lemon
1 bayleaf (optional)
1 wineglass dry white wine or vodka
6 rashers streaky bacon
salt to taste
6 peppercorns
6 juniper berries
2 slices stale white bread
milk
butter for cooking
1 onion

Half cook the game, ie for about 20 minutes in butter in a medium hot oven at about 200°C (400°F) Mark 6. Save juices. Cool. Remove flesh from the bones and discard skin. Either mince or chop finely.

Peel and chop onion, remove crusts from bread

and soak in milk. Squeeze out lightly and put the belly of pork or sausagemeat, the onion and bread through the mincer.

Add the egg, game with juices, salt, peppercorns, juniper berries, a little grated nutmeg, strained juice of ½ lemon and wine or vodka if you like. Blend all ingredients thoroughly. Line a large pudding basin with half the streaky bacon. Cover with the mixture and finish by laying the streaky bacon on top and the bayleaf if you are using it. Place dish in a tin with water and cook for 1¼-1½ hours at 150°C (300°F) Mark 2.

Smaller quantities of game pâté can of course be made from left-overs or portions of rabbit, hare, etc, which one can buy in supermarkets.

Use the equivalent weight of pork of the uncooked game. Domestic duck is already fat and needs less pork. You can add a little minced veal instead.

Serve the pâté on a bed of lettuce. Garnish with slices of hard boiled egg, wedges of lemon, salted cucumbers cut in quarters or pickled grapes or plums (page 149).

Haunch of venison with sour cream

serves 10-12

1 haunch of venison 2.7-3.6 kg (6-8 lb)
butter or oil for cooking
salt to taste
6 juniper berries
2 bayleaves
6 peppercorns
3 cloves
1 onion
100g (4 oz) larded bacon
500 ml (1 pt) 2½ cups vinegar
1.25 l (2 pt) 5 cups water
250 ml (½ pt) 1¼ cups sour cream

Trim off the haunch, beat it, wash, dry and rub all over with salt and the crushed peppercorns, cloves and juniper berries. Place in a glass dish and sprinkle with bay leaves and chopped onion. Cover with marinade. (Marinade 500 ml (1 pt) 2½ cups vinegar to 1.25 l (2 pts) 5 cups water, bring to the boil and cool.) Leave for 24 hours in a cool place turning the meat from time to time.

Remove from dish and wipe with cloth, make incisions with sharp knife and insert fat bacon into them. Brush with butter or oil. Put into roasting tin and brush with oil or butter and add the remainder of the bacon. Cover with lid. Put into oven at 180°C (350°F) Mark 4. Allow 25 minutes to the 400 g (1 lb). Baste frequently.

Remove the lid 1 hour before taking out and allow the joint to brown. Pour the sour cream over, half an hour before serving. This will form the sauce, and go a pale brown colour.

Slice the venison across the grain. When ready serve on a hot dish with the sauce separately. Make sure the plates are also hot as there is nothing that congeals more rapidly than venison fat.

Accompaniments: mashed or roast potato, hot beetroot (page 68), red cabbage (page 66) or chestnut purée. Serve with either cranberry sauce (page 94) cherry sauce (page 92) or apple sauce (page 95). Any left-over venison can be eaten cold with salad. Try chicory fruit salad (page 84), fruit salad (page 87), beetroot salad (page 82), Russian salad (page 83), potato salad (page 83). You can substitute kvass for marinating or dry red wine if you wish. Also dry cider.

The season for venison is: *Buck* July – September *Doe* October – December.
In the US it is 30 to 90 days from 1 December.

Venison should always be well hung before cooking. The best part of the animal is the haunch, ie leg and loin in one joint. Plenty of creamy white fat is an indication of good quality meat. The buck is considered superior to the doe. Neck and shoulder are usually made into stews and pies.

Hare in sour cream

serves 6-8

1 hare
2 carrots
1 parsnip
500 ml (1 pt) 2½ cups sour cream
250 ml (½ pt) 1¼ cups vinegar
1.25 l (2 pt) 5 cups water
oil for frying
2 onions
1-2 bayleaves
6 peppercorns
salt to taste
bunch of parsley

Cut prepared hare into portions and wash. Put into earthenware dish and cover with marinade.

MARINADE
Take 250 ml (½ pt) 1¼ cups vinegar, 1.25 l (2 pt) 5 cups water, 3 peppercorns and bring to the boil. Cool and cover the hare. Leave for 1½ hours.

After marinating remove the hare and dry with cloth. Put into a large frying pan and add the cleaned chopped carrots, parsnip, onions and butter or oil. Salt. Fry on both sides turning all the time and basting with the juices formed. When ready put into a saucepan. Add the cream to the juices in the frying pan and boil through. Transfer the sour cream sauce to the saucepan and add 3 peppercorns and bayleaves. Cover with lid and cook slowly for a further 30 minutes or till ready.

SECOND METHOD

Use half sour cream and half water when stewing the hare. Thicken the sauce with 1 tablespoon butter and 1 tablespoon flour.

Eat with boiled potatoes and garnish with chopped parsley. Serve with blackcurrant jam, cranberry sauce, or chestnut purée, red cabbage (page 66), hot beetroot (page 68), or beetroot salad or red cabbage salad (page 82) if you prefer a salad.

This recipe is suitable for a young hare only. Older animals need to be cooked longer. If you shoot your hare yourself and do not get it from the butcher. the best season is from September to March. Hang the hare in the skin for at least three days before paunching, longer if possible. It should be skinned two days before it is needed and soaked in marinade before cooking. See previous recipe.

Use dry red wine in place of the vinegar and water for the marinade if you wish.

Roast pigeons

serves 5-6

5-6 pigeons
3 medium onions
500 ml (1 pt) 2½ cups vinegar
1.25 l (2 pt) 5 cups water
150 g (6 oz) ¾ cup butter or oil
1 glass port or madeira
1 stick celery
250 ml (½ pt) 1 cup stock
6 rashers fat bacon
salt to taste
1 bayleaf
2 cloves
1 sprig parsley
1 tablespoon flour
1 carrot
6 peppercorns

Wash trussed pigeons thoroughly and put into large glass dish to marinate overnight.

MARINADE

Clean the carrot and onion and chop finely. Wash and chop the celery, add the milled peppercorns, bayleaf, cloves, 1.25 l (2 pt) 5 cups water and 500 ml (1 pt) 2½ cups vinegar, salt and boil thoroughly. Cool.

When cold pour the marinade over the pigeons and cover. Leave overnight. Take out next day and dry with a towel, inside and out. Put a piece of fat bacon inside each bird. Place in large saucepan with 150 g (6 oz) ¾ cup butter or oil and fry. Cover with lid and fry slowly for 1 hour turning the birds frequently. When cooked remove from pan and make the following sauce:

Using 2 tablespoons of fat from the pan sprinkle in 1 tablespoon flour, blend with wooden spoon and add 250 ml (½ pt) 1¼ cups stock and 1 glass port or madeira. The stock can be made from the juices left in the saucepan after the pigeons are cooked. Just add water and boil through, after removing excess fat.

Young pigeons do not need marinating. Just roast in saucepan in butter for about 30 minutes.

Pigeons should be eaten fresh, ie 12-24 hours after killing. If you use the marinade substitute dry red wine if you like. Serve with mashed potatoes and cucumber salad with sour cream (page 81).

Any left over can be made into game pancakes. Put the flesh through a mincer, moisten with any left-over sauce or sour cream and add a few fried and chopped mushrooms instead of mincemeat. See page 108 for pancakes.

Stuffed pigeons

serves 5-6

5-6 pigeons
1 small french loaf
milk or stock
salt to taste
2 eggs
oil for cooking or 150 g (6 oz) ¾ cup butter
1 tablespoon melted butter
25-50 g (1-2 oz) 3-6 tablespoons currants
grated nutmeg

Wash trussed pigeons and dry with towel. Stuff with the following stuffing:

Take one small stale french loaf, remove crusts and soak in milk or stock. Squeeze out excess liquid and add 2 beaten eggs, 1 tablespoon melted butter, the currants and a little grated nutmeg and salt. Mix thoroughly. Salt the inside of the birds, stuff and tie with string. Place on a greased baking sheet, dot with butter or brush with oil.

Roast the birds at 180°C (350°F) Mark 4, for 20-30 minutes till tender. Baste frequently. Serve with the juices left in the pan after cooking.

Accompaniments: mashed potatoes and fresh cucumber salad (page 81).

Care should be taken to dry the inside of the birds with a dry towel or the stuffing will be wet. Only young birds are suitable for roasting.

Red sauce with wine

125 ml (¼ pt) ⅔ cup light french white wine
juice of ½ lemon
1-2 teaspoons sugar
2 tablespoons breadcrumbs

Pour off the fat from the bird when ready, into a

saucepan. Bring to the boil and add 2 tablespoons stale breadcrumbs, fry lightly. Add the white wine, lemon juice and the juices left in the pan. Also 1 teaspoon sugar or more if necessary, also a bouillon cube to the sauce if you wish, stir well, check for seasoning. Boil through and serve.
Suitable for turkey or cotletti.

Turkey stuffed with rice and currants

STUFFING
150 g (6 oz) 1 cup carolina rice
2 tablespoons butter
a little stock
2 tablespoons currants
2 eggs (optional)
a little grated nutmeg
salt and pepper to taste

Put the rice into a saucepan and cover with water so that there is 1 finger more water above the rice. Boil till half ready, about 10 minutes, stirring frequently. Transfer into a colander and pour over cold water. Allow to drain. Return to saucepan. Add 2 tablespoons butter, a little stock, cook under a lid slowly for a further 10 minutes. Add the currants, salt and pepper, grated nutmeg and eggs if liked. Combine all ingredients thoroughly. Stuff the bird with this stuffing.

For cooking turkey (page 55).

This makes a change from the traditional stuffing and is cheaper than the other stuffings in this book.

Turkey with walnut and kidney stuffing

STUFFING
100 g (4 oz) 1 cup shelled walnuts
400 g (1 lb) veal kidneys
3 tablespoons butter
½ stale vienna loaf
2 eggs
salt and pepper to taste

Put the walnuts into a bowl and pour over boiling water to cover. Allow to stand till the skins come off easily. Remove skins. Skin the kidneys and split lengthwise without quite separating the two parts. Remove the cores and then soak in cold water for 5 minutes. Melt 1 tablespoon of butter and fry the kidneys lightly. Put the kidneys and the nuts twice through the mincer. Remove crusts from bread and soak in milk. Wring out excess moisture and mix with the nuts and kidneys. Add the eggs and the remainder of the butter. Season with salt and pepper. Combine all ingredients. Stuff the turkey.

This turkey with walnut and kidney stuffing should be eaten with the red sauce with wine (page 62).

Vegetables

Potato cutlets

serves 6

8 medium potatoes
salt and pepper to taste
3 eggs
25 g (1 oz) 2 tablespoons butter
40 g (1½ oz) $\frac{1}{3}$ cup flour
dry breadcrumbs
butter or oil for frying
1 sprig parsley
500 ml (1 pt) 2½ cups mushroom sauce (page 90)

Wash the potatoes and boil them in their skins in salted water until ready. Peel them and put through a sieve. Mash with the butter. Add two beaten eggs, flour, salt and pepper and form into rissoles. Dip in beaten egg, coat in breadcrumbs and fry for a few minutes on each side. Garnish with parsley and serve with mushroom sauce.

This is a favourite dish in Lent. Can be eaten as a main dish with a side plate of salad. Choose either a green salad or Caucasian salad.

Also can be served with grilled chops.

Potatoes with mushroom sauce

serves 6

12 medium potatoes
salt to taste
1 sprig parsley

SAUCE
300 g (12 oz) 3 cups chopped mushrooms
1 onion
2 tablespoons butter
1 teaspoon flour
500 ml (1 pt) 2½ cups fresh or sour cream

SAUCE
Clean and chop the mushrooms. Peel the onion and chop finely. Fry the mushrooms and onion in butter for about 20 minutes. Season. Stir in the flour, cook for a few minutes and add the cream.

Meanwhile, wash the potatoes and boil them in their skins in salted water until they are cooked. They should be ready at the same time as the sauce. Peel and slice. Pour the sauce over the potatoes and garnish with chopped dill or parsley.

Potatoes done this way go well with cotletti (page 41). They can be either beef, pork, veal or a mixture of pork and veal.

Also good with fried fish, preferably white.

Potatoes with sour cream

serves 4

6 medium potatoes
salt and pepper to taste
25 g (1 oz) 2 tablespoons butter
165 ml ($\frac{1}{3}$ pt) ¾ cup sour cream
25 g (1 oz) ¼ cup grated cheese (optional)
1 sprig parsley

Peel the potatoes and boil them in salted water until they are cooked. Strain and slice them and arrange them in layers in a buttered fireproof dish. Add salt and pepper to the sour cream and pour it over the potatoes. Dot with butter and sprinkle with grated cheese. Bake in a fairly hot oven 200°C (400°F) Mark 6 for about 20 minutes or until brown. Garnish with chopped parsley before serving.

Potatoes done this way go well with cold roast beef or cotletti (page 41) or boiled white fish.

Potatoes with sour cream (2) *serves 6*

8 medium new potatoes
salt to taste
125 ml (¼ pt) ⅔ cup sour cream
1 sprig dill

Wash the potatoes and boil them in salted water until cooked. Peel. Strain off any excess water and return them to the saucepan. Add the sour cream. Warm through and serve garnished with chopped dill.

Potatoes done this way go well with any roast meat, chicken, boiled or fried white fish. It is a very delicious way of cooking the humble potato even though a bit fattening.

Kasha *(Buckwheat)*

Kasha is part of the staple Russian diet and when well cooked is a delicious accompaniment to lamb, pork or goose. It is traditionally served with borshch and shchi.

Use two parts water to one part kasha when cooking. The kasha will increase in bulk like rice when cooked. Pick over the kasha to remove any husks and cook in one of the following ways:

(1) Roast the kasha in a frying-pan without fat, stirring all the time with a wooden spoon until it starts to pop. Transfer to a fireproof dish, allowing plenty of space for the kasha to increase in bulk. Add boiling water and salt. Put plenty of butter on top as this will soak in. Cover with a lid and bake in a moderate oven 180°C (350°F) Mark 4 for 40-45 minutes. Dark hard grains will form on top. Serve with plenty of butter.

(2) Roast the kasha in a frying-pan as above. Add the boiling water and salt and cook in a double saucepan on top of the stove for about 45 minutes.

(3) Use 1½ times water to volume of buckwheat. This makes the grains separate. However, this is a matter of taste. This type of kasha is better if used for stuffing or heated up with milk for breakfast.

Kasha also means pudding in Russia. Any type of milk pudding, whether rice, sago, or semolina, is also called kasha. It is very popular in Russia and often takes the place of potatoes.

Sauerkraut *serves 6*

800 g (2 lb) sauerkraut
100 g (4 oz) ½ cup butter
4 medium cooking apples
strawberry or apple juice (optional)

If the sauerkraut is very sour pour cold water over it and squeeze out the excess liquid. Melt the butter in a saucepan and add the sauerkraut and the peeled, cored and chopped apples. Cover and simmer for 30-40 minutes, stirring frequently. A little strawberry or apple juice can be added, if available. Otherwise a little stock or water may be necessary to keep it moist during cooking.

Serve with goose, duck, pork, veal, sausages, chicken and fried fish (white).

There are two types of sauerkraut. One is very sour and made with vinegar and the other made with salt and much milder. It is best to test to see which one you have managed to buy.

Red cabbage *serves 6*

1 red cabbage
1 teaspoon salt
pepper to taste
25 g (1 oz) 2 tablespoons butter
1 large cooking apple
1 tablespoon sugar
2 tablespoons lemon juice or wine vinegar

Discard the outer leaves and cut out any thick veins. Wash the cabbage, shred and put in a saucepan. Cover with boiling water and leave to stand for about 20 minutes. Strain and add salt. Melt the butter in a saucepan. Add the cabbage and stir well. Peel, core and slice the apple and add it to the cabbage. Cover and cook slowly for about 30 minutes, stirring from time to time. The cabbage should remain moist, otherwise it will burn. Before serving, adjust the seasoning and add the sugar and lemon juice or vinegar.

Red cabbage is very popular in Russia and Eastern Europe. In fact it is eaten as often as green cabbage is in England. This is a neglected vegetable and should be eaten more often. Serve with game, pork, sausages, chicken, veal or cotletti.

Cauliflower with butter and breadcrumbs

serves 4

1 medium cauliflower
1 teaspoon salt
50 g (2 oz) 4 tablespoons salted butter
1 tablespoon dry breadcrumbs

Wash the cauliflower and put it in boiling salted water in a saucepan. Cover and simmer for about 20 minutes until cooked. Transfer to a warm dish. A few minutes before the cauliflower is ready melt the butter in a small saucepan. Add the breadcrumbs and cook gently for a few minutes until the breadcrumbs have absorbed the butter. Serve with the cauliflower.

This is an easy sauce and quick too. Serve the cauliflower with any type of hot meat, also good with boiled fish (white).

SWEET CORN

Preparation and cooking: Only young cobs are suitable for boiling. They can be cooked with or without the leaves. Wash and simmer for 15-20 minutes in salted water until tender. Be careful not to overcook. Serve with butter or white sauce (page 89).

Sweet corn with sour cream

serves 3-4

4 corn cobs
3 tablespoons sour cream
25 g (1 oz) ¼ cup grated cheddar or gruyère cheese
25 g (1 oz) 2 tablespoons butter

Cook the sweet corn as above. Remove the grains from the cobs and mix them with the sour cream. Put into a buttered fireproof dish, sprinkle with cheese and dot with butter. Cook in a moderate oven 180°C (350°F) Mark 4 for about 15 minutes or until brown. Garnish with chopped parsley.

Serve this as a separate dish before the main course. Sweet corn is in season from August to September. It should be eaten when young and tender with the grains a greeny-white in colour. If any corn is left over the kernels are good in a salad.

ASPARAGUS

Preparation and cooking: Cut off the hard end of the stalk with a sharp knife. Scrape or peel the white part. Wash, drain and tie in bundles of 8 to 10. Cook, lying flat, in boiling salted water in a saucepan with a large base. Simmer, with the lid on, for 20-25 minutes, according to size. Be careful not to overcook. When tender, transfer to a warm plate and serve with hollandaise sauce (page 90).

Asparagus

serves 4

200 g (8 oz) asparagus
salt to taste
250 ml (½ pt) 1¼ cups white sauce (page 89)
25 g (1 oz) 2 tablespoons butter
40 g (1½ oz) ⅓ cup cheddar or gruyère cheese

Prepare asparagus as above. Cut into 50 mm (2 in.) lengths and boil in salted water until tender. Meanwhile, prepare the white sauce. Butter a fireproof dish and pour in half the sauce. Lay the asparagus carefully in the dish and cover with the rest of the sauce. Grate the cheese and sprinkle on top. Dot with knobs of butter and bake in a fairly hot oven 200°C (400°F) Mark 6 for 15 minutes or until brown or, alternatively, brown for a few minutes under the grill.

Serve as a separate course or with roast beef or cotletti (page 41).

Asparagus is at its best and cheapest from May to July but you can use canned asparagus if you wish. It can also be served plain with melted butter. Any left over use for a mixed salad.

BEETROOT

Preparation and cooking: Wash the beetroot carefully, making sure that the skin is not damaged or cut in any way as this will cause the beetroot to 'bleed' or lose colour. Leave about 25-50 mm (1-2 in.) of the top on until the beetroot is cooked.

BOILING

Cover with boiling salted water and simmer gently with the lid on for about an hour. The cooking time will, of course, depend on the size and age of the beetroot. If the beetroot is to be used for salad, leave in the water to cool before peeling off the skin.

BAKING

Young beetroots are especially good baked as this method retains all the juice and flavour. Wrap the beetroot in greased paper or aluminium foil and bake in a moderate oven 180°C (350°F) Mark 4 for about an hour, depending on size and age.

Beetroot with sour cream

serves 4

4 medium raw beetroots
knob of butter
1 teaspoon vinegar
1 dessertspoon flour
salt to taste
1 teaspoon sugar
125 ml (¼ pt) $\frac{2}{3}$ cup sour cream

Peel and wash the beetroot. Slice them and cut into thin strips. Put into a saucepan with the butter, vinegar and enough water to prevent them catching. Cover and simmer for about 40 minutes until tender. Stir in the flour, salt and sugar. Add the sour cream. Bring to the boil and serve.

This is one of the most popular vegetables in the USSR owing to the fact that it keeps in winter. Beetroot with sour cream can be served with almost any plain dish, ie cotletti, steak, roast beef, pork, chicken, veal, game or fried white fish.

Beans with beetroot in sour cream

serves 6

200 g (8 oz) 1 $\frac{1}{3}$ cups beans (kidney, butter or flageolets)
salt to taste
2 medium raw beetroots
25 g (1 oz) 2 tablespoons melted butter
165 ml ($\frac{1}{3}$ pt) ¾ cup water
1 teaspoon sugar
1 teaspoon vinegar
2 tablespoons sour cream
parsley

BEANS

Soak the beans overnight in cold water. Discard the water and transfer the beans to a saucepan. Cover with fresh, cold salted water and simmer with the lid on for about an hour or until the beans are tender.

BEETROOT

Peel the beetroot and cut it into small cubes. Put it in a saucepan with the melted butter, water and salt about 20 minutes after the beans so that they are both ready at the same time. Cover and simmer for about 30-40 minutes until cooked. Add the sugar and vinegar and mix thoroughly. (Ready-cooked beetroot can be used. If so, peel, cut into cubes and heat through in the butter. Add sugar, salt and vinegar.)

Mix the strained beans with the beetroot. Add the sour cream and warm through if it is to be served hot. Garnish with parsley. Serve hot or cold with any type of meat.

The beans for this recipe can of course be canned, also the beetroot. It will save cooking time. The flavour, of course, will not be the same but what can one do, even cooks have to compromise sometimes! Try the beans with venison or pheasant.

Swedes in white sauce

serves 6

2 medium swedes
salt to taste
500 ml (1 pt) 2½ cups white sauce (page 89)

Wash and peel the swedes and cut them into cubes. Boil them in salted water for about 30 minutes until almost cooked. Pour off the liquid and use to make the white sauce: one part vegetable stock to one part milk. Cook the sauce for a few minutes. Add the swedes and cook for a further 5 minutes or so.

Carrots can be cooked in this way, in which case they should be peeled and sliced thinly.

Swedes in white sauce can be eaten with any roast meat, game, chicken or with fried fish (white).

Turnips in cream

serves 3

1 medium turnip
salt to taste
15 g (½ oz) 1 tablespoon butter
4 tablespoons double cream
1 teaspoon sugar

Peel the turnips and cut into cubes or strips. Boil in salted water for about 30 minutes until tender. Strain. Melt the butter in a saucepan. Add the turnips, cream, sugar and a little salt. Stir until heated through. Serve with roast meat.

This can also be made with carrots. Young carrots will only need scraping and can be cooked whole.

The best time for turnips is of course in the spring when they are small and young. You can also serve them with cream when serving roast chicken or game.

Pumpkin in sour cream *serves 6*

400 g (1 lb) pumpkin
½ teaspoon salt
1 tablespoon flour
50 g (2 oz) 4 tablespoons butter
3 tablespoons sour cream
1 teaspoon sugar

Peel the pumpkin and remove the seeds. Slice thinly, salt and coat lightly in flour. Fry in butter till golden brown. Test with a fork to see if the pumpkin is tender. Add the sour cream and sugar and heat through.

Serve with roast veal or chicken.

Russians have a craze for sour cream as you can see by the recipes, but this makes the food more digestible and not nearly as fattening. Use home-made sour cream for this recipe.

Pumpkin in sour cream is also suitable for game if roasted since it is inclined to be dry.

Celery in sour cream *serves 4*

1 large head celery
salt to taste
1 sprig dill or parsley

SAUCE
¼ onion
15 g (½ oz) 1 tablespoon butter
1 teaspoon tomato purée
3-4 tablespoons sour cream
salt and pepper to taste

Cut off the leaves, trim the root and scrape the outer stalks of the celery. Cut sticks into four and wash thoroughly. Tie together in small bundles with cotton thread. Put into a pan in salted water, cover and simmer for about an hour until tender. About five minutes before serving prepare the sauce.

SAUCE
Peel the onion and chop it very finely. Fry in butter till golden brown. Add the tomato purée, the sour cream and a little salt and pepper and warm through.

Strain the celery, remove the thread and transfer to a warm serving-dish. Pour over the sauce and garnish with chopped dill or parsley.

Serve this dish with any type of roast meat, chicken, game or fried white fish.

Celery is at its best in the winter after the first frost.

Cucumber in sour cream *serves 4*

½ large fresh cucumber
salt and pepper to taste
1 tablespoon flour
butter or butter and oil for cooking
1 egg
3 tablespoons sour cream

Peel the cucumber and divide it lengthways and across. Sprinkle with salt and pepper and coat in flour. Fry gently in butter or oil until brown and transfer to a buttered fireproof dish. Mix the sour cream with the egg and pour it over the cucumber. Bake in a moderate oven 180°C (350°F) Mark 4 for about 15 minutes. Serve as a separate dish or with roast meat.

You can use the small cucumbers for this. If you serve it as a separate dish allow 1 cucumber per head. Since cucumbers in sour cream are rather rich they also go well with game, ie pheasant, venison, grouse, etc.

Ukrainian stewed vegetables *serves 8*

1 onion
3 tablespoons olive oil
3 medium carrots
6 medium tomatoes
2 green peppers
1 large aubergine
1 teaspoon sugar
salt to taste
2 teaspoons lemon juice

Peel the onion and chop fairly finely. Fry very slowly in oil for about five minutes taking care not to let it brown. Peel the carrots and slice them, if young, or dice if old. Add them to the onion and cook slowly for a further five minutes. Peel and quarter the tomatoes. Remove the stalk and all the seeds from the peppers and cut them into fairly small pieces. Cut stem off the aubergine and cut into large pieces. Add the tomatoes, peppers and aubergine to the onion and carrots. Cover and cook slowly for about 40 minutes until the carrots are tender, stirring frequently. Ten minutes before serving add the sugar, salt and lemon juice. Serve hot or cold.

This dish is called ratatouille in France and is eaten mostly along the Mediterranean but now it has become popular both in restaurants and in the home in England and elsewhere. The Russian version is slightly different however. Can be eaten with any type of meat or chicken.

Potatoes stuffed with meat *serves 4*

8 large potatoes
salt to taste
butter or fat for cooking
6 medium tomatoes
2 tablespoons sour cream

STUFFING
400 g (1 lb) 2 cups raw minced/ground beef
1 onion
oil for frying
salt to taste

STUFFING
Peel and chop the onion and fry it lightly for a few minutes. Add the minced beef and cook for about 20 minutes until brown. Season.

Peel and wash the potatoes and boil them for a few minutes in salted water. Cut the tops off and scoop out the centres. Fill the potatoes with stuffing and replace the tops. Transfer the potatoes to a greased baking-tin, add a knob of butter to each potato and cook in a moderate oven 180°C (350°F) Mark 4 for about half an hour. Wash and slice the tomatoes and put them in the tin with the potatoes. Cook for a further 20 minutes or until the potatoes are ready, basting from time to time. Remove the potatoes and keep them warm. Sieve the tomatoes and juice from the tin, adding a little water. Adjust the seasoning and stir in two tablespoons sour cream. Heat through and pour over the potatoes.

This is an economical dish and easy to prepare. Serve a green vegetable with this or a green salad on a side plate.

Green peppers with minced beef *serves 4*

8 green peppers
6 medium ripe tomatoes or 2-3 tablespoons tomato purée
1 teaspoon cornflour (optional)
2 tablespoons sour cream

STUFFING
400 g (1 lb) 2 cups raw minced/ground beef
1 onion
1 tablespoon cooked rice
salt
oil or butter for frying

Peel the onion and chop finely. Fry lightly in butter or oil. Add the minced meat and cook for a further 20 minutes, adding a little water if it gets too dry. Mix with the cooked rice and salt to taste.

Cut the tops off the peppers and make sure that all the seeds are scooped out. Stuff the peppers with the above mixture and put them into a saucepan or greased casserole-dish. Meanwhile, cook the tomatoes separately in a little salted water and sieve when ready. If tomato purée is used instead dilute it with about 375 ml (¾ pt) 2 cups water. The tomato sauce can be thickened with a teaspoon of cornflour mixed with a little water. Pour the sauce over the peppers. Cover the saucepan and simmer for about an hour or bake in a moderate oven 180°C (350°F) Mark 4. When ready, add the sour cream to the sauce and warm through.

Cook this dish slowly or it will burn. Serve with potatoes either boiled or mashed. Green peppers are at their best from August to November.

Aubergines *(egg plants)* with vegetable stuffing *serves 3*

3 aubergines/egg plants
salt to taste
oil for cooking
6 medium tomatoes
sugar to taste
lemon juice to taste

STUFFING
2 carrots
2 sticks celery
½ parsnip or turnip
1 onion
1 sprig parsley
oil for cooking

Cut the ends off the aubergines and remove the centre part. Rub well with salt both inside and out.

STUFFING
Clean and chop the vegetables finely. Cook them slowly in oil, with the parsley, for about 10 minutes. Do not allow them to brown. Stuff the aubergines with this mixture.

Put the stuffed aubergines into a saucepan with a little more oil and salt. Cook the tomatoes in a little salted water for a few minutes. Strain and sieve and add to the aubergines. Cover and simmer for 30-40 minutes until the aubergines are tender. Before serving, add a little sugar and lemon juice to the sauce and more salt, if necessary. Serve hot or cold.

This can be given as a separate dish or served with hot or cold meat.

Aubergines are very popular in the Ukraine where there is an abundance in the summer months. Hence there are many ways of doing them, not all contained in this book.

Aubergines *(egg plants)* stuffed with beef or chicken

serves 4

4 aubergines /egg plants
salt to taste
125 ml (¼ pt) ⅔ cup sour cream

STUFFING
200 g (½ lb) 1 cup finely minced raw beef or chicken
2 tablespoons breadcrumbs
1 egg
salt and pepper

Slice the ends off the aubergines, remove the centre part and salt both inside and out.

STUFFING
Mix the finely minced beef or chicken with the beaten egg, breadcrumbs and salt and pepper.

Stuff the aubergines with the mixture and put them in a well-greased casserole in a slow oven 150°C (300°F) Mark 2 for about an hour until ready. Pour over the sour cream five minutes before serving.

Serve this as a main course with roast potatoes, or as a hot zakuska on its own. You can of course, use any left-over meat or game for this dish.

Stuffed marrow

serves 4

1 medium sized marrow
oil or butter for cooking
500 ml (1 pt) 2½ cups tomato sauce (page 89)
2 tablespoons sour cream

STUFFING
1 large onion
oil or butter for cooking
400 g (1 lb) 2 cups fresh minced beef
salt and pepper to taste
1 tablespoon rice

STUFFING
Fry the finely chopped onion. Add the minced/ground beef and fry for about 20 minutes until brown. Add salt and pepper. Meanwhile, boil the rice in salted water until cooked. Strain and add to the mince.

Peel the marrow, cut it in half lengthwise and remove all the seeds. Fill with the stuffing and tie the halves together again with thread. Put the marrow in a greased baking-tin with plenty of oil or butter and bake in a moderate oven 180°C (350°F) Mark 4 for about an hour or until ready. Baste frequently. Prepare the tomato sauce while the marrow is cooking. Pour the sauce over the marrow and then the sour cream on top a few minutes before serving.

This is very popular in the South where people have their own gardens and grow vegetables. Serve with roast potatoes.

Parboil the potatoes first, ie boil for a few minutes and then put round the marrow with additional oil. Baste frequently.

Baked stuffed onions

serves 4

4 spanish onions
salt and pepper to taste
butter for cooking
1 tablespoon dry breadcrumbs
15 g (½ oz) 1 tablespoon butter

STUFFING
3 rashers streaky bacon
50 g (2 oz) calf's liver
salt and pepper to taste
15 g (½ oz) 1 tablespoon butter
¼ teaspoon grated nutmeg

Choose onions of equal size. Peel them and cut off the tops with a sharp knife. Scoop out the centres carefully and salt and pepper the insides.

STUFFING
Cut off the rind and chop the bacon. Wash the liver, removing any skin or membrane and chop, together with a little of the onion cut out from the centres. Add to the bacon. Season and fry lightly in butter for 5-10 minutes. Put through a mincer, add the nutmeg and mix together thoroughly.

Stuff the onions and tie them securely with cotton. Put them in a large saucepan in a little boiling salted water. Cover and cook for about 10-15 minutes. Grease a baking-tin and carefully transfer the onions. Sprinkle with breadcrumbs, dot with butter and cook in a moderate oven 180°C (350°F) Mark 4 for about an hour or until ready. Serve as a separate course.

This could be served as a hot zakuska before the main course or with kidneys in sour cream (page 44) in which case serve potatoes either boiled or mashed.

Pumpkin, marrow or carrot pancakes olady

serves 6

200 g (8 oz) 1¾ cups flour
1 egg
200 g (8 oz) either pumpkin, marrow or carrot
1 tablespoon sugar
125 ml (¼ pt) ⅔ cup sour milk
½ teaspoon cooking salt
½ teaspoon baking powder or bicarbonate of soda
oil for frying

Peel the vegetables and wash. Cut into fairly small pieces and cook in a small amount of water till tender. When ready put through the blender or sieve. Whilst the vegetable purée is still warm beat in the egg, add the salt, sour milk and stir in the sifted flour together with the raising powder or bicarbonate of soda. Mix all the ingredients to form a smooth batter.

Brush a thick-based frying pan (omelette pan) or griddle with oil and drop tablespoons of batter on to it. Fry on both sides till brown, lifting them out with a palette knife. These are thicker than the usual pancakes so take longer to cook. Reduce the heat once they start frying or they will burn. As they are small you can cook two or three at the same time. Serve with jam, honey, maple syrup or sugar and sour cream.

Remember to keep the pancakes warm whilst you are still frying and serve on hot plates. They are best if eaten straight from the pan. A good dish to serve for breakfast on a cold day. Purée the vegetables the day before and warm the purée when making the batter or the dough will not rise. 'Olady' means a thick pancake in Russian.

Purée of squash

600 g (1½ lb) squash (summer squash or yellow crookneck)
1 tablespoon butter
½ tablespoon flour
1-2 lumps sugar
salt to taste
3 tablespoons milk

Trim the squash. Cut into small pieces and put into boiling water with salt to just cover, cook slowly under a lid for 20-30 minutes. When ready remove from saucepan and put through a sieve. Add sugar. Make a roux with the butter and flour. Add 3 tablespoons milk and blend with the purée. Heat through stirring all the time.

Use this as a garnish for beef cotletti, liver, roast or boiled beef. Can be made with small marrows. Only remove seeds and rind.

Stuffed squash, butternut

serves 4

4 butternut squashes
300 g (12 oz) 1½ cups minced beef (ground)
150 g (6 oz) 1 cup rice or millet
1 onion
2 tablespoons sour cream
2 tablespoons tomato purée
1 tablespoon flour
2 tablespoons butter
salt and pepper to taste
chopped dill or parsley

STUFFING

Fry the minced meat in the butter. Peel and chop the onion and add to the meat. Cook slowly for about 20 minutes. Add salt and pepper. Cook the rice or millet separately in boiling salted water for 20 minutes. Strain. Mix the millet or rice with the cooked mince and onion. Add chopped dill or parsley.

SQUASH

Peel and cut the squash crosswise. Remove the seeds. Stuff the squash and cover. Make a roux of the butter and flour and combine with 1 cup of boiling water or stock. Add the sour cream, tomato purée and mix thoroughly. Pack the squashes in a large saucepan and cover with the sauce. Cook for 30-40 minutes under a lid slowly or in the oven at 180°C (350°F) Mark 4 for 30-40 minutes.

Serve with roast potatoes or mash.

This recipe can be adapted to small marrows.

Lady's fingers

125 g (5 oz) 1¼ cups flour
8 medium potatoes
100 g (4 oz) ½ cup butter or margarine
½ teaspoon salt
1 egg
caraway seeds
egg for glazing

Peel and boil the potatoes in salted water under a lid till ready, about 20 minutes. Strain and mash. Whilst the potatoes are still hot cut the butter into small pieces and combine with the mashed potatoes so that the butter melts and there are no lumps. Add the flour gradually mixing with a wooden spoon all the time. Finally add the lightly beaten egg. Mix all ingredients and add a little salt to taste. If the mixture is too wet to roll out add a little more flour. Put on a floured board and roll out to fit a 23 cm (9 in.) square tin. It should be about 15 mm (½ in.) thick. Brush with egg and scatter caraway seeds on top. Cut into lady's fingers. Cook for 15-20 minutes at 200°C (400°F) Mark 6, till golden.

This is best done when potatoes are in season. Not suitable for young new potatoes. Can be eaten before the main course or with the roast joint or grills. You can save a little of the egg for the glaze if you wish or use a left-over white of egg if you have one.

Armenian bean purée with raisins and almonds

serves 6

250 g (10 oz) 1⅔ cups white beans (haricot or butter)
40 g (1½ oz) 4 tablespoons seedless raisins
75 g (3 oz) ¾ cup shelled almonds
1 lemon
salt to taste
1 sprig parsley

Put the beans in a bowl in water to soak overnight. Discard water and put into fresh water in a saucepan with a little salt. Cover with lid and cook slowly for about 1½ hours or till tender. Put through a sieve. Pour boiling water over the almonds and allow to stand for 5 minutes. Remove the skin and chop finely. Mix together the purée of beans, the chopped almonds and the seedless raisins. Brush a casserole dish with oil and put the mixture in it. Even out the top. Cook for a further 10-15 minutes in the oven at 135°C (275°F) Mark 1-2. Slice lemon and chop parsley.

Garnish with the sliced lemon and chopped parsley. Serve with boiled ham, lamb, boiled salted brisket.

Jardinière

serves 6

6 potatoes
3 carrots
2 onions
½ swede
salt to taste
400 g (1 lb) green peas or fresh beans
1 large cabbage stalk from white cabbage
½ cauliflower (optional) or 1 squash (optional)
50 g (2 oz) butter or 2 tablespoons sunflower oil

Peel potatoes, carrots, onion and swede. Slice. Shell garden peas or top-and-tail and slice beans if used. Cut cabbage stalk in large chunks. Divide cauliflower in flowerets. Peel squash, remove seeds and slice. Put into a large casserole with a tight lid. Thus: 1 layer of potatoes then a layer of onions, layer of swede until the vegetables are used up. Cover with water. Cook for 45 minutes at 180°C (350°F) Mark 4. Remove from stove and add salt. Pour over the melted butter or oil and serve in the same dish with a napkin round it.

These vegetables are delicious. In the winter substitute white hard cabbage in place of the peas or beans and use turnip if not bitter. It is best to use a transparent casserole then you can see what is going on. In place of the butter or oil use a cream sauce.

CREAM SAUCE
1 tablespoon butter
1 teaspoon flour
1 cup cream

Melt the butter and combine with the flour, add the cream gradually till all ingredients are well blended and hot.

Green peas and cauliflower with hollandaise sauce

serves 4-6

400 g (1 lb) green peas
1 cauliflower
salt to taste

Hollandaise Sauce (page 90)

Shell peas and put into a saucepan. Add the cauliflower to the peas. Add water and salt. Cover with lid and cook for 20 minutes or till both peas and cauliflower are ready. Strain. Put the green peas in the middle of the dish and garnish with the cauliflower cut into flowerets. Pour over the hollandaise sauce and serve.

This can be eaten wherever you would use green peas, ie grilled steak, cotletti, roast beef, etc.

Split peas à la Russe

serves 4

200 g (8 oz) 1⅓ cups split peas
1 onion
1 dried mushroom
½ teaspoon salt
1-2 teaspoons sugar
1 teaspoon flour
1 tablespoon butter

Soak the peas in warm water overnight to swell. Rinse and put in a saucepan with the peeled onion, dried mushroom and the sugar, cover with cold unsalted water and cook on a low flame for at least an hour. Strain, put into salted boiling water and simmer till done. Melt the butter and blend with the flour, add strained peas, mix and serve.

Eat with boiled ham, boiled mutton, or boiled beef.

Beans with walnuts

serves 6

150 g (6 oz) 1 cup dried beans (butter, haricot or flageolets)
4-5 spring onions
50 g (2 oz) ½ cup shelled walnuts
1 tablespoon butter
1 tablespoon chopped parsley
salt and pepper to taste

Soak the beans in cold water overnight. Pour off the water and put into hot water in a saucepan with a little salt with lid on. Cook slowly for 2-2½ hours.

Meanwhile prepare the onions. Remove the outer leaves and root. Chop finely. Add to the beans when they are cooked. Boil through and strain. Either pound the walnuts in a mortar or put through a mincer twice. Add the butter, salt and pepper. Mix all ingredients. Heat through. Transfer to dish. Sprinkle with chopped parsley and serve.

Serve with roast and boiled beef, boiled ham or mutton. Can be eaten either hot or cold.

Parsnips in sour cream

serves 4

600 g (1½ lb) parsnips
2 tablespoons vinegar or lemon juice
50 g (2 oz) 4 tablespoons butter
1 tablespoon flour
1 teaspoon salt
250 ml (½ pt) 1¼ cups sour cream

Scrape the parsnips and keep in cold water with a little vinegar or lemon juice till needed. Rinse in cold water, slice and put in a buttered casserole dish. Melt the butter, blend with the flour and add the sour cream. Season with salt, pour over the parsnips. Bake in the oven for about 45 minutes at 200°C (400°F) Mark 6, or till cooked.

Serve as a second vegetable when eating roast beef, boiled ham, game, etc.

Potato and ham pudding

serves 6

600 g (1½ lb) boiled potatoes
½ chopped cooked ham
100 g (4 oz) ½ cup butter
3 egg yolks
3 whole eggs
salt and pepper to taste
2 tablespoons grated cheese

Beat the butter till it turns white, blend with the 3 egg yolks and the 3 whole eggs. Mash the potatoes and add the chopped ham, eggs and butter. Grease a casserole dish. Put the mixture into it and bake at 200°C (400°F) Mark 6, for 20-30 minutes or till brown. Take out of the oven and sprinkle with cheese, pour a little melted butter over the top and serve in the same dish.

This is a good supper dish and I have made it successfully with only 3 whole eggs and minced ham. Serve with a green salad or tomato salad.

Turnips with malaga wine

serves 6

6-8 small turnips
1½ teaspoons salt
1 tablespoon butter
1 tablespoon flour
375 ml (¾ pt) 2 cups stock
2 teaspoons sugar
1 wineglass malaga wine

Wash the turnips. Bring to the boil once without peeling. Rinse. Cut off the stalk end and the peel. The peel should be cut off quite thickly as it is rather bitter. Slice and put into salted boiling water. Boil for two or three minutes. Strain. Add the melted butter blended with the flour. Combine with the hot stock. Stir to get out any lumps. Add the sliced turnips. Cover with lid and cook till the turnips are done and the stock thickens. About 15-20 minutes.

Before serving sprinkle in the sugar, season with salt to taste and add the wine, stir and cook through.

Serve as a second vegetable when eating roast beef, lamb, or veal.

Zucchini/courgettes with cheese

serves 6

6 zucchini/courgettes about 15 cm (6 in.) long
1 egg
200 g (8 oz) 2 cups sharp cheddar cheese coarsely grated
50 g (2 oz) ¼ cup cottage cheese (small curd)
½ teaspoon salt
pepper
25 g (1 oz) 2 tablespoons butter
about 2 tablespoons dry breadcrumbs or cracker crumbs

Cut off end of zucchini/courgettes. Cook covered with water and salt for about 12 minutes till almost done. Remove from water and cut in halves lengthwise. Scoop out centre pulp of the zucchini. Mix the cottage cheese with the coarsely grated cheddar, add pepper (this gives it a lot of flavour) and the egg. Stuff the zucchini/courgettes and put the cheese on top. Melt butter; and add the crumbs. Sprinkle this mixture over the zucchini/courgettes. Put into a greased tin and bake at 180°C (350°F) Mark 4 for about 25 minutes.

This is a good idea when all the zucchini or courgettes ripen at the same time. Have as a starter to a meal when eating a salad on a hot day. If cooking for one do not use the oven but boil the zucchini/courgettes until they are tender, ie try with a fork and if ready stuff and put under the grill with the breadcrumbs. Very quick to do. I have done this successfully for one without the egg. The mixture should be fairly stiff.

Potato roll with meat

serves 4

900 g (2¼ lb) potatoes
1 large egg
3 teaspoons flour
1 tablespoon dry breadcrumbs
oil for frying
4 tablespoons sour cream
300 g (12 oz) 1½ cups fresh minced/ground beef
1 onion
1 tablespoon milk
50 g (2 oz) 4 tablespoons butter
salt and pepper to taste
dry dill weed

Peel and boil potatoes of equal size in salted water with lid on for about 20 minutes or till done. When cooked strain and put through a sieve or mash. Add the egg beaten in the milk, 25 g (1 oz) 2 tablespoons of butter and 3 teaspoons flour. Adjust seasoning. Mix thoroughly.

Whilst the potatoes are cooking peel the onion and chop finely. Fry the mince and the onion in a little oil for about 15 minutes. If the mixture dries add a little water stirring all the time till it is absorbed. The mixture should be moist but not wet or too dry. Add salt and pepper to taste and a little dry dill. Lay out the mashed potato on a damp tea towel and roll out into an oblong shape about 15 mm (½ in.) thick. Spread the meat mixture down the centre of the potato and roll up the cloth. Press ends together. Put the roll on to a greased baking sheet with seam downwards. Brush with a little milk, dust with breadcrumbs and dot with butter. Cook at about 200°C (400°F) Mark 6, for 25-30 minutes or till it browns. Baste.

Serve the sour cream separately. This can also be made from left-over meat. To do this put the cooked meat either boiled or roasted through a mincer and add the fried chopped onion together with a little water to make it a moist mixture. Follow instruction as above.

Accompaniments: green vegetables, such as sprouts, cabbage, or green salad. Tomato salad, (page 81) also goes well with this dish.

Vegetable and potato roll

2 carrots
1 onion
few mushrooms
2 sticks celery
½ turnip
oil
salt and pepper

Take 400 g (1 lb) of mixed vegetables as suggested above. Peel, wash and cut pretty finely. Cook in a little oil and add salt and pepper. Do not allow the vegetables to brown. Just cook through.

Follow the instructions for the potato and meat roll for the rest of the recipe only using vegetables instead of meat. See opposite.

As this is not a filling main meal for vegetarians a suggested pudding to follow is cheese baba (page 136) or tvorozhniky (page 135).

Potatoes with cucumber sauce

serves 4

8 medium potatoes
4 salted cucumbers
6 mushrooms
500 ml (1 pt) 2½ cups water
1 tablespoon flour
1 sprig parsley
1 tablespoon butter
1 onion

Peel the cucumbers, cut into cubes or strips. Clean the mushrooms and boil in 500 ml (1 pt) 2½ cups of salt water with the cucumber peel, sprig of parsley and the peeled onion for about 20 minutes or till the mushrooms are ready. Strain and retain stock. Chop the mushrooms.

Boil potatoes of equal size in their skins in salted water under a lid for about 20 minutes or till ready. Peel and keep hot.

Make a roux from the butter and flour. Dilute 500 ml (1 pt) 2½ cups of hot stock stirring all the time to prevent lumps. Add the diced cucumbers and chopped mushrooms to the sauce. Heat through and pour over the hot potatoes.

Eat with roast beef or boiled beef, cotletti from beef, veal or pork. You can if you wish use some of the salted water from the cucumbers for the sauce and add a little burnt sugar.

Sauerkraut with sour cream and mushrooms

serves 6

400 g (1 lb) sauerkraut
6 mushrooms
125 ml (¼ pt) $\frac{2}{3}$ cup sour cream
1 tablespoon butter
½ tablespoon flour

Clean mushrooms, cover with water and boil with a little water and salt for 20 minutes. Strain. Cut mushrooms in small pieces. Try the sauerkraut. If it is too sharp, pour boiling water over it and squeeze out before using.

Put the sauerkraut into a saucepan, add the mushroom stock and chopped mushrooms, cream, salt. Cook slowly for 20 minutes. Add the flour blended with melted butter. Stir well and cook till ready a further 10 minutes or so. Stirring frequently.

Eat with roast or boiled chicken, turkey, fried or boiled fish.

Stuffed acorn squash

serves 4

4 acorn squashes
2 tablespoons stale breadcrumbs
2 hard boiled eggs
1 tablespoon butter
4 kidneys or 300 g (12 oz) 1½ cups minced veal
2 tablespoons sour cream
salt and pepper to taste

Peel and wash squash. Carefully remove top and scoop out inside. If using kidneys soak them in tepid salt water for 15 minutes. Wash well, skin if necessary, remove the core and any fat and cut the kidneys into small pieces.

STUFFING

Fry the veal or chopped kidneys in butter till lightly brown about 5 minutes stirring with a wooden spoon. Add the breadcrumbs and cook for a further 10 minutes slowly. Set aside. Add salt, pepper, 2 tablespoons sour cream and the chopped hard boiled eggs.

Now stuff the squash. Cover with top and tie with thread. Put into a large saucepan and add a little water or stock. Cook slowly with lid on for about 30-40 minutes or till squash and stuffing are cooked. Remove thread before serving.

Serve with mashed potatoes and the sauce in the pan.

Tovchenka

serves 4

3 medium potatoes
½ cup beans (haricot or butter beans)
2 tablespoons poppy seeds
2 tablespoons sugar
1 onion
2 tablespoons chopped parsley
salt and pepper to taste

Soak the beans overnight in boiling water. Drain them and cover well with cold salted water. Simmer under a lid for 2 hours or till done. Strain. Soak poppy seeds in boiling water till they double in size. Strain. Put through a mincer.

Boil the potatoes in their skins until tender; peel and mash. Peel onions, quarter and put through the mincer. Combine all ingredients whilst still hot, ie the ground poppy seeds, the mashed beans, the mashed potatoes, the minced onion, salt, pepper, sugar and chopped parsley. Stir till you get a smooth paste. Cook and serve cold.

Serve with cold meat and green salad. *Tovchenka* means to grind in Ukrainian. Hence the name, since all things were ground in a mortar in the old days. This is a famous Ukrainian dish.

Potato baba with curd cheese

serves 4-6

9 medium potatoes
150 g (6 oz) ¾ cup curd cheese
2 eggs
1 tablespoon breadcrumbs
1 tablespoon cream
2½ tablespoons flour
3 tablespoons butter
1 tablespoon sugar
125 ml (¼ pt) $\frac{2}{3}$ cup sour cream

Wash potatoes of equal size and put in cold water in a saucepan with a little salt. Cover with a lid and cook for 20 minutes or till ready. Peel and mash. Mix the potato purée with 1 tablespoon butter, cream the egg yolks blended with sugar, flour and salt. Mix thoroughly. Whip the whites till they stand in peaks and fold into the mixture. Transfer to buttered soufflé dish. Sprinkle with breadcrumbs, dot with butter. Bake at 200°C (400°F) Mark 6, for 20-30 minutes or till brown. Serve with sour cream.

This pudding can be eaten with ham, or boiled fish if liked or as a separate dish for supper or an entrée with a green salad.

Potato loaf with curd cheese

serves 6

8 medium potatoes
200 g (8 oz) 1 cup curd cheese
2 eggs
1½ tablespoons butter
1½ tablespoons sugar
1 tablespoon breadcrumbs
125 ml (¼ pt) $\frac{2}{3}$ cup sour cream

Mash peeled and cooked potatoes (see above). Put through a sieve. Mix 1 raw egg with the cream and add to the purée. Sieve the curd cheese if it is hard. Blend the cheese with the remaining egg, sugar and salt.

Butter a loaf tin or oblong casserole dish. Place a layer of potatoes then a layer of cheese alternately till you finish with a layer of potatoes. Brush with egg, dot with butter and sprinkle with the breadcrumbs. Bake at 200°C (400°F) Mark 6, for 30 minutes, or till well browned.

Serve cut in slices with the sour cream. This is filling and could be the main course with a green salad or eaten as an entrée to a light meal.

Pumpkin with apples

serves 6

800 g (2 lb) pumpkin
4 medium apples
2 tablespoons butter
2 tablespoons sugar
125 ml (¼ pt) $\frac{2}{3}$ cup water
100 g (4 oz) 1 cup nuts
pinch of cinnamon

Remove rind and seeds from pumpkin and wash. Cut into cubes. Put in saucepan. Peel, core and cut apples into small pieces and add, also sugar, butter, and water. Bring to the boil and reduce heat to simmering point. Cook under a lid for 30 minutes or till done.

Meanwhile prepare the garnish. Chop nuts and mix with 1 teaspoon sugar and a little cinnamon. Combine the nuts with the cinnamon. Transfer the pumpkin to warm dish. Sprinkle with the nut mixture.

Serve with roast beef, cotletti, roast chicken, turkey, etc.

Pumpkin au gratin with sour cream

serves 6

800 g (2 lb) pumpkin
1 tablespoon butter
3 tablespoons sour cream
2 tablespoons sugar
1 tablespoon breadcrumbs (dry)
2 tablespoons grated cheddar
1 tablespoon plain flour
salt to taste

Peel and remove seeds from pumpkin. Wash and cut into cubes. Salt. Dredge with flour and fry lightly in butter. Butter a casserole dish and sprinkle with dry breadcrumbs. Transfer the pumpkin to the dish, add the sour cream and sprinkle with grated cheese. Dot with butter and cook in a fairly hot oven 220°C (425°F) Mark 7, for about 30 minutes or till well browned.

This can be served as a separate dish to start a meal or as a vegetable with roast beef, cotletti, or fish.

Marrow or squash purée

serves 4

400 g (1 lb) marrow or squash
1 onion
1 tablespoon oil
100 g (4 oz) $\frac{1}{3}$ cup tomato purée
1 tablespoon wine vinegar
salt and pepper to taste
1 clove garlic

Peel marrow and remove seeds. Cut in cubes. Fry lightly in oil. Peel onion, chop finely and add to the marrow. Cook slowly till both are cooked. Add the tomato purée. Salt. Cook through. Chill and pass through a mincer. Mix with the vinegar, oil, pepper and crushed garlic.

Serve as a cold vegetable with cold meat, ham, etc or spread on small pieces of black bread and butter and serve with drinks. Best with chilled vodka.

Onion sauce with caraway seeds

5-6 onions
½ tablespoon flour
½ tablespoon butter
1½ teaspoons caraway seeds
1 teaspoon vinegar and made mustard (optional)
1 tablespoon burnt sugar (optional)
250 ml (½ pt) 1¼ cups beef or chicken stock

Peel onions and cut off root. Put into cold water

and bring to the boil, strain if a mild flavour is required. Then transfer to boiling stock, reduce heat and cook gently under a lid for 1½-2 hours or till ready.

Strain and put the onions through a sieve. Melt the butter and mix with the flour adding 250 ml (½ pt) 1¼ cups of the hot stock gradually stirring all the time to avoid lumps. Add the sauce to the purée of onion and the caraway seeds. A little burnt sugar, 1 teaspoon vinegar and 1 teaspoon made mustard can also be added for flavour if liked. Boil through and stir.

Serve with roast lamb, beef cotletti, roast beef, etc.

Runner beans with hard boiled eggs

serves 6

800 g (2 lb) runner beans	1 tablespoon butter
2 hard boiled eggs	½ teaspoon salt
125 ml (¼ pt) $\frac{2}{3}$ cup sour cream	2 sprigs parsley or dill
	180 ml ($\frac{3}{8}$ pt) 1 cup water

Wash the beans, trim them and remove any strings. Slice. Cook in 1 cup of boiling salted water with lid on for 15-20 minutes.

Meanwhile peel the eggs and chop. When the beans are ready strain and add the butter. Heat through. Combine the chopped hard boiled eggs and sour cream with the beans. Transfer to dish. Sprinkle with chopped dill and serve at once.

Eat with roast beef, cotletti, veal or chicken.

Millet kasha

serves 4-6

400 g (1 lb) 2 $\frac{2}{3}$ cups millet	salt
800 ml (2 pt) 5 cups water	2 tablespoons butter

Pick over the grain of the millet. Wash and drain. Put into a saucepan with the water, salt and 1 tablespoon butter. Cook the kasha till it thickens and then add the rest of the butter and transfer to a casserole with a lid and cook for a further hour in a slow oven to dry off. 135°C (275°F) Mark 1-2.

This may be eaten instead of potatoes with meat or as a separate dish for breakfast.

Croûtons for spinach and other dishes

4 thick slices white bread	½ teaspoon sugar
125 ml (¼ pt) $\frac{2}{3}$ cup milk	butter for frying
1 egg	

Combine the egg, milk and sugar. Remove the crusts from the bread. Dice and soak in the egg and milk mixture. Fry in butter till golden brown.

Croûtons can be served with purée of other vegetables if liked.

Runner beans in sour cream and tomato sauce Georgian

serves 4-6

400 g (1 lb) runner or french beans	1 teaspoon basil
50 g (2 oz) 4 tablespoons butter	1 teaspoon salt
2 onions	½ teaspoon ground black pepper
1 small green pepper	180 ml ($\frac{3}{8}$ pt) 1 cup sour cream
3 medium sized tomatoes	1 egg

Prepare beans. Trim and remove strings. Slice. Peel onion and chop. Remove stalk and seeds from the green pepper and cut into 15 mm (½ in.) pieces.

Pour boiling water over tomatoes. Allow to stand and then peel and cut in half and remove seeds. Chop finely.

Bring 3 l (5 pt) 6¼ cups salted water to boil in a pan. Add beans slowly and bring to the boil. Reduce heat and cook uncovered for 10 minutes. Drain, wash under cold running water in a sieve and put to one side.

Melt butter in a large frying pan. Turn temperature to high and add onion and green pepper, reduce heat and cook for 5 minutes until vegetables are tender. Add tomatoes, and boil rapidly for 1-2 minutes till most of the juices in the pan have evaporated. Add the beans and simmer for 2 minutes. Beat together the egg, sour cream, salt and pepper in a mixing bowl. Stir into the beans. Serve immediately.

Buckwheat kasha with curd cheese

serves 4-6

200 g (8 oz) 1¼ cups buckwheat
375 ml (¾ pt) 2 cups milk
200 g (8 oz) 1 cup curd cheese
180 ml ($\frac{3}{8}$ pt) 1 cup sour cream
2 eggs
2 tablespoons butter
1 tablespoon dry breadcrumbs
½ teaspoon salt

Bring the milk to the boil. Add the buckwheat and cook till it thickens stirring from time to time. It should be like porridge. Put the cheese through a sieve if hard or lumpy. Remove from the stove and add the cheese, the raw eggs, salt and sugar. Combine all ingredients thoroughly. Pour into a buttered baking dish which has been dusted with breadcrumbs. Brush the top with sour cream and pour over a tablespoonful of melted butter. Bake for 40-50 minutes at 180°C (350°F) Mark 4.

Cut into portions and serve with melted butter or sour cream. This is sometimes served with borshch in which case it can take the place of the main course.

Potato galushki

serves 4

4 medium potatoes
2 eggs
1 tablespoon butter
1 tablespoon flour
2 tablespoons butter (melted)

Wash and cook potatoes in their jackets for 20 minutes under a lid. Peel and mash. Add the eggs, flour and mix. Make the galushki. Dust a pastry board with flour and roll out. Cut into small squares If the dough is too soft add a little grated raw potato. Boil in salted water for 6 to 8 minutes. minutes.

Serve with melted butter or add to clear soups, ie chicken, beef, etc.

Salads

Cucumber salad with sour cream

serves 4

1 fresh cucumber
salt to taste
125 ml (¼ pt) ⅔ cup sour cream sauce (page 92)
2 sprigs dill or parsley

Wash and peel the cucumber. Slice thinly and salt. Leave to stand for a few minutes. Add the sour cream sauce and garnish with chopped dill or parsley. Chill for a few minutes and serve.

This salad can be eaten with any cold meat or fish. Try it with cold salmon or game. Can also be served as a separate course to start a meal. To keep cucumber crisp salt first and leave for about 20 minutes. Pour off the liquid and proceed to make the salad.

Tomato salad with onions and green peppers

serves 3

6 medium tomatoes
¼ spanish onion
½ green pepper
french dressing (page 92)
salt (optional)

Slice the tomatoes and peel and slice the onion finely. Remove the seeds from the green pepper and chop into fairly small pieces. Pour the dressing over the tomatoes, onion and pepper and toss. A little extra salt can be added, if necessary.

If you wish, peel the tomatoes first by plunging them in boiling water. This salad can be eaten with any type of meat or cold fish (white or salmon). Cucumber or celery can be substituted instead of green peppers for this salad.

Kidney bean salad

serves 4

200 g (8 oz) 1¼ cups kidney beans
sprig parsley
salt and pepper to taste
1 small onion
2 tablespoons olive oil
1 tablespoon lemon or gooseberry juice

Soak the beans overnight in cold water. Cook in salted water with the onion and parsley for about an hour until tender. Drain. Put into a bowl and add pepper, oil, lemon or gooseberry juice and more salt, if necessary. Serve with cold mutton. This salad can be made with small red or white haricot beans or flageolets.

This salad can be made from canned beans to save cooking time. A useful standby if you have a tin in your store cupboard. Beans are second class protein.

Spring salad

serves 4-6

1 lettuce
1 boiled new carrot
2 tomatoes
2-3 boiled new potatoes
1 bunch radishes
½ fresh cucumber
2 hard boiled eggs
2 spring onions
sour cream sauce (page 92)

Wash the fresh vegetables. Strain the lettuce, pat dry and tear into small pieces. Put into the middle of a large salad bowl. Slice the carrot, tomatoes, potatoes, radishes and cucumber and arrange round the lettuce. Garnish with slices of egg and finely chopped spring onions. Serve the sour cream sauce with the salad.

This is a very good salad if you do not have much to eat. The hard boiled eggs and potatoes make it a bit more filling. Serve with any cold meat, chicken or cold white fish.

In France where salad is eaten every day they have a good way to drain away the excess water. If you pass a hamlet or village you will see the women swinging a wire basket with the lettuce leaves in a circular motion. This can only be done out of doors of course. You will drench the kitchen if you make any attempt to do it indoors!

Red cabbage salad

serves 6-8

1 medium red cabbage
1 teaspoon cooking salt
french dressing (page 92)
2 teaspoons sugar

Wash the cabbage and remove the outer leaves, thick stems and veins. Cut into strips and rub the cooking salt in well. Leave for an hour. Drain off the liquid. Add the french dressing with two teaspoons of sugar and mix well.

This salad can be eaten with hot cotletti (any type including fish) or any cold meat. A good winter salad which is much neglected. The only difficulty with red cabbage is that it stains your hands so wear gloves if you can.

Radish salad

serves 3-4

2 bunches of radishes
salt and pepper to taste
1 hard boiled egg
sour cream sauce (page 92)

Wash and trim the radishes and cut them into thin slices. Add salt and pepper. Put the egg yolk through a sieve and mix it with the sour cream sauce. Pour the sauce over the radishes and mix well. Garnish with chopped egg-whites. Chill and serve.

This can be served separately as a zakuska before the main course or with other salads when eating cold meat.

Caucasian salad

serves 3-4

1 bunch of radishes
½ fresh cucumber
2 spring onions
salt and pepper to taste
3 tablespoons sour milk
  or yoghurt
pinch of sugar (optional)
1 sprig dill

Wash and trim the radishes and slice them thinly. Cut the cucumber in thin slices. Clean the spring onions and chop them finely. Season. Add the sour milk or yoghurt and a pinch of sugar. Mix all the ingredients thoroughly. Garnish with chopped dill and chill for half an hour before serving.

This can be served as a starter to the main course for lunch or with an evening snack of sandwiches.

Beetroot salad

serves 4

4 medium cooked beetroots
2 tablespoons olive oil
3 tablespoons wine vinegar
1 teaspoon sugar
salt to taste
1 sprig dill or parsley

Peel and slice the beetroot and cut into thin strips. Mix the oil, vinegar, sugar and salt and pour over the beetroot. Mix well and leave to stand for about half an hour before serving. Garnish with chopped dill or parsley

This is one of the most popular salads in Russia owing to the fact that beetroots are obtainable all the year round. It will go with most hot or cold meats or game and also with cold white fish.

Russian salad

serves 4

4 medium potatoes
1 salted or pickled cucumber
1 cooked carrot
2 medium cooked beetroots
1 teaspoon finely chopped onion (optional)
1 tablespoon cooked green peas
french dressing (page 92)

Slice the potatoes and slice and quarter the cucumber and carrot. Cut the beetroot into cubes. Put them in a bowl together with the onion and peas. Pour over the french dressing and mix well. Chill before serving.

Russian salad or Salade Russe is called *vinegrette* in Russian. The main ingredients are potatoes, beetroot and cucumber yet these are the very ingredients which are often omitted when it is prepared abroad. The beetroot and salted cucumber give it the true Russian flavour so please do not forget them. It can of course be eaten with any type of cold meat or cold white fish.

Sauerkraut and cranberry salad

serves 6

400 g (1 lb) sauerkraut
1 tablespoon olive oil
1 tablespoon sugar
1 eating apple
2 stalks celery (optional)
100 g (4 oz) 1 cup cranberries

If the sauerkraut is very sour, pour cold water over it and squeeze out the liquid. Add the oil and sugar to the sauerkraut. Peel, core and chop the apple and clean the celery and cut it into strips. Wash the cranberries. Add the apple, celery and cranberries to the sauerkraut and mix well. This salad is particularly good with cold poultry or cold roast pork.

This can also be done with blue or red bilberries in place of the cranberries.

Cod salad with horseradish

serves 6

400 g (1 lb) cooked fillet of cod
½ fresh cucumber
2 medium cooked potatoes
25 g (1 oz) 4 tablespoons grated horseradish
125 ml (¼ pt) $\frac{2}{3}$ cup mayonnaise (page 91)
salt to taste
2 teaspoons wine vinegar
2 spring onions
1 sprig parsley

Remove the skin and cut the boiled cod into small pieces. Peel and slice the cucumber and slice the potatoes. Put most of the grated horseradish in a bowl. Add the mayonnaise, vinegar, and salt. Mix in the fish, potatoes and most of the cucumber and transfer to a salad bowl. Garnish with pieces of cucumber, chopped spring onion, grated horseradish and parsley

Eat this salad as a light lunch with black bread and butter or as an *hors d'oeuvre* before the main course. It should be enough for 3 if it is eaten for lunch.

Follow with a filling pudding such as: sweet omelette with fruit sauce (page 130), tvorozhniky (page 135) or zapekanka of cream cheese (page 135).

Rice salad

serves 6

150 g (6 oz) 1 cup rice
salt to taste
125 ml (¼ pt) $\frac{2}{3}$ cup french dressing (page 92)
2 cooked carrots
1 tablespoon cooked green peas
2 sprigs parsley
1 tablespoon sultanas (optional)
1 tablespoon chopped red or green pepper

Boil the rice in salted water. Transfer to a sieve and run cold water through. Put in a bowl and pour over the french dressing. Chop the carrots into small cubes. Add the carrots, peas, chopped parsley, pepper and sultanas to the rice. Serve with cold meat.

You may add ½ fresh green pepper cut into small strips to this salad and substitute sweet corn in place of the green peas if you have any left over.

This salad goes with any cold meat or fish.

Potato salad

serves 4-5

4 medium boiled potatoes
2 spring onions
½ teaspoon made mustard
french dressing (page 92) or mayonnaise (page 91)
1 sprig dill or parsley

Slice the cooked potatoes and put them in a bowl with the finely chopped spring onions, the mustard and the french dressing or mayonnaise. Mix. The flavour is improved if the dressing is added while the potatoes are still hot. Garnish with chopped dill or parsley.

Potato salad can be eaten not only with every type of cold meat, chicken, game or cold boiled fish but also with hot boiled beef from the soup (See soups pages 17-28) with plenty of mustard. Have it on a side plate or it will cook the beef too quickly.

Celery and pineapple salad *serves 4*

100 g (4 oz) 1 cup fresh pineapple
2-3 sticks celery
2 tablespoons french dressing (page 84)
1 teaspoon sugar
½ lettuce
2 slices cooked beetroot

Remove the skin from the pineapple and wash and trim celery. Cut them both into thin strips and mix with a tablespoon of the french dressing and the sugar.

Wash the lettuce, drain and pat dry. Tear into small pieces and arrange in a salad bowl. Put the celery and pineapple round the edge. Cut the beetroot into cubes and place in the centre. Pour the rest of the french dressing over the salad. Serve with cold meat or poultry.

If tinned pineapple is substituted for fresh the sugar should be omitted.

This is a good winter salad when celery is in season. It is excellent with ham or cold game.

When lettuce is poor and out of season, ie in the winter, omit, but double the other ingredients.

Chicory and fruit salad *serves 3-4*

2 heads of chicory (endive)
1 orange
1 apple or banana
grated lemon or orange rind
2 tablespoons mayonnaise or mayonnaise with sour cream (page 91)

Remove the outer leaves of the chicory, cut off the base, wash and slice. Peel the orange, slice thinly and remove the pips. Peel and core the apple or peel the banana and cut in fine slices. Mix all the ingredients with the mayonnaise and garnish with coarsely grated lemon or orange rind.

Serve with cold meat or poultry.

Chicory need not be washed but if you do, wipe with a cloth so that no water remains or it will spoil the flavour. This is a good winter salad especially suitable for cold game.

Bean and asparagus salad *serves 4*

1 handful runner beans
1 handful asparagus
1 tablespoon green peas
1 handful cauliflower
salt and pepper to taste
½ lettuce
1 tomato
¼ fresh cucumber
2 tablespoons french dressing (page 92) or mayonnaise with sour cream (page 91)
1 sprig parsley or dill

Trim the beans and string them. Remove the hard ends from the asparagus and cut into 25 mm (1 in.) pieces. Wash the beans, asparagus, peas and cauliflower and boil them in salted water, with the lid on, for 20 minutes or till cooked. Leave them to cool in the water they have been cooked in. When cool, drain, divide the cauliflower into flowerets and slice the beans. Wash and divide the lettuce. Pat dry and tear into small pieces. Peel and slice the tomato and cucumber. Mix all the vegetables in a bowl, season and add the french dressing or mayonnaise with sour cream. Garnish with chopped parsley or dill.

Asparagus is at its best in spring and summer and since green beans are also included this is a summer salad. The best way to try this salad is to reserve some asparagus and green beans one day and make the salad the next since such a small quantity is used. This type of salad can be eaten with any type of cold meat which is not fat, or chicken.

Kazan salad *serves 6*

100-150 g (4-6 oz) cold roast beef
1 medium cooked potato
1 salted or pickled cucumber
1 cooked carrot
1 tablespoon cooked peas
½ lettuce
2-3 tablespoons mayonnaise (page 91) or mayonnaise with sour cream (page 91)
1 hard boiled egg
1 eating apple
1 sprig parsley or dill

Cut the beef, potato, cucumber and carrot into

small, thin slices. Add the green peas and mix well with the mayonnaise. Wash the lettuce, drain and pat dry. Slice the egg and peel, core and slice the apple. Chop the dill or parsley. Tear the lettuce into small pieces and arrange in a bowl. Put the dressed meat salad in the middle. Garnish with the egg, apple and parsley or dill.

This salad can be eaten any time of the year since the ingredients are easily available. You can either serve it as a zakuska before a main course or as a light lunch in which case there is enough for 2-3. Eat with rye bread and butter.

Fruit salad with mayonnaise

serves 4

3 eating apples
1 pear
1 orange
1 mandarin
1 teaspoon sugar
pinch of salt
4 tablespoons mayonnaise (page 91)
juice of ¼ lemon

Peel and slice the fruit, discarding the cores and pips where necessary. Put in a bowl and sprinkle with sugar and salt. Add the mayonnaise mixed with lemon juice. Garnish with grated orange rind. Grapes, blackcurrants, redcurrants or cooked prunes can also be used for decoration.

Serve with hot or cold meat, poultry or game.

As mandarins are not always available, drain the juice from a can and use the segments. Add the juice from the can to a lemon or orange jelly (jello).

Spinach salad

serves 6

200 g (8 oz) spinach
3 tablespoons oil
2 tablespoons vinegar
1 tablespoon breadcrumbs
½ teaspoon salt

Wash and drain spinach thoroughly. Remove stalks. Chop finely and transfer to salad dish. Combine the vinegar, oil, breadcrumbs and salt and mix with the salad.

It is difficult to get spinach in England suitable for this salad. However, if you grow some in the garden, young leaves make an excellent salad.

Beetroot, bean and apple salad

serves 4-6

1 cup cooked beans (haricot, or butter beans)
1 beetroot (cooked)
2 eating apples
3 tablespoons olive or sunflower oil
2 tablespoons vinegar
salt and pepper to taste
pinch of sugar

Peel beetroot and cut into strips. Reserve some for garnish. Peel apples, core and cut into small pieces. Combine beetroot, apples and cooked beans and add black pepper, a little sugar, salt and the oil and vinegar.

Serve with cold meat, chicken, cold fish and ham. This is a good way of using up any cooked beans left over after a meal.

Green pepper salad

serves 6

400 g (1 lb) green peppers
125 ml (¼ pt) $\frac{2}{3}$ cup salad dressing or mayonnaise

Cut peppers in half and remove seeds and stalks. Wash. Plunge in boiling salted water and boil for 5 minutes. Cool and drain.

Cut into strips and combine with the mayonnaise. Transfer to salad bowl and serve with cold meat or fish.

Spring onion salad sauce

serves 4

1 good bunch spring onions
60 ml ($\frac{1}{8}$ pt) ¼ cup sour cream
½ tablespoon vinegar
salt to taste
parsley or dill

Peel off the outer leaves of the onions and remove the root. Chop finely. Cover and leave for 1 hour or so.

Mash gently with a wooden spoon. Add salt. Combine with the vinegar, sour cream and chopped parsley or dill.

This is a sauce rather than a salad. Serve with chopped radishes or with curd or cottage cheese.

Runner bean and walnut salad

200 g (8 oz) runner beans
25 g (1 oz) ¼ cup walnuts
1 tablespoon vinegar
2 tablespoons parsley
salt and pepper to taste

Wash and trim the beans. Do not cup up french beans or young runner beans as they lose their flavour. For older Scarlet runners slice thinly in a slanting direction. Cook with lid on in boiling salted water with just enough water to cover, 15-20 minutes. Drain and cool.

Mix in the vinegar. Check seasoning. Chop the nuts finely or grind. Combine all ingredients. Transfer to suitable dish. Garnish with chopped fresh parsley.

This is suitable to eat with fried fish or boiled river fish which has a mild flavour.

Green salad with hard boiled eggs

serves 4-6

1 head lettuce
2 hard boiled eggs
1 teaspoon sugar
1 tablespoon vinegar
180 ml ($\frac{3}{8}$ pt) 1 cup sour cream
salt to taste
dill

Cut off stump of lettuce and discard outside leaves. Separate all the leaves and wash thoroughly. Drain. Tear leaves into small pieces and put into a bowl. Peel and slice hard boiled eggs. Chop dill.

Mix the sugar, vinegar, and salt with the sour cream and pour the dressing over the lettuce. Mix thoroughly and transfer to salad bowl. Peel eggs and slice. Chop dill. Garnish with sliced hard boiled eggs and the chopped dill. Eat immediately.

This can be eaten with any cold meat if it is not too fat, ie cold ham, chicken, beef, game, turkey or veal.

Beetroot caviar

serves 4

4 medium cooked beetroots
2 tablespoons oil
2 tablespoons sugar
juice and rind of ½ lemon

Peel the beetroot and put through a mincer. Put into a saucepan with the oil, grated rind and juice of half a lemon and the sugar. Cook through for 5 minutes stirring frequently. Cool and put into a salad dish.

This can be eaten with any cold meat or fish.

Bean salad

serves 4

400 g (1 lb) french or runner beans
2 tablespoons oil
1 tablespoon vinegar
1 teasooon sugar
salt and pepper to taste

Trim the beans and slice. Cook for 15-20 minutes with lid on in salted water. Drain. Mix the oil, vinegar, sugar, salt and a little pepper together and pour over the salad. Mix all ingredients and transfer to salad bowl.

This salad can be eaten with any cold meat. Good way of using up left-over beans.

Chicory salad

serves 4-6

400 g (1 lb) chicory (endive)
1 clove garlic
3 tablespoons olive oil
1½ tablespoons lemon juice
salt and pepper to taste

If the chicory is bitter, soak in salted water for a few hours. Pick off outside leaves, rinse and dry on a cloth. Chop.

Peel a clove of garlic and crush with a wooden spoon in a bowl. Add the salt, pepper, lemon juice and olive oil. Blend well. Put the chicory in a salad bowl. Pour over the dressing and mix well.

This salad can be served when cold meats are on the table.

Tomatoes with carrot stuffing

serves 4

6 medium tomatoes
5 medium carrots
1 tablespoon sugar
4 tablespoons sour cream
1 tablespoon chopped parsley
4 lettuce leaves
salt to taste

Cut the tops off the tomatoes and scoop out the inside. Salt and turn upside down to drain. Peel and wash carrots and grate on rough grater. Add the sour cream, sugar, and salt. Fill the tomatoes and cover. Arrange lettuce leaves on a dish and put the tomatoes on it. Garnish with the chopped parsley.

Serve with cold meats.

Cabbage, tomato and carrot salad

serves 6

1 medium cabbage
3 medium tomatoes
1 carrot
1 onion
3 tablespoons oil
1 tablespoon vinegar
1½ tablespoons sugar
2 tablespoons chopped parsley
salt

Remove outside leaves of cabbage. Grate rest coarsely. Put into a saucepan, add salt and vinegar and heat. Cook till the cabbage settles to the bottom of the pan. Do not over cook. Strain off any liquid. Cool. Peel carrot and onion. Grate carrot on coarse grater, and chop the onion finely. Add the carrot and onion to the cabbage and the oil and sugar. Blend all ingredients together.

Transfer to salad dish, garnish with slices of tomatoes and chopped parsley. Eat with any cold meat.

FRUIT SALADS

Apricot fruit salad

serves 4

6-8 fresh apricots
3 tablespoons sugar
1 lemon
125 ml (¼ pt) ⅔ cup sweet white wine

Remove the skins of the apricots by plunging in boiling water and peeling with a sharp knife. Cut into quarters and discard the stones. Cover with sugar and add the juice of the lemon or wine. Allow to stand for at least 1 hour before serving. Best eaten chilled.

As the season for apricots is short try this with golden plums. Eat with fresh cream if liked. If using apricots use vanilla sugar, this enhances the flavour.

Ukrainian fruit salad

serves 4

1 pear
5 medium peaches
100 g (4 oz) ½ cup sugar
1 lemon

Peel the peaches and cut into cubes. Discard stones. Peel and core pear and likewise cut into cubes. Squeeze juice from lemon and add the strained juice to the fruits and the sugar. Mix thoroughly. Allow to stand for at least 1 hour before serving.

This is best eaten chilled with cream. All fruit tastes better when in season.

Ukrainian apple and nut fruit salad

serves 4

4 medium eating apples
100 g (4 oz) ½ cup sugar
10 shelled walnuts
½ teaspoon vanilla essence
125 ml (¼ pt) ⅔ cup cherry, cranberry or orange juice
125 ml (¼ pt) ⅔ cup cream

Peel and core the apples. Either coarse grate or chop finely. Add the chopped nuts, sugar, vanilla and fruit juices. Stir thoroughly till the sugar has dissolved. Allow to stand for at least 1 hour before serving. Serve with whipped cream.

Cranberry juice and cherry juice can be bought in many delicatessen shops. If you have vanilla sugar use this in preference to the essence. The apples should be as tart as possible to provide a good flavour.

Carrot and apple salad

serves 4

6 medium carrots
1 eating apple
50 g (2 oz) ½ cup shelled walnuts
2 tablespoons oil
1 tablespoons lemon juice
1 dessertspoon sugar or honey
salt to taste
1 stalk celery

Peel carrots and grate on coarse grater. Peel and core apple and chop finely. Mix the lemon juice, sugar and oil. Combine the french dressing with the apples and carrots. Chop nuts. Transfer the salad to a bowl and sprinkle with the nuts and garnish with parsley.

Eat with cold meats.

Sauces

Basic white sauce

25 g (1 oz) 2 tablespoons butter
25 g (1 oz) ¼ cup flour
500 ml (1 pt) 2½ cups milk
salt and pepper

Melt the butter in a saucepan. Stir in the flour. Mix well and cook gently for 1-2 minutes. Remove from the heat and gradually add the milk, which may be warm, stirring to obtain a smooth consistency. Return to the heat, season and cook gently for about five minutes.

White sauces should always be made in a heavy bottomed enamelled, stainless steel or tin-lined copper saucepan. A thin pan will burn the sauce and ruin the flavour. Aluminium can discolour a white sauce, especially if you use wine or egg.

Caper sauce

25 g (1 oz) 2 tablespoons butter
25 g (1 oz) ¼ cup flour
500 ml (1 pt) 2½ cups milk
salt to taste
2 tablespoons capers

Make a white sauce as in the previous recipe and add a few capers.

This sauce can be served with any type of white boiled fish or with cotletti made from fish.

Pickled mushroom sauce

25 g (1 oz) 2 tablespoons butter
25 g (1 oz) ¼ cup flour
500 ml (1 pt) 2½ cups milk
salt and pepper to taste
6 small pickled mushrooms

Make a white sauce and add salt, pepper and the finely chopped pickled mushrooms. This sauce is served with fried fish cutlets or boiled white fish.

This sauce is more interesting than the ordinary mushroom sauce which is often served with fish. It is well worth trying.

Tomato sauce

½ onion
15 g (½ oz) 1 tablespoon butter
2 teaspoons flour
5 medium ripe tomatoes or 3 tablespoons tomato purée
250 ml (½ pt) 1¼ cups water
1 teaspoon sugar
lemon juice or wine vinegar to taste
½ teaspoon salt

Peel and chop the onion and fry it lightly in butter. Stir in the flour. Then add the water and tomatoes and simmer slowly for about 30 minutes. If tomato purée is used, double the amount of water will be necessary, but it will only need a few minutes' cooking. Sieve and add sugar and lemon juice or vinegar and salt.

Fresh tomatoes are of course best for this. Choose ripe tomatoes or the sauce will be a poor colour. If you use the purée it is a good idea to add 1 chopped fresh tomato for flavour. First of all peel it and remove the seeds.

Tomato sauce can be served with boiled potatoes if you have a grill, or with boiled or fried fish or potato or fish cutlets.

Tomato sauce with capers or pickled mushrooms

Make basic tomato sauce (see above) substituting either two tablespoons of capers or a few pickled mushrooms for the lemon juice or vinegar.

If you go picking mushrooms and find you have more than you can eat, pickle them. Then you will always be able to make a sauce or have them with drinks.

This sauce is good with white boiled fish or fish cutlets also cotletti (page 41).

Hollandaise sauce

3 tablespoons lemon juice
salt to taste
6 peppercorns
3 egg yolks
2 tablespoons water or stock (chicken or fish)
100 g (4 oz) ½ cup butter

Put the lemon juice, peppercorns, salt and water into a small pan and heat till reduced to 2 tablespoons of liquid. Strain and put in a double saucepan. Stir the egg yolks in gradually and then add the softened butter in small pieces, stirring all the time until it thickens. Season delicately.

This is an international sauce but eaten in Russia as elsewhere. Serve with boiled fish, vegetables or boiled chicken.

White wine sauce

1 medium onion
1 sprig chopped parsley
50 g (2 oz) ¼ cup butter
25 g (1 oz) ¼ cup flour
500 ml (1 pt) 2½ cups fish stock
1 egg yolk
salt to taste
2 tablespoons dry white wine
squeeze of lemon juice

Peel and chop the onion and fry the onion and parsley lightly in half the butter. Stir in the flour to make a roux. Gradually add all the hot fish stock, stirring all the time. Simmer for several minutes and take off the heat. Blend in the egg yolk and the rest of the butter. Add salt and sieve. Add the wine and lemon juice. Heat through, being careful not to let it boil. Serve this sauce with fish katushki.

If you have no parsley handy try a pinch of dry dill or tarragon. Use only small quantities of herbs or it will ruin the flavour.

This sauce can also be served with fish pâté (page 13) if served hot or any boiled white fish if eaten hot.

Mushroom sauce

200 g (8 oz) mushrooms
1 onion
butter for frying
salt and pepper to taste
1 dessertspoon flour
1 cup fresh or sour cream

Clean and chop the mushrooms and stalks. Chop the onion finely and brown it lightly in butter. Add the chopped mushrooms and cook over a low heat for about 20 minutes. Add salt, pepper and flour and stir well. Add the sour cream and heat through. Serve with meat, fish or potato cutlets and kasha.

For a different flavour put 1 sprig parsley or dill in a muslin bag with 1 bay leaf, 2 peppercorns, one clove and a small piece of cinnamon (very small) tie up and heat the mushroom sauce through with these herbs. Omit pepper if you add the herbs. When ready lift out the bag and serve.

This sauce is a great favourite in Russia since mushrooms grow wild in the woods and are there for the picking. Now, however, with women working there is less time but mushrooms are still very popular.

Mushroom sauce with wine

200 g (8 oz) mushrooms
25 g (1 oz) 2 tablespoons butter
juice of ¼ lemon
3 tablespoons water or bouillon
1 tablespoon flour
125 ml (¼ pt) ⅔ cup water
salt and pepper
1 teaspoon sugar
1-2 wineglasses dry white wine
2 egg yolks

Clean the mushrooms, including the stalks, and cut into fairly large pieces. Stew gently in a saucepan in 15 g (½ oz) 1 tablespoon of melted butter for a few minutes. Add the lemon juice and 3 tablespoons water or bouillon and simmer for about 20 minutes until soft. In a separate saucepan make a roux from a dessertspoon of flour and 15 g (½ oz) 1 tablespoon butter. Do not let it brown. Gradually add 125 ml (¼ pt) $\frac{2}{3}$ cup water, salt, pepper and sugar. Stir in the wine and bring to the boil. Remove from the heat and stir in the egg yolks. Warm through, stirring all the time. Do not allow it to boil or the egg yolks will curdle. Add the mushrooms. Serve with roast goose, duck or game.

In the old days many people picked their own mushrooms. The woods in Russia abound in mushrooms of all kinds. In fact, we have done this in England. You must be very careful however, not to pick toadstools and you should seek guidance in this. My father was an expert and knew all the names of the different types. However, my husband would not trust him and never touched the mushrooms when we cooked them. He was sure they were poisonous. As you can see I am still alive to tell the tale!

Mustard sauce

3 egg yolks
1 dessertspoon sugar
2 tablespoons olive oil
2 tablespoons wine vinegar
1 tablespoon either capers or chopped olives
1 small teaspoon made English mustard

Put the yolks, sugar and mustard into a bowl and mix thoroughly with wooden spoon. Add the olive oil gradually beating all the time until it is all used up and the mixture thickens. Dilute with the vinegar and add the capers or chopped olives. The capers give a sharper flavour. This sauce is excellent with cold salmon or halibut, fish pâté (page 13), grilled herrings or mackerel. If the capers or olives are omitted it can be used as a dressing for Russian salad (page 83).

Remember not to overcook the eggs, ie 8 minutes and to plunge them into cold water to cool immediately or the yolks will be discoloured and ruin the colour of this sauce.

Horseradish with sour cream

1 horseradish root
1-2 tablespoons vinegar
125 ml (¼ pt) $\frac{2}{3}$ cup sour cream
1 teaspoon sugar
salt to taste

Grate the horseradish and pour the mixture of vinegar, sour cream, sugar and salt over it. Serve with studen and fish pâté.

Horseradish is difficult to get fresh but it can sometimes be bought in jars already grated. This sauce should be served very cold. You can also make it with fresh thick cream. If so, whip it before adding the vinegar. Horseradish cream is also good with ham or roast beef.

Mayonnaise

1 egg yolk
1 teaspoon sugar
pinch of salt, pepper
1 teaspoon English made mustard
up to 125 ml (¼ pt) $\frac{2}{3}$ cup olive oil
1 tablespoon wine vinegar or lemon juice

Mix the egg yolk with the sugar, salt, pepper and mustard. Add the olive oil drop by drop, stirring all the time. Use up to 125 ml (¼ pt) $\frac{2}{3}$ cup with each yolk. The mixture should be very thick before you add the vinegar or lemon juice. Keep in the fridge in an airtight jar.

The eggs and oil should be at the same temperature and not too cold so take them out of the fridge well in advance. See that there is no trace of egg white left in the yolk. Use a thick heavy basin which will stand vigorous beating or a mixer. If the mixture curdles add a fresh yolk and start again. To use after storing add a little more vinegar and whisk again.

Mayonnaise with sour cream

125 ml (¼ pt) $\frac{2}{3}$ cup mayonnaise (see above)
125 ml (¼ pt) $\frac{2}{3}$ cup sour cream
1 sprig parsley
1 tablespoon wine vinegar or lemon juice

Mix the above ingredients in a large cup and use immediately as it will not keep.

This sauce is much richer than mayonnaise so watch your figure! It is useful however, if you have not got enough mayonnaise left in the fridge. By adding a little sour cream you will double the quantity.

Sour cream sauce for salads

4 tablespoons sour cream
1 tablespoon lemon juice or wine vinegar
pinch of salt
½ teaspoon sugar (optional)

Mix the above ingredients in a large cup and use immediately as it will not keep.

This sauce is a welcome change from the french dressing usually used. It is not very rich and well worth trying. Mostly used for green salad, ie lettuce.

French dressing

8 tablespoons olive oil
4 tablespoons wine vinegar or lemon juice
salt and pepper to taste
1 clove garlic (optional)

Peel the clove of garlic and crush it in a basin with the salt. Add the other ingredients and mix well. Use immediately or store in a bottle in the fridge.

If you wish to include the garlic use a wooden spoon, a metal spoon will not do.

Some like sugar in french dressing. Add ½ teaspoon if you like.

Use medium priced olive oil, the cheapest has too much flavour and the dearest is too refined. Sunflower oil is excellent too for salad dressing.

Egg and caper dressing

2 hard boiled eggs
½ tablespoon English made mustard
½ teaspoon sugar
salt to taste
2 tablespoons olive oil
¾ tablespoon wine vinegar or lemon juice
1 tablespoon capers

Sieve the egg yolks and beat them with the mustard until they are white. Add the sugar and salt and stir in the oil gradually. Add the vinegar or lemon juice and mix thoroughly. Finally, add the chopped egg whites and the capers. Serve with cold fish.

Olive oil should be at room temperature. It goes hard in the fridge so take out well in advance of making the sauce.

Morello cherry sauce

400 g (1 lb) morello cherries
500 ml (1 pt) 2½ cups water
sugar to taste
1 tablespoon potato flour or cornflour
1 wineglass port or madeira (optional)
clove (optional)
cinnamon (optional)

Wash, stalk and stone the cherries and stew them in the water and sugar for about 10 minutes or until cooked. Stir in the potato flour mixed with a little water to thicken the juice. If the port or madeira is added a little more potato flour will be needed. Heat the sauce through again. Cinnamon and clove will give a spicy taste. Serve with veal, poultry and game, and with cherry charlotte (page 129).

This can be made from canned or frozen cherries, of course, because the season is so short. If you make the sauce with dessert cherries add a little lemon juice or the sauce will be too sweet.

Turnip or swede sauce

1 medium turnip or swede
1 tablespoon sugar
2 tablespoons butter
1 egg white
1 tablespoon lemon juice
a little lemon rind

Peel and cut turnip in cubes. Boil till tender. Put through a sieve. Add sugar, lemon juice, rind and butter. Cook till it thickens. Cool slightly and add the egg white which should be whipped thoroughly beforehand so that it stands in peaks.

Blend all ingredients thoroughly but do not reboil. Serve hot.

Turnips vary according to season so may take from 15-30 minutes to cook depending on age and time pulled from the ground. Serve with roast meat, cutlets and game.

Soufflé wine sauce

serves 4

3 eggs
2 wineglasses of dry white wine
50 g (2 oz) 4 tablespoons sugar
small rind of lemon or orange

Separate eggs. Put the whites into a large mixing bowl so that you can whisk them later. Beat the yolks with sugar till white. Add the wine, lemon or orange rind and cook in double boiler till the mixture thickens, whisking all the time.

Remove the rind and whip the whites till they stand in peaks. Fold into the egg mixture and cook for a further few minutes.

This sauce can be used instead of custard, hot or cold, with stewed or tinned fruit or as a separate dish. If served as a dessert garnish with fresh strawberries or raspberries. This quantity is enough for 3 only if used as a dessert and best eaten chilled.

Almond milk

1 teaspoon castor sugar
125 ml (¼ pt) ⅔ cup milk
2 teaspoons almond flavouring

Combine ingredients and heat through. Cool. Use with fruit kissel.

Almond milk is very popular in Russia and used for sauces too. It is difficult to make nowadays since it involves the use of bitter almonds which are not easily available, so I have included this simple version.

Cream sauce for puddings

250 ml (½ pt) 1¼ cups thin cream or sour cream
50 g (2 oz) 4 tablespoons sugar
2 yolks of eggs
vanilla essence or pinch of cinnamon

Bring cream to the boil. Add essence or cinnamon. Whip the sugar with the yolks till white. Add to the hot cream. Blend thoroughly. Do not allow to boil but heat through to boiling point. Stir all the time it is cooking.

Serve with puddings. If cold it can be served with stewed fruit or fresh raspberries or strawberries or curd cheese.

White sauce with sour cream

1 tablespoon butter
750 ml (1½ pt) 3¾ cups chicken stock
1½ tablespoons flour
250 ml (½ pt) 1¼ cups sour cream
15-20 marinated gooseberries
salt to taste
sugar to taste

Melt butter in a small pan. Add flour gradually till it forms a roux. Dilute with the hot chicken stock slowly stirring all the time to prevent lumps forming. Add the sour cream, gooseberries, salt and sugar to taste.

Serve in a large dish as there is plenty of it. Eaten with either boiled chicken, turkey, sucking pig or fish.

You can also pour this sauce over individual plates with the chicken, etc. Serve boiled potatoes with this dish.

Redcurrant sauce

200 g (8 oz) redcurrants
125 ml (¼ pt) ⅔ cup red wine
a little gravy
100 g (4 oz) ½ cup sugar
a little cinnamon
1 teaspoon potato flour

Wash the redcurrants and pick over. Remove the stalks. Put through a sieve. Add a little gravy, 125 ml (¼ pt) ⅔ cup wine, 100 g (4 oz) ½ cup sugar and a little cinnamon. Transfer to saucepan and bring to the boil. Add 1 teaspoon potato flour mixed in 1 tablespoon water. Allow to boil, stirring all the time to thicken and prevent lumps. Serve with wild boar, wild goat, lamb, etc.

This recipe is from an Old Imperial Russian Cookbook and I am afraid some of these animals are almost extinct! Try boiled ham, chicken or venison.

Cream sauce for vegetables

165 ml (⅓ pt) ¾ cup thin cream
6 g (¼ oz) ½ tablespoon butter
2 tablespoons dry breadcrumbs
2-3 pieces sugar
a little grated nutmeg
165 ml (⅓ pt) ¾ cup vegetable stock
salt to taste

Take vegetable stock and cream, a little salt, grated nutmeg, 2-3 lumps sugar, butter and boil through. Add the dry breadcrumbs and stir well till absorbed. Sauce should be like thick cream.

Use for boiled carrots, white cabbage, turnip, swede or cauliflower.

Salted herring sauce

serves 4

½ small salted herring fillet
1 large egg
1 teaspoon sugar
2 tablespoons cream
1 tablespoon vinegar
1 tablespoon oil
½ small onion
½ teaspoon mustard powder

Hard boil the egg for 7 minutes. Cover with cold

water to cool. Peel the onion and chop very finely. Remove any remaining bones and skin from the fish. Chop flesh very finely. When the egg is quite cool remove the shell and white and combine the yolk with the oil first and then with the rest of the ingredients with a wooden spoon. Chill.

This sauce is thick but if you wish it to be thinner add a little more vinegar. Eat with cold meat.

This is quite original and the taste of the fish is not very strong. Can be eaten with cold chicken, game, veal, pork and turkey as well as cold beef. Slice the pieces of meat and pour the sauce over to cover before serving.

Tkemaly sauce *(plum sauce)*

200 g (8 oz) tart plums
1 clove garlic (optional)
60 ml ($\frac{1}{8}$ pt) ¼ cup water
½ teaspoon salt
pinch of dry dill
pepper to taste

Stew the plums in water till tender. About 5 minutes. Remove stones. Put the plums through a sieve. Add the salt, pepper, crushed garlic and dill. The consistency should be like thick cream. Add more water if necessary. Cool. Serve with shashlik or any grilled meat or chicken.

Tkemaly is the Georgian name for the wild plums which grow in the Caucasus. They are a tart plum. This sauce can of course be made from frozen or canned plums if they are tart enough and contain no sugar. This is a typical Georgian sauce as they put garlic in everything!

Walnut sauce, Caucasian *serves 4-6*

100 g (4 oz) 1 cup shelled walnuts
1 clove garlic
1 teaspoon coriander seeds
chilli pepper and salt
60 ml ($\frac{1}{8}$ pt) ¼ cup water
60 ml ($\frac{1}{8}$ pt) ¼ cup wine vinegar

Crush the nuts and garlic and rub together with the salt. Add the wine vinegar mixed with the water, the coriander seeds and chilli pepper. Mix thoroughly. Serve with white fish, poultry or fried eggplant.

If you find the sauce too thick test for sharpness and add water or vinegar, whichever you prefer. You can crush the nuts with a rolling pin on a hard surface or in a pestle and mortar if you have one. If you do not like the strong flavour of garlic substitute spring onions instead. Pull off outer leaves and chop finely including some of the green part.

Cranberry sauce *serves 4*

200 g (8 oz) cranberries
125-250 ml (¼-½ pt) $\frac{2}{3}$- 1¼ cups water
50 g (2 oz) 4 tablespoons sugar
knob of butter (optional)

Put the cranberries with the water into a saucepan and cook slowly till the berries start to pop. Put through a sieve, add the sugar and butter and cook through. For the sake of economy you can add 1 small cooking apple peeled, cored and chopped, to the above but add more sugar.

This is, as is well known, excellent with turkey, chicken and all game, ie hare, venison, pigeon, etc. It can also be made with bilberries for a change. Serve with pancakes too (page 108).

Rum sauce

15 g (½ oz) 1 tablespoon butter
1 tablespoon flour
375 ml (¾ pt) 2 cups water
100 g (4 oz) ½ cup sugar
3 tablespoons white wine
3 tablespoons rum

Make a roux from the butter and flour. Gradually add the water, stirring all the time to obtain a smooth consistency. Boil gently for a few minutes. Add the sugar, wine and rum and bring back to the boil, still stirring.

Serve with rice pudding or the soufflé with wine or rum (page 129).

In Russia rum is more popular than brandy for cooking. In France, however, they use more brandy. If you prefer you can alter this recipe and use the brandy. If no brandy is available however, substitute whisky instead.

Apple sauce or purée

6 medium cooking apples
75 g (3 oz) 6 tablespoons sugar
1 tablespoon water

Peel and core the apples and cut them into slices. Put them in a saucepan with the sugar and water. Cover and cook slowly for 10-20 minutes until tender. Stir from time to time. Sieve.

This quantity makes about 500 ml (1 pt) 2½ cups sauce or purée.

Serve with roast goose or use for making pastila (page 114).

Apple sauce is also good with roast chicken or turkey. Add a little lemon juice to improve the colour.

Lemon madeira sauce

1 tablespoon butter
1½ tablespoons flour
500 ml (1 pt) 2½ cups stock
1 wine glass madeira or white wine
3 yolks
juice of ½ lemon and rind
1 teaspoon sugar
salt and pepper to taste

Prepare as for basic white sauce using the butter, flour and stock from chicken or meat or fish for fish dishes. Season with salt and pepper. Remove from heat. Add the lemon rind and juice. Blend the yolks with the wine, add to the hot sauce, together with the sugar and re-heat without allowing it to boil. Stir well.

To be eaten with boiled chicken, turkey, pigeons, and fish.

Eggs

Breakfast eggs

serves 6

2 rusks
40 g (1½ oz) 3 tablespoons butter
6 eggs
salt and pepper to taste
1 spring onion or sprig parsley

Crush the rusks into fine crumbs with a rolling-pin. Brush the bottom and sides of a frying-pan with melted butter and dust with crumbs. Break the eggs into the pan. Salt and pepper each egg separately. Sprinkle with finely chopped spring onion or parsley and put a knob of butter on each egg. Fry quickly until set. Serve from the pan.

Have absolutely fresh eggs or you will find that the yolk breaks and you will ruin the appearance of this dish. To make home-made breadcrumbs, slice bread thinly and put into a slow oven about 150°C (300°F) Mark 2, till the bread is crisp and dry. Put through a mincer and keep in an airtight tin.

Breakfast eggs with mushrooms

serves 4

100 g (4 oz) mushrooms
bacon fat
1 slice black bread
50 g (2 oz) 2 slices Polish sausage
50 g (2 oz) 2 slices ham
2 tomatoes
4 eggs
salt and pepper to taste

Wash and slice the mushrooms and fry them in bacon fat for about ten minutes until tender. Discard the crust and cut the bread in cubes. Skin the sausage, cut it in slices and divide each slice in four. Chop the ham and cut the tomatoes in half. Add the bread, sausage, ham and tomatoes to the mushrooms and fry for a few minutes. Break four eggs into the pan. Salt and pepper each egg and cook till set. Serve from the pan.

It is as well to invest in a good frying pan with a thick base. See that the pan is absolutely hot before you start to fry. A good dish if you have any little bits of left-over ham.

Eggs with black bread

serves 6

100 g (4 oz) 4 slices ham
2 spring onions
1 slice black bread
6 eggs
salt and pepper to taste
25 g (1 oz) 2 tablespoons butter

Chop the ham and the spring onions finely. Discard the crusts and cut the bread into cubes. Beat the eggs and season. Melt the butter in a thick frying-pan. Fry the ham, onions and bread lightly. Pour in the eggs and cook till firm.

Have the family sitting at table whilst you are cooking and make *them* wait for the eggs and not the eggs for the family as the eggs will spoil.

This would make a good supper dish with green salad.

Eggs in cream

serves 4

125 ml (¼ pt) $\frac{2}{3}$ cup sour cream
4 slices french bread
25 g (1 oz) 2 tablespoons butter
4 eggs
salt and pepper to taste
parsley or dill for garnish

Grease a fireproof dish and pour in half the cream. The french bread slices should be about 25 mm (1 in.) thick. Discard the soft part of the bread and fry the crusts lightly in butter. Place them in the dish. Beat the eggs, season and pour into the crusts. Alternatively, break a whole egg into each crust and sprinkle with salt and pepper. Cover with the rest of the sour cream and bake in a moderate oven 180°C (350°F) Mark 4 till set. Garnish with parsley or dill.

This makes a good supper dish. Serve with mashed potatoes and some green vegetable, or green salad with french dressing (page 92).

Eggs with courgettes or marrow

serves 4

4 small courgettes or 8 slices marrow
oil for frying
4 tomatoes
4 slices bacon
4 eggs
salt and pepper to taste

Trim the courgettes, and slice thinly, or peel marrow, remove seeds, slice and cut each slice in half. Brown on both sides in a little oil. Add the peeled and chopped tomatoes and the bacon and cook for a few minutes. Add the eggs. Salt and pepper well and cook until set.

This was a favourite dish of mine during the war when food was scarce. It makes bacon go a long way. You can serve this dish with potatoes.

Omelette Hutsul style

serves 3-4

4 eggs
180 ml ($\frac{3}{8}$ pt) 1 cup fresh cream
180 ml ($\frac{3}{8}$ pt) 1 cup sour cream
75 g (3 oz) ½ cup corn meal
½ tablespoon chopped parsley
salt and pepper to taste
50 g (2 oz) 4 tablespoons butter

Blend the fresh cream with the sour cream in a bowl. Whip the eggs and add. Combine with the corn meal, add salt and pepper. Heat a heavy frying pan till it is very hot. Melt the butter. As soon as the foaming subsides and the butter is on the point of changing colour pour in the omelette. Shake the pan back and forth over the heat at the same time scrape the bottom of the pan with a large fork held flat in your right hand, back and forth several times in one direction then in the other and bringing in the sides so that the eggs cook evenly. Continue for a few seconds and then let the omelette set.

The surface should be soft and moist when you lift it out. Fold the omelette and turn out onto a hot plate. Garnish with chopped parsley.

This is rather rich and could be a main course with different salads.

Omelette with nuts and honey

serves 3-4

4 eggs
50 g (2 oz) ½ cup shelled walnuts
2 tablespoons butter
100 g (4 oz) 1 cup candied fruit or 200 g (8 oz) raspberries
2 tablespoons stale breadcrumbs
2 tablespoons cream
1 tablespoon honey
1 tablespoon icing sugar (for raspberries)

If using raspberries, wash and strain. Chop the nuts finely, mix with the breadcrumbs and fry in a tablespoon of butter for 2-3 minutes. Stir in the honey, heat and remove from the stove. Beat the eggs and combine with the cream. Put the pan again on the stove and heat till the butter sizzles. Pour in the omelette. Cook as any other omelette (see this page Omelette Hutsul style). When ready either sprinkle with the candied fruit or the raspberries. Dust with icing sugar, fold and serve on a warm plate.

It is easier to make two omelettes out of the quantity suggested. This is an interesting pudding for a light lunch.

Omelette with spring onions

serves 2

3-4 eggs
1 tablespoon butter
1 tablespoon milk
1 tablespoon chopped spring onions
salt and pepper to taste

Break the eggs into a bowl, season with salt and pepper, add the spring onions and milk and whisk lightly. Melt butter in a heavy frying pan and pour in the omelette. (Instructions for cooking the omelette *see* Omelette Hutsul style page 98).

Serve with sauté potatoes and your favourite salad for lunch.

Omelette with jam à la russe

serves 6-8

8 eggs
4 tablespoons sugar
rind of ¼ lemon or a little cardamom
50 g (2 oz) 4 tablespoons butter
250 g (10 oz) 1 cup jam

Divide all ingredients into two and cook two omelettes. Beat 4 yolks with 2 tablespoons sugar till white, add the lemon rind or pinch of cardamom. Whip the whites till they stand in peaks. Fold into the yolks and sugar. Grease a skillet or large frying pan. Pour in the omelette. Put into a hot oven 200°C (400°F) Mark 6, cover with a plate and wait till it sets, about 8 minutes.

Turn upside down on to a warm plate and spread with jam. Repeat with the remaining ingredients.

The best jam for this is raspberry or blackcurrant. Best served after a light lunch since it is rather filling.

Stuffed eggs with mashed potatoes

serves 4

4 eggs
2 slices white bread
1 small onion
4 medium potatoes
50 g (2 oz) 2 slices ham
50 g (2 oz) ½ cup grated cheddar cheese
125 ml (½ pt) 1¼ cups milk
3 tablespoons butter
sprig of parsley
salt and pepper to taste
water

Boil the eggs for 7 minutes. Pour over cold water and cool. Shell. Cut in half lengthwise and remove the yolks. Mash the yolks. Chop the ham finely, chop parsley, peel and chop onion and fry in butter. Mix the ham, fried onion and the yolks. Add bread soaked in 125 ml (¼ pt) ⅔ cup milk, a pinch of salt and pepper and 1 raw egg. Fill the whites with this mixture making the shape of a whole egg. Boil the potatoes in salted water under a lid for 20 minutes. Strain and mash with the rest of the milk. Lay out the purée in a buttered baking dish and place the stuffed eggs on it. Sprinkle with grated cheese and melted butter and bake in a hot oven 200°C (400°F) Mark 7, for 10 minutes.

Garnish with chopped parsley and serve.

This could be a starter to a meal or a light lunch if 2 eggs are served per head.

Ukrainian eggs

serves 4

4 eggs
125 ml (¼ pt) ⅔ cup sour cream
parsley or dill
salt and pepper to taste

Hard boil the eggs for 8 minutes. It is best to put them carefully into boiling water (as long as they are not straight out of the fridge) and count the time from the moment they reboil.

Plunge them at once into cold water before shelling. Slice the eggs and put into small saucepan. Add salt and pepper. Cover with the sour cream and heat through. You can also put these in the oven if you have other dishes cooking. Sprinkle a little chopped dill or parsley before serving.

This can be eaten as a snack with vegetables, ie boiled carrots, spinach etc, or as a hot zakuska.

Pastry

Yeast pastry

15 g (½ oz) fresh yeast or 1 packet dried yeast
1 tablespoon sugar
250 ml (½ pt) 1¼ cups milk
550 g (1 lb 5 oz) 5 cups plain flour (approx)
pinch of salt
50 g (2 oz) 4 tablespoons butter
3 eggs

Cream the yeast and the sugar with a little warm water. Gradually add the warm milk and about half the sifted flour. Beat well with a wooden spoon until the consistency resembles a rather thick pancake batter. Cover with a cloth and leave in a warm place to rise for about half an hour. When the dough has risen to double its original quantity and is full of bubbles add the salt, melted butter, beaten eggs and the rest of the flour. Knead by hand for about half an hour until the dough comes away from the bowl without sticking. The mixture should be firm enough to roll out. Cover with a cloth and leave to rise a second time in a warm place. This may take anything from 1-4 hours depending on the room temperature. When it has doubled in bulk again remove from the bowl and knead lightly on a floured board.

Yeast baking is the most difficult subject in this book. It requires patience and practice. My first attempts when married were terrible and I confess I was in tears. It looked so easy when my mother did it and I helped her. However, I soon found out that it depends on the temperature of the room. (I had a cold kitchen in the North of England.) You should have a warm temperature since, if it is cool it will take twice as long. It also depends on the quality of the flour. It should be dry. If damp, the results will not be so good. If the dough is heavy, ie more flour, it will take twice as long as the dough which is soft and light, ie less flour. The best dough is like cake, not too hard. This is the easiest to handle.

To make pirog (pie): Roll the pastry out about 3 mm (1/8 in.) thick and line a greased baking-tin with half of it. Spread the filling evenly and cover with the rest of the pastry. Pinch the edges and prick with a fork. Leave to rise again for a further half-hour before putting into the oven. Brush with beaten egg if you wish and bake in a fairly hot oven 200°C (400°F) Mark 6 for about 20 minutes until golden brown. When ready transfer to a suitable dish, brush with melted butter and cover with a tea-cloth to prevent the crust from hardening.

To make piroshki (small pies): The quantity of pastry given above will make about 15 piroshki but will only need a third as much filling as the larger pirog. Form the pastry into a roll about 50 mm (2in.) in diameter and cut off 25 mm (1 in.) pieces. Press each piece in the middle to form a small circle and put into each one heaped teaspoonful of filling. Pinch the edges together over the filling and put the piroshki on a greased baking-sheet. Leave them for about half an hour to rise again. Brush with beaten egg, if you wish, and bake in a fairly hot oven 200°C (400°F) Mark 6 for 10-20 minutes until golden brown. Transfer to a suitable dish when ready, brush with melted butter and cover with a tea-cloth.

Piroshki made with yeast pastry can also be fried in deep oil. They should be lifted out with a perforated spoon when they turn golden.

Pirog and piroshki may be eaten hot or cold. If hot, they are always served with butter. They may be served with soup or eaten as a separate course. Pirog and piroshki made from meat, cabbage or mushroom may be eaten with beef or chicken bouillon. Meat pirog makes a specially good accompaniment for shchi. All types of pirog are served with borshch, the only exception being cabbage pirog which is never served with Ukrainian borshch.

Short pastry

450 g (1 lb) 3½ cups self-raising flour
225 g (8 oz) 1 cup butter
pinch of salt
water to mix

Sift the flour into a basin and add a pinch of salt. Cut the butter into small cubes and rub them into the flour using the tips of your fingers until the mixture resembles fine breadcrumbs. Add only enough water to make a stiff dough. Mix with a knife. Roll out very lightly on a floured board. When used for pirog bake in a fairly hot oven 200°C (400°F) Mark 6 for about 20 minutes until golden brown.

The ideal thing is to have a marble slab. We used to have one but now there is less space there is no room to keep it. However, a pastry board is a must. It is difficult to get one now but well worth the effort. Short pastry is best if kept in the fridge for 30 minutes after you have rolled it out. This will minimise the danger of shrinking.

Puff pastry

350 g (12 oz) 2 ⅔ cups plain flour
pinch of salt
350 g (12 oz) 1½ cups unsalted butter
juice of ½ lemon
cold water to mix

Sift the flour into a basin and add the salt and lemon juice. Rub in 25 g (1 oz) 2 tablespoons of butter. Add enough cold water to mix to a soft dough. Knead on a floured board until smooth. Roll out into a square. Form the butter into an oblong and place it on one half of the pastry. Fold over the other half and seal the edges. Roll out slightly. Fold in three and put aside in a cold place for 20 minutes. Repeat this process five or six times being careful not to press out the air bubbles which form.

When ready it can be rolled out to the required thickness and made into a pirog. Put the pirog into the fridge for about 20 minutes and then transfer it immediately to a very hot oven 240°C (475°F) Mark 9 and bake for about 20 minutes or until brown.

The secret of good puff pastry is to have all the ingredients cold and to put it into a really hot oven. If you have warm hands it is said that you are no good as a pastry maker. Hence the saying 'she has a light hand with pastry'.

Sour cream pastry

450 g (1 lb) 3½ cups self-raising flour
100 g (4 oz) ½ cup butter
275 ml (½ pt) 1¼ cups sour cream
½ teaspoon salt
1 tablespoon sugar
2 eggs

Cut the butter into small cubes. Sift the flour into a basin. Make a well in the centre and add the butter, sour cream, salt, sugar and eggs. Mix the ingredients very thoroughly with a wooden fork. Turn out on to a floured board and knead quickly by hand until the dough is of a smooth, stiff consistency. Leave in a cold place for about 40 minutes.

Roll out and use for pirog or piroshki. Brush with beaten egg and bake in a fairly hot oven 200-230°C (400-450°F) Mark 6-8 for about 20 minutes until brown.

This pastry is especially recommended for mushroom pirog.

This is a good way to use up cream which has gone sour and makes excellent pastry. For pastry you can use sour cream which has been kept and is not very fresh.

Plain pastry *(for Lamb pirog)*

4 tablespoons oil
water
450 g (1 lb) 3½ cups plain flour
½ teaspoon salt

Add enough water to the oil to make up 250 ml

(½ pt) 1¼ cups. Sift the flour into a basin and add the salt. Add the liquid gradually, stirring all the time with a wooden spoon. When it is fairly stiff turn out on to a floured board and knead by hand until it is a smooth, firm consistency. Roll out fairly thinly and make into a pirog. Bake in a hot oven 230°C (450°F) Mark 8 for about 25 minutes until brown.

This type of pastry is stiff and needs a heavy rolling pin to roll out properly. I keep two rolling pins in the kitchen, one light, and one heavy for difficult work.

Fillings for pirog and piroshki

The quantities of pastry given in each of the above recipes are sufficient to make a large pirog or about 15 small piroshki. The quantities of fillings given below are also sufficient for a large pirog. Piroshki made from the stated amounts of pastry, only need about a third as much of the filling as a pirog.

Rice and mushroom pirog

serves 4-5

150 g (6 oz) 1 cup rice
salt and pepper
1 large onion
150 g (6 oz) mushrooms
butter for frying

Boil the rice in salted water until cooked. Strain. Meanwhile, peel and chop the onion and clean the mushrooms. Fry the onion and mushrooms lightly in butter for about 20 minutes. Mix the cooked rice with the onions and mushrooms and season. Cool and use for the pirog.

You can also make this pirog omitting the rice. It is a good time to try it when you have pickled your own mushrooms and have too many for a sauce or to fry up with bacon. The quantity should not be less than 450 g (1 lb) 3½ cups for 225 g (8 oz) 1 cup fat for short pastry. If you have not got enough pickled mushrooms add a few cultivated ones.

This is a favourite dish in Lent.

Rice and egg pirog

serves 4-5

150 g (6 oz) 1 cup rice
salt and pepper to taste
25-50 g (1-2 oz) 2-4 tablespoons butter
2 hard boiled eggs

Boil the rice in salted water until cooked. Strain and rinse in cold water. Return to the saucepan and add the butter. Cook over a low heat until it has melted. Stir lightly, season and add the chopped hard boiled eggs. The ingredients should be well mixed but too much stirring will spoil the rice. Cool and fill the pirog with the mixture.

This is also popular in Lent since it has no meat. However, if you have any left-over cooked beef you can mince (grind) it and add to the pirog. Do not forget to add a little stock or water to the meat or the pirog will be too dry. I put a few dabs of butter on top of my stuffing before covering it with pastry to ensure the mixture is moist.

Serve with soup.

Beef pirog

serves 4-5

400 g (1 lb) 2 cups fresh minced beef or beef boiled for stock
1 onion
butter for frying
salt and pepper to taste
2 hard boiled eggs

Peel and chop the onion and fry it lightly in butter. If fresh mince is used add it to the onion and fry for about 20 minutes until brown. If the meat has already been cooked put it through a mincer and mix with the fried onion. Season. Add 2-3 tablespoons water or bouillon and the chopped hard boiled eggs. Make into the pirog.

This is a popular way of using up the beef you have left over after making stock or soup. Some add a little cooked rice if there is not enough stuffing. You can also add a few knobs of butter on top of the stuffing before covering it with pastry to ensure the pirog does not dry in the oven.

This is a Russian national dish and eaten with borshch or clear soup on any festive occasion such as birthday parties, etc.

Salmon pirog with rice and egg

serves 4-5

150 g (6 oz) 1 cup rice
salt to taste
50 g (2 oz) 4 tablespoons butter
2 hard boiled eggs
1 sprig parsley
600 g (1½ lb) salmon

Boil the rice in salted water until it is cooked. Strain, rinse in cold water and return to the saucepan. Add 25 g (1 oz) 2 tablespoons butter; stir over low heat until melted. Add the chopped hard boiled eggs and chopped parsley and mix well. Cool. Line a greased tin with the pastry. Spread half the rice mixture over the pastry. Clean and bone the salmon and put small pieces of fish on top of the rice. Season and dot with butter. Cover with the rest of the rice mixture and the pastry.

For a more economical dish substitute halibut for salmon.

Serve this dish with borshch or clear soup. It can also be served with fish soup.

Salmon is in season in England and Scotland from February to August. In Ireland from January to September. It is much cheaper when in season. You can substitute tinned salmon for this recipe. Drain off the liquid first and remove bones and skin. It will not taste as good but I add a little good fresh white fish to it to improve the flavour.

Cabbage and egg pirog

serves 4-5

1 medium white Dutch cabbage
50 g (2 oz) 4 tablespoons butter
1 onion
salt and pepper to taste
2 hard boiled eggs

Discard the outer leaves and the thick veins. Wash and drain the cabbage and shred it finely. Melt the butter and fry the chopped onion lightly. Add the cabbage gradually and cook on a low heat, stirring frequently to prevent burning. The cabbage may turn slightly golden, but it should not be allowed to brown. It will take about 45 minutes to cook. Add salt and pepper about 15 minutes before it is ready. Cool. Chop the hard boiled eggs and mix with the cabbage. Fill the pie with this mixture.

This is a Russian national dish and can be served with clear soup or Moscow borshch. It is very tasty and a great favourite in Lent when meat is not eaten. I have a story about this: I had a student once (a young boy) and I used to give him some sponge or cabbage pirog after the lesson. When my book came out I asked him if he had tried my Russian sponge since he was interested in cooking. His reply was "I prefer the cabbage pie!" I was very flattered that a young boy should take the trouble to make this dish.

Liver and buckwheat pirog

serves 8

300 g (12 oz) liver (lamb's, pig's or calf's)
150 g (6 oz) 1 cup kasha
50-75 g (2-3 oz) 4-6 tablespoons butter
1 onion
salt and pepper to taste
2 hard boiled eggs

Cook the kasha (see page 66). Meanwhile, prepare the liver. Remove any skin or membrane and wash meat in cold water. Cut in small pieces and fry in butter. Peel and chop the onion and cook slowly with the liver for 5 minutes. When ready, chop the liver finely and season. Mix the cooked kasha and the chopped hard boiled eggs with the liver and onion, adding a little more butter if it is dry. Cool and make into a pirog.

This is a useful way of using up any left-over kasha. Remember to cook the liver very lightly or it will be hard. This pirog is rather filling and if you serve it with borshch, have a light pudding to follow such as ice cream.

Caucasian lamb pirog
Cherbureki

serves 6

600 g (1½ lb) fillet of lamb
1 onion
2-3 tablespoons water
1 clove garlic
salt and black pepper to taste
50 g (2 oz) ½ cup cooked rice
1 beaten egg

Make the plain pastry indicated on page 102. Chop the lamb with a sharp knife into very small pieces or put through a coarse mincer. Add the finely chopped onion, crushed garlic, rice and water. Also plenty of salt and pepper. It should be highly seasoned. Roll out the pastry very thinly. Cut out circles of pastry with the aid of a small saucer. Put the mixture on one half of the pastry. Brush the edges with beaten egg and fold over and seal. Fry in a deep frying pan in oil and serve very hot.

This pastry is like pasta and should be rolled out wafer thin. Use a heavy rolling pin. This makes the work easier.

These little pirogi are sold hot in the streets of Moscow.

Kouliabaka

Kouliabaka is a rich type of pirog. It has more filling than the ordinary pirog and is made either with puff pastry (page 102) or a rich yeast pastry. The ordinary yeast pastry in this book (page 101) can be adapted by adding 50 g (2 oz) 4 tablespoons extra butter and a little more flour. The pastry should be rolled out thicker than for a pirog as there is more weight in the filling. The actual pie will be smaller, but thicker. Kouliabaka can be made in the same shape as a pirog or in the shape of a thick, fat sausage. The same stuffings can be used as for an ordinary pirog. If it is made from fish, two or more varieties are usually used and one of these would be a more expensive type of fish such as salmon or sturgeon.

Kouliabaki are served on special occasions.

Fish kouliabaka

serves 6-8

PUFF PASTRY (page 102)

FILLING
200 g (8 oz) white fish or bream
200 g (8 oz) halibut
200 g (8 oz) salmon
1 onion
25 g (1 oz) 2 tablespoons butter
1 sprig parsley or dill
560 ml ($1\frac{1}{8}$ pt) 2¾ cups water
150 g (6 oz) 1 cup coarse grained semolina
salt and pepper to taste
1 egg

Prepare the pastry in the quantity given (page 102). Remove the skin and bones and wash the fish. Peel and chop the onion finely and fry it lightly in butter with the chopped parsley or dill. Add to the white fish or bream and chop the fish with the onion as finely as possible. Meanwhile, bring the water to the boil and add the salt and semolina. Stir quickly to prevent lumps from forming. Remove from the heat when cooked and fold in the beaten egg. Return to the heat and warm through, stirring all the time. Make sure that it does not boil. Remove from the heat and add the chopped white fish, onion and parsley. Adjust the seasoning and leave to cool.

Roll out the pastry. It should be slightly thicker than for an ordinary pirog as there is more filling. Line a baking-tin with half the pastry and spread half the semolina filling over the bottom. Slice the raw halibut and salmon and put the slices on top of the semolina. Season and put in with rest of the semolina and fish mixture. Cover with the rest of the pastry. Trim and pinch the edges and prick with a fork. Brush with beaten egg, if you wish, and put in a hot oven 230-260°C (450-500°F) Mark 8-10 turning down to 200°C (400°F), Mark 6 when it starts to brown. Bake for 35-45 minutes.

This is a party dish and takes time to prepare but is well worth it. Use tinned salmon if fresh is not available. The taste will not be the same but it is a good substitute.

Serve with clear soup.

Sprat shangi

serves 4-5

yeast pastry (page 101)
600 g (1½ lb) fresh sprats
butter
salt to taste

Make the yeast pastry as for a pirog. Wash the fish, trim head and tail; salt fish. Roll out the dough on a floured board and cut into 15 cm (6 in.) squares. Place three fishes top-to-tail on each tart and turn up the edges. Put the shangi on greased baking-sheets and leave in a warm place to rise for another half an hour. Place in a fairly hot oven 200°C (400°F) Mark 6 for about 20 minutes. Add a knob of butter to each shangi before serving. This is a dish from Archangel.

Sprat shangi is an inexpensive dish and most original. It was a great favourite of my father's and one which we always had in Lent. You can substitute any small fish in these tarts.

Paste for pelmeni and vareniki

225 g (8 oz) 1¾ cups plain flour
salt to taste
2-3 tablespoons water
1 egg

Sift the flour into a basin. Add the salt. Make a well in the centre and break in the egg. Mix to a fairly stiff paste with a fork, adding a little water at a time. Knead on a floured board until it is smooth and all the flour is worked in. Roll out thinly and use for pelmeni or vareniki. This is the correct amount of paste for the fillings given in the following recipes.

Siberian pelmeni

serves 4

PASTE

FILLING
300 g (12 oz) top rump
salt and pepper to taste
2 tablespoons water
1 tablespoon finely chopped onion (optional)

Make the paste as in the previous recipe.

Mince the meat very finely. Season and add the onion and water. Mix well. Cut the thinly rolled paste into small rounds with a wineglass and put a teaspoonful of the filling on to each round. Pinch the edges together to make small 'pies'. Use a little water if the pastry will not stick. Drop the pelmeni into boiling salted water, bone stock or bouillon (see page 17), and simmer for 10-15 minutes. Serve in the liquid or lift out and transfer to a dish with melted butter and serve with sour cream or vinegar and mustard.

Eat as a main course.

This dish was invented in Siberia as the name suggests. It is very convenient as they can be made in advance and frozen. In fact many housewives say that they are better if frozen first. If you prepare them in advance and decide to keep them in the fridge they must not touch each other unless frozen hard or they will stick.

When boiling they will float to the surface when ready but a little extra cooking does no harm if you are talking at the dinner table.

This is a favourite dish for men so make enough. Allow 15 per head as a main course.

The tastiest way to eat them is with vinegar and mustard. There are many other fillings for these little pies. When made very small they are called 'Oushki' which means little ears in Russian. When made with a fruit filling they are called Vareniki. In the south they make them slightly larger and sometimes fry the mince.

Vegetarian fillings were used during Lent and other great religious feasts, ie before Christmas. These were often served on Christmas Eve with soup in preparation for all the lovely food to come, ie sucking pig, goose, etc.

Pork and beef filling
Use slightly less pork than beef. Remember to have only very fine lean pork mince. If the butcher will not oblige bring the mince home and put it through the grinder once more yourself.

Mushroom filling
These can be made with fresh or dried mushrooms. Boil the mushrooms first then chop and mix with finely chopped fried onion. Dried mushrooms can be bought in delicatessen shops.

Potato filling
Use mashed potato in place of the mince.

Cabbage filling
Use finely chopped hard white cabbage (Dutch) and a small amount of minced pork and onion to flavour. This is eaten in eastern parts of Russia.

Lamb filling
Use lean lamb filling, ie from the leg. It should be finely minced as above. Serve with yoghurt and melted butter or sour cream. These are eaten in Uzbek and other eastern parts of Russia where beef is scarce.

Vareniki with curd cheese *serves 4*

PASTE

FILLING
300 g (12 oz) 1½ cups curd cheese
1 egg
40 g (1½ oz) 3 tablespoons sugar
25 g (1 oz) 2 tablespoons butter
salt to taste
165 ml ($\frac{1}{3}$ pt) ¾ cup sour cream

Make the paste (page 105). Sieve the cheese to remove any lumps. Add the egg yolk, sugar and 15 g (½ oz) 1 tablespoon melted butter. Home-made cheese (page 147) may need a little salt, but bought cheese is usually salty enough. Mix thoroughly with a wooden spoon. Cut the thinly rolled paste into small rounds with a wine or sherry glass. Put a teaspoonful of the mixture on to each round. Dab the edges with beaten egg white and pinch them together to form small 'pies'. Drop the vareniki into boiling salted water and simmer for 10-15 minutes until they rise to the surface. Lift them out with a perforated spoon. Melt the remaining butter and pour into a warm dish. Put in the vareniki and serve with sour cream.

If sugar is omitted this is a main course and eaten in Lent. With sugar it becomes a pudding.

Vareniki with damsons or cherries *serves 6*

PASTE

FILLING
300 g (12 oz) morello cherries or damsons
165 ml ($\frac{1}{3}$ pt) ¾ cup water
pinch of salt
250 ml (½ pt) 1¼ cups sour cream
castor sugar

Make a paste (page 105). Stone the cherries or damsons and cover them with the sugar. Leave for several hours in the sun, if possible, to absorb the sugar. Remove the kernels from a few of the stones and crush them. Boil them in 165 ml (1/3 pt) ¾ cup water for a few minutes and strain. When the fruit is ready add any of the juice which has formed and any of the sugar which has not been absorbed and boil for a few minutes to make a syrup.

Cut the thinly rolled paste into rounds. Put either 1 damson or 2 cherries on each round and pinch the edges firmly together. Drop them into boiling salted water and simmer until they float to the top. Lift out with a perforated spoon and drain off all the water. Transfer to a warm dish and pour over the hot syrup. Serve with sour cream and castor sugar.

This is of course a summer dish. It is rather filling so if you decide to do it have a light salad for the main course.

You can substitute cherry plums instead of damsons or cherries. These are small red plums which have a short season in the summer.

Moscow pastry

225 g (8 oz) 1 cup butter
100 g (4 oz) ½ cup vanilla sugar
1 egg
450 g (1 lb) 3½ cups self-raising flour
rind of 1 lemon

Cream the butter and vanilla sugar until white. Add the beaten egg and grated lemon rind. Beat. Gradually fold in the sifted flour and mix with the hands to a firm dough. It will not be as stiff as English short pastry and is more difficult to handle but it is worth the extra trouble. Use for vatrushka (this page) and all tarts. Bake in a fairly hot oven 200°C (400°F) Mark 6 for 20 minutes until golden brown.

This pastry is very rich and short. It never goes hard like short pastry so you will find you will have to use your hands to press it into shape.

Sweet yeast pastry

15 g (½ oz) fresh yeast or 1 packet dried yeast
1 teaspoon sugar
575 g (1¼ lb) scant 4½ cups plain flour
275 ml (½ pt) 1¼ cups milk
75 g (3 oz) 6 tablespoons butter
2 eggs and 1 yolk
75 g (3 oz) 6 tablespoons vanilla sugar
pinch of salt

Cream the yeast with a teaspoon of sugar and a little warm water. Warm the milk and add it to the yeast mixture together with half the sifted flour. Beat well to make a batter. Cover with a cloth and leave in a warm place to rise for about half an hour. When it has doubled its original size and there are bubbles on top add the melted butter, eggs, vanilla sugar, salt and the rest of the sifted flour. Knead well for about half an hour until the dough comes away from the sides of the bowl without sticking. Cover with a cloth and leave to rise a second time in a warm place. When it has doubled its bulk again knead lightly on a floured board and roll out. Make into a tart and leave to rise a third time for half an hour before putting in the oven. Bake in a fairly hot oven 200°C (400°F) Mark 6 for about 20 minutes. Use for making vatrushka (see below) and all tarts.

Remember when making all yeast dough that it takes time to rise so allow enough time. The warmer the temperature the quicker it will start bubbling. You may have to adjust the amount of flour since flour varies so much. The texture should be like cake, not too soft or too hard. If you do it in a mixer test it with your hand.

Vatrushka

serves 4-6

Moscow or sweet yeast pastry (this page)

FILLING
600 g (1½ lb) 3 cups curd cheese
150 g (6 oz) ¾ cup vanilla sugar
rind of 1 lemon
a few sultanas (optional)
2 eggs
2 tablespoons fresh cream

Make Moscow or sweet yeast pastry in the quantities given.

FILLING
Sieve the cheese to remove any lumps and add the vanilla sugar. The amount of cheese used can be varied and the amount of sugar needed depends on whether the cheese is home-made or bought. Bought cheese usually needs more sugar. Add the grated lemon rind, sultanas, beaten eggs and cream and mix well.

Roll out the pastry and line a large tin. Spread the cheese mixture evenly and turn up the edges of the tart. Strips of pastry can be laid across the tart. Brush the pastry with beaten egg if you wish. If sweet yeast pastry has been used leave the pastry to rise for half an hour before putting it in the oven. Bake in a fairly hot oven 200°C (400°F) Mark 6 for about 20 minutes. Moscow pastry should also be cooked for about 20 minutes but will need a slightly hotter oven 220°C (425°F) Mark 7.

This is a great favourite for tea in all Russian households. You will see that it is different from the cheese cake sold in the shops. However, this cheese tart originated in Eastern Europe.

Blini

Blini are pancakes made with yeast. They are served very hot with plenty of melted butter, sour cream and a large selection of salted fish and caviar. Although in Russia they are served as an extra dish they are sufficiently filling to be served as a main course. Blini are traditionally eaten in the week before Lent (most people have two helpings, so be prepared) and clear soup is served after the blini as the salted fish makes one thirsty.

Blini are now world famous and mostly eaten in restaurants but it is quite easy to do them at home if you follow the instructions. By tradition a blini party should be the week before Lent. Have a 'run through' before the party trying out just how long it takes before you can start frying the pancakes then you will be more confident. When frying the blini have a heavy-based pan, in fact, you should have at least two or three going at the same time or you will never finish. My mother and I used to have 4 frying pans going at the same time. You will have to be quick, of course.

Use a mixture of oil and melted butter to grease the pan. A pastry brush is best for this. Make the pan very hot before the first pancake. By tradition the first pancake is supposed to be fat and only good enough for the dog. The second pancake should be all right. Use a soup ladle, one half measure should be enough to spoon the batter out of the bowl. Remember that the salted fish, caviar, etc, should be on the side of the plate and not inside the pancake. Vodka is drunk all the time the pancakes are eaten.

To serve, put 2 or 3 blini at a time on warm plates and pour over as much melted butter and sour cream as required. The blini should be folded over or rolled and eaten with one of the varieties of salted fish or caviar.

Blini

serves 8

700 g (1 lb 9 oz) 5½ cups plain flour
50 g (2 oz) fresh yeast or 4 packets dried yeast
700 ml (1¼ pt) 3 cups warm water
50 g (2 oz) 4 tablespoons melted butter
3 eggs
1 teaspoon salt
25 g (1 oz) 2 tablespoons sugar
575 ml (1 pt) 2½ cups milk
butter or oil for frying

Mix the yeast with a little warm water to a smooth paste. Add the rest of the warm water and half the sifted flour. Mix with a wooden spoon, cover and leave in a warm place for about half an hour. It should rise to approximately double its original quantity and be full of bubbles. Gradually add the rest of the sifted flour, beating until the mixture is smooth. Stir in the melted butter, egg yolks, sugar and salt. Warm the milk and add it gradually until a smooth batter is obtained. Leave in a warm place to rise a second time. Beat the egg whites until they stand in peaks and fold them in when the mixture has doubled. Allow it to rise a third time. The batter should be full of bubbles. Heat two small frying-pans with thick bases and brush them with melted butter or oil. Pour tablespoons of the batter into the frying-pans. The blini should be very thin when cooked and full of holes like lace. The first blini are often rather thick and can be discarded. If the batter seems too thick a little more warm milk can be added carefully. Keep the first blini in a warm dish while you are frying the others. The rest of the batter can be left for a short time while you are eating the first batch. These quantities should make about 32 blini.

Blini can also be made from a mixture of buckwheat and plain white flour. The method and other ingredients are exactly the same. Add 450 g (1 lb) 3½ cups of sifted buckwheat flour in the first stage and 250 g (9 oz) 2 cups of sifted white flour in the second. A little more salt can be used.

Basic pancakes

10 pancakes

115 g (4 oz) scant 1 cup self-raising flour
pinch of salt
1 teaspoon sugar
1 egg
275 ml (½ pt) 1¼ cups milk
butter or oil for frying

Sift the flour and salt into a basin with the sugar. Add the egg. Beat with a wooden spoon, gradually adding the milk. Leave for half an hour. Heat a frying-pan, brush with oil or melted butter and pour in about two tablespoons of batter, tilting the pan so that it is evenly covered. Fry on one side until brown. Turn or toss carefully and fry on the other side. Put aside to keep warm while the other pancakes are cooking. If the first pancake is too thick dilute the batter with a little warm milk. Serve with jam or lemon juice and castor sugar.

This pancake mixture is suitable for making blinchati piroshki (see opposite page) or quick pancakes with cream cheese (see opposite page).

Pancake batter is best if left in a warm place before you start frying. Remember to have the pan very hot. A thick-based pan is essential (omelette pan) for good results and it is well worth investing in one or two.

Russians love stuffing everything and pancakes are no exception. Try pancakes with apple sauce (page 95). Put the sauce at one end of the pancake and roll up. Dust with castor sugar mixed with cinnamon. Serve with cream or sour cream.

Cranberry sauce can be used in the same way (page 94). Serve with fresh double cream and castor sugar.

Pancakes get cold very quickly and are best if served straight from the pan. See that the plates are warm too.

Pancake pie

You can make a savoury or sweet pie if you wish with the basic pancakes. Use either minced/ground beef (this page), blinchati piroshki, curd cheese (page 147) apple (page 95) or cranberry. Butter a large soufflé dish about the same diameter as the pancakes. Put one pancake at the bottom with the uncooked side down, cover with a layer of filling, continue till the pancakes are used up. Finish with a pancake on top, dot with butter and breadcrumbs. Bake in a hot oven to brown. Turn out on a dish and cut wedges of pancake pie. Serve the meat with soup and the sweet pie with sugar and sour cream.

Blinchati piroshki

10 pancakes

basic pancake batter (see opposite page)
butter
dry breadcrumbs

FILLING
200 g (8 oz) 1 cup minced meat (beef, veal or pork)
1 small onion
butter for frying
salt and pepper to taste
1 hard boiled egg
1 sprig dill or parsley

Make the basic pancake batter in the quantities given (see opposite).

FILLING

Fry the peeled and chopped onion lightly in butter. If fresh mince is used add it to the onion and fry for about 20 minutes until brown. If the meat is already cooked put it through the mincer and add the fried onion. Add a little water too or the stuffing will be too dry. Season and add the chopped hard boiled egg and chopped dill or parsley. Heat through. The filling should be ready at the same time as the pancakes.

Cook the pancakes but leave one side fairly white. Put a tablespoon of the filling on to the brown side. Turn the edges over to form a small 'envelope', sprinkle with dry breadcrumbs, dot with butter and brown for a few minutes under the grill. Serve with bouillon.

These piroshki are very popular in Russia because they use up the left-over meat after making soup. They are quick and easy. You can also serve them with borshch or have them as a supper dish with green vegetables.

Quick pancakes with cream cheese

10 pancakes

basic pancake batter (see opposite page)
125 ml (¼ pt) $\frac{2}{3}$ cup sour cream
sugar

FILLING
200 g (8 oz) 1 cup curd cheese
1 small egg
25 g (1 oz) 2 tablespoons vanilla sugar
a few sultanas (optional)

FILLING

Sieve the cheese to remove any lumps. Add the beaten egg, vanilla sugar and sultanas and mix well.

Make the pancakes. When they are all cooked put a tablespoon of the filling on to each pancake and roll up. Brown on both sides for a few minutes under the grill. Sprinkle with sugar and serve with sour cream.

The pancakes can be prepared in advance if you wish. Place a piece of greaseproof paper between each pancake. They can also be stored in a plastic bag in a refrigerator for up to four days. You can sprinkle these with sugar mixed with cinnamon before serving.

Cream pancakes

10 pancakes

2 large eggs
1 tablespoon sugar
50 g (2 oz) 4 tablespoons butter
115 g (4 oz) scant 1 cup self-raising flour
1 tablespoon milk
115 ml (scant ¼ pt) ½ cup single cream
butter or oil for frying

Beat the eggs and sugar well with a fork. Melt the butter and beat it into the mixture. Sift the flour into another basin and mix with the milk and cream. Gradually add the mixture of eggs, sugar and butter to the flour, beating all the time until it is smooth. Leave for 1-2 hours. Heat a frying-pan with a thick base and brush with oil or butter. Pour in about two tablespoons of batter and fry on one side until brown. Turn or toss carefully and fry on the other side. If the first pancake is too thick, dilute the batter with a little warm milk. Serve with jam or castor sugar and lemon juice.

These can be made in advance and stacked with greaseproof paper between each pancake. Cover with a cloth and they will keep for a few hours till needed. To reheat put into fireproof dish with a lid and brush the top pancake with melted butter. Put into the oven at 200°C (400°F) Mark 6 for about 7 minutes. These are good for a dinner party as they are rich and a little bit different from the ordinary pancakes.

Remember to use only a little oil or butter for frying or you will spoil the delicate flavour.

Mlintzi *(pancakes)* with wild strawberries

8 small pancakes

2 eggs
15 g (½ oz) 2 tablespoons flour
25 g (1 oz) 2 tablespoons sugar
125 ml (¼ pt) $\frac{2}{3}$ cup milk
pinch of salt
oil for frying
2 cups strawberries
1 tablespoon icing sugar for dredging

Wash and hull strawberries. Drain. Dredge with icing sugar. Leave for at least 1 hour.

Separate eggs. Beat egg yolks till white with the sugar. Stir in half the milk and the flour. Blend to a smooth batter. Add the remaining milk and stir. Whip the whites till they stand in peaks and fold into the batter. Heat a heavy frying pan. Brush with oil and take 1 tablespoon of batter and pour into the pan. Tip from side to side to distribute the batter. Fry slowly. Turn the pancake and put the strawberries in the middle leaving the sides free. Turn the pancake quickly and cook the other side. Turn on to a hot plate. Serve with more sugar if liked and the juices from the strawberries.

You can do these from cultivated strawberries or raspberries. If using strawberries cut into small pieces since the pancakes are quite small. This is quite complicated to do, so if you are not experienced just roll the strawberries in the pancake. They are very light and the batter cannot be kept long so it is advisable to cook straight away and not to do large quantities at the same time or the white of egg tends to drop.

Ukrainian little cheese pancakes

8 pancakes

150 g (6 oz) ¾ cup curd cheese
1 dessertspoonful sugar
1 egg
25 g (1 oz) ¼ cup self-raising flour
1 tablespoon flour for dredging
oil for frying
60 ml ($\frac{1}{8}$ pt) $\frac{1}{4}$ cup sour cream

Put the cheese through a sieve if necessary (see instructions). Separate the egg. Beat the yolk with the sugar till white. Blend the cheese, the yolk, sugar and flour together. Whip the white till it stands in peaks. Fold into the mixture. Heat a heavy frying pan and put in oil. When very hot, drop tablespoons of the mixture in and fry on both sides. Keep warm. The temperature should be reduced immediately so that they do not burn but they must catch. If you find the batter running add a little more flour or dredge the pancakes whilst they are still cooking. The best way is to have plenty of oil for them to fry in and to see the pan is hot enough to start with.

These are similar to Scotch pancakes in appearance and the batter should be the same consistency. They are very light and have a cheese flavour. Eat with castor sugar or jam immediately. They are quick to prepare and should be fried at once and not kept to rise like ordinary pancakes.

Cakes

Pryanik *(honey cake)*

2 eggs
50 g (2 oz) 4 tablespoons sugar
70 ml ($\frac{1}{8}$ pt) ¼ cup vegetable oil
2 tablespoons honey
pinch of baking powder
175 g (6 oz) 1 $\frac{1}{3}$ cups self-raising flour
½ teaspoon powdered cinnamon

Beat the egg yolks with the sugar. Warm the oil and honey a little and add to the egg yolks. Mix in the flour, baking powder and cinnamon. Beat the egg whites until they stand in peaks and fold them into the mixture. Transfer to a greased baking-tin and bake in a moderate oven 180°C (350°F) Mark 4 for about 40 minutes.

This pryanik will keep in a tin for several days.

Pryaniki

375 g (15 oz) 3¼ cups self-raising flour
½ teaspoon powdered cloves
½ teaspoon powdered nutmeg
½ teaspoon powdered cinnamon
½ teaspoon powdered ginger
¼ teaspoon powdered cardamom
¼ teaspoon baking powder
2 eggs
225 g (8 oz) 1 cup brown sugar

GLAZE
125 ml (¼ pt) $\frac{2}{3}$ cup water
300 g (12 oz) 1½ cups sugar
2 egg whites

Sift the flour, baking powder and spices into a bowl. Beat the eggs and sugar for about five minutes and add them to the flour mixture. Mix well. The dough should be stiff and fairly sticky. Roll into balls of about 25 mm (1 in.) in diameter. Put on a greased baking-sheet and bake in a moderate oven 190°C (375°F) Mark 5 for about 15 minutes.

GLAZE
Meanwhile, boil the water and sugar to form a syrup. Beat the egg-whites until stiff and pour the syrup into the egg-whites. Beat well. Dip the pryaniki in the glaze while they are still hot. Cool on a wire tray.

This quantity will make about 40 pryaniki.

When breaking the eggs it is safer, in case the yolk breaks, to break them into two cups and then transfer the yolks and whites. If you have the tiniest particle of yolk in the white it will not beat up so well and ruin the cake.

Vanilla, lemon or peppermint pryaniki

225 g (8 oz) 1 cup castor (verifine) sugar
2 large eggs
275 g (10 oz) 2¼ cups self-raising flour
½ teaspoon baking powder
flavouring

Beat the eggs with the sugar till white, add flavouring (see page 112). Blend in the flour and finish by kneading on a floured board by hand. The dough should be stiff enough to handle. Grease 3 large tins if you are doing the full amount and make balls of the mixture by hand. They should be the size of a teaspoon of the mixture. Place the balls in rows on a baking sheet well apart as they will rise and spread. If they touch they will spoil their shape. Cook for 7-10 minutes at 200°C (400°F) Mark 6.

These are suitable to serve with coffee after dinner or with afternoon tea instead of biscuits. They should not be overcooked or they will become crisp. They should be soft throughout.

For vanilla pryaniki: Use vanilla sugar instead of ordinary sugar.

For lemon pryaniki: Add the grated rind of one lemon to the above mixture.

For peppermint pryaniki: Add two saltspoonfuls of oil of peppermint to the mixture.

This recipe will make about 36 pryaniki.

This is a simplified recipe from a Soviet book but it is not like the commercial pryaniki you buy in the shops. However, the flavour is good and I always put these on the table to have with coffee after dinner when I have a party.

Khvorost

1 egg	225 g (8 oz) 1¾ cups plain flour
25 g (1 oz) 2 tablespoons sugar	butter and/or oil for frying
150 ml (¼ pt) ⅔ cup milk	icing sugar
1 sherry glass rum	
½ teaspoon salt	

Beat the egg with the sugar until white. Stir in the milk, rum and salt. Sift in the flour and mix well to a stiff paste. Knead on a floured board until smooth. Roll out thinly and cut into strips of about 100 mm x 25 mm (4 in. x 1 in.) Make a slit down the middle and thread one end through the slit (see diagram). Deep fry in oil or butter or a mixture of the two until golden brown. Remove with a perforated spoon and drain on greaseproof paper. Dredge with sifted icing sugar before serving and eat on the same day.

The secret of deep fat frying is to have the fat very hot and allow the fat to reheat before cooking another batch. Have a lid handy in case the fat catches fire. Strain the fat after use.

Serve with Russian tea. The ladies drank their tea in cups in Russia but the men always in glasses. The head of the household had a silver holder with his initials.

Moscow doughnuts

15 g (½ oz) fresh yeast or 1 packet dried yeast	50 g (2 oz) 4 tablespoons butter
25 g (1 oz) 2 tablespoons sugar	pinch of salt
150 ml (¼ pt) ⅔ cup milk	pinch grated nutmeg, cinnamon or cardamom
250 g (10 oz) 2¼ cups plain flour	jam for filling
2 egg yolks	oil or butter for frying
	icing or castor sugar for coating

Mix the yeast with a teaspoonful of sugar and a little water to a smooth paste. Add the warm milk and about half the sifted flour. Cover with a cloth and leave to rise in a warm place for about half an hour until it has doubled its bulk and is full of bubbles. Gradually add the yolks and sugar, beating all the time. Melt the butter and allow it to cool slightly. Add the butter to the yeast mixture together with the rest of the sifted flour, salt and spice. Knead for about half an hour until the dough leaves the sides of the bowl without sticking. Cover and leave to rise a second time. When it has doubled its bulk again roll out on a floured board to about 15 mm (½ in.) thick. Cut in rounds with a glass. Put a teaspoonful of jam on each round and cover with another round. Pinch the edges to form a ball. Leave for another half an hour to rise. Deep fry in very hot oil or butter until brown. Drain on greaseproof paper. Coat in icing or castor sugar before serving.

See hints opposite for deep fat frying. These should be started early in the morning as they will not keep. All cakes made with yeast dough should if possible, be eaten the same day.

Krendel *(birthday cake)*

40 g (1½ oz) fresh yeast or 3 packets dried yeast
200 ml ($\frac{3}{8}$ pt) 1 cup milk
475 g (1 lb 1 oz) 3¾ cups plain flour
6 eggs
140 g (5 oz) $\frac{2}{3}$ cup butter
150 g (6 oz) ¾ cup vanilla sugar
pinch of salt
75 g (3 oz) ¾ cup sultanas
2 tablespoons icing sugar
50 g (2 oz) ½ cup blanched almonds

Mix the yeast with a teaspoonful of sugar and a little warm water to a smooth paste. Add the warm milk and half the sifted flour. Beat well. Cover with a cloth and leave in a warm place to rise until it has doubled its bulk and has bubbles on top. Add the yolks and the vanilla sugar, stirring all the time. Melt the butter and allow it to cool slightly. Add gradually to the yeast mixture together with the salt, sultanas and remaining flour. Knead well by hand for about half an hour until the dough leaves the sides of the bowl without sticking. Cover with a cloth and leave in a warm place until it has again doubled in bulk. Knead lightly on a floured board. Roll out into a long sausage shape with tapering ends. Make a figure-of-eight by looping the two ends round to the middle of the sausage. Leave on a greased baking-sheet for a further half an hour to rise again. Brush the top of the krendel with beaten egg and sprinkle with chopped almonds. Bake in a moderate oven 180°C (350°F) Mark 4 for 40-50 minutes. When cool, sprinkle with sifted icing sugar.

This is by tradition eaten at a birthday tea party with the samovar at the head of the table where the hostess pours out the tea. The quantity is rather large but there should be enough for everyone. The appearance of this cake is really attractive.

Start early in the morning so there will be no panic and the cake is ready in time. Krendel will not really keep but if any is left over put in a tin to prevent it drying. In this way it will keep for several days.

Sour cream rusks

2 eggs
115 g (4 oz) ½ cup sugar
50 g (2 oz) 4 tablespoons butter
150 ml (¼ pt) $\frac{2}{3}$ cup sour cream
350 g (12 oz) 2$\frac{2}{3}$ cups self-raising flour

Beat the eggs with the sugar until they are white. Beat the butter until it is soft and add it to the eggs and sugar. Fold in the sour cream. Add the sifted flour gradually until the mixture is stiff enough to roll out. Roll out on a floured board making long sausage shapes about 50 mm (2 in.) in diameter. Bake in a moderate oven 190°C (375°F) Mark 5 for about 15-20 minutes until brown. Cool on a wooden board and cut in slices 20 mm (¾ in.) thick. Put on baking-sheets and dry in a slow oven 100°C (200°F) Mark ¼ for 1-2 hours. Store in an airtight tin.

These rusks will keep for weeks in a tin and are a useful standby to serve with coffee or morning tea.

Remember that these rusks must be made with real sour cream, ie cream that has gone sour in the kitchen or you have soured yourself. The shop variety will not do. There is not enough fat content.

Vanilla rusks

25 g (1 oz) fresh yeast or 2 packets dried yeast
140 ml (¼ pt) $\frac{2}{3}$ cup plus 2 tablespoons milk
700 g (1 lb 9 oz) 5½ cups flour
pinch of salt
4 eggs
175 g (6 oz) ¾ cup butter
175 g (6 oz) ¾ cup sugar
vanilla essence
grated nutmeg (optional)

Mix the yeast with a teaspoon of sugar in a little warm water to a smooth paste. Gradually add the warm milk and about half the sifted flour. Beat well with a wooden spoon until it resembles a thick pancake batter. Cover with a cloth and leave in a warm place to rise for about half an hour until it has doubled its original bulk and is full of bubbles. Mix together the eggs and sugar and melt the butter and allow it to cool slightly. Add these together with the rest of the sifted flour, salt, vanilla essence and nutmeg. Knead by hand for about half an hour until the dough comes away from the sides of the bowl. Cover with a cloth and leave in a warm place to rise a second time. When it has doubled its bulk again turn it out on to a floured board. Butter two meat-tins and form the dough into four sausages the length of the tins. Leave them to rise a third time in the tins. Bake in a moderate oven 180°C (350°F) Mark 4 for about 20 minutes until well browned and risen. Cool on a wooden board. The following day cut into slices about 6mm (¼ in.) thick and put on baking-sheets to dry for 2-3 hours in a slow oven 100°C (200°F) Mark ¼. When ready the rusks will be golden and dry all the way through. Store in airtight tins.

These rusks are not only suitable for babies but interesting enough to serve with morning coffee or cocoa at night.

Pastila

250 ml (½ pt) 1¼ cups apple purée (see page 95)
1 egg white
100 g (4 oz) ½ cup sugar

Make the apple purée. Beat the egg white until it stand in peaks and fold it into the purée with the sugar. Spread about 15 mm (½ in.) thick on a greased baking-sheet and dry in a very slow oven 100°C (200°F) Mark ¼ for 3-4 hours. Cut into squares. Serve with Russian tea.

This is a good way to use up extra apples if you have them in your garden. Fallen apples can be used in this way. Use the yolk to enrich a milk pudding.

Rum babas

15 g (½ oz) fresh yeast or 1 packet dried yeast
25 g (1 oz) 2 tablespoons sugar
150 ml (¼ pt) cup milk
250 g (9 oz) 2 cups plain flour
115 g (4 oz) ½ cup butter
3 eggs
pinch of salt
25 g (1 oz) 3 tablespoons currants (optional)

SAUCE
575 ml (1 pt) 2½ cups water
150 g (5 oz) ⅔ cup castor sugar
2 wineglasses rum

Mix the yeast with a teaspoonful of sugar and a little warm water to a smooth paste. Add the warm milk and half the sifted flour. Cover and leave to rise in a warm place for about half an hour until it has doubled its bulk and there are bubbles on top. Add the sugar and eggs, stirring all the time. Melt the butter and cool slightly. Add the butter to the yeast mixture together with the rest of the sifted flour, and the salt and currants. Beat well with a wooden spoon for 5-10 minutes until the dough is smooth and shiny. Cover and leave in a warm place to rise a second time. When it has doubled its bulk again stir lightly to remove air bubbles and transfer to a greased cake-ring or small greased cake-tins. Leave to rise again for half an hour before putting in the oven. Bake in a moderate oven 180°C (350°F) Mark 4 for 25-30 minutes for the cake-ring or 15-20 minutes for the small tins.

This is quite easy and quick to do compared with some yeast recipes as the quantities are so small. The finished effect is very professional and the taste is infinitely better. You can taste the eggs. This is very suitable to give after a dinner party in place of a pudding. I have made the sauce not too sweet as I find the shop variety is rather sickly. If you prefer a sweeter sauce use 225 g (8 oz) 1 cup sugar.

SAUCE
Dissolve the sugar in boiling water and add the rum. Turn out the baba when cooked and pour the sauce over while it is still hot. Glaze with sieved apricot jam, if you wish. Decorate with whipped cream when cool.

Bulka *(yeast cake)*

25 g (1 oz) fresh yeast or 2 packets dried yeast
250 ml (½ pt) 1¼ cups milk
550 g (1 lb 6 oz) 5½ cups plain flour
100 g (4 oz) ½ cup butter
3 eggs
175 g (6 oz) ¾ cup vanilla sugar
pinch of salt
2 tablespoons sultanas
2 tablespoons mixed peel
pinch of nutmeg or cardamom

Mix the yeast with a teaspoonful of sugar and a little warm water to a smooth paste. Add the warm milk and half the sifted flour. Beat well. Cover with a cloth and leave to rise in a warm place for about half an hour until it has doubled its original bulk and is full of bubbles. Melt the butter and add it together with the remainder of the flour and the other ingredients. Knead well by hand for about half an hour until the dough leaves the sides of the bowl. Cover with a cloth and leave to rise in a warm place until it has again doubled its bulk. Line a tin with buttered greaseproof paper. Knead the mixture lightly and transfer it to the tin. Leave for about half an hour to rise again and bake in a moderate oven 180°C (350°F) Mark 4 for 1-1¼ hours. Serve with or without butter for breakfast or afternoon tea.

This is a rich bun and best started early in the morning. It is quite large so if you have any left over it will keep in a tin.

Poppy seed roll

PASTRY
25 g (½ oz) fresh yeast or
2 packets dried yeast
275 ml (½ pt) 1¼ cups milk
600 g (1 lb 5 oz) 5½ cups
plain flour (approx)
pinch of salt
115 g (4 oz) ½ cup butter
115 g (4 oz) ½ cup sugar
3 eggs

FILLING
675 g (1½ lb) poppy seeds
200 g (8 oz) 1 cup sugar or
honey
25 g (1 oz) 3 tablespoons
sultanas
25 g (1 oz) ½ cup chopped
walnuts
1 tablespoon icing sugar

Cream the yeast with a teaspoon of sugar and a little warm water. Warm the milk and add it to the yeast mixture together with half the sifted flour. Beat well until the consistency resembles a thick batter. Cover with a cloth and leave in a warm place to rise for about half an hour. When it has doubled its original size and there are bubbles on top, add the melted butter, sugar, eggs, salt and the rest of the flour. Knead well by hand until the mixture comes away from the sides of the bowl without sticking. Cover with a cloth and leave to rise for a second time in a warm place. When it has doubled its bulk again knead lightly on a floured board and roll out to about 5 mm (1/3 in.) thick.

FILLING
Meanwhile, cover the poppy seeds with boiling water and leave them to stand for about half an hour. Squeeze out all the liquid. Put the seeds through a mincer two or three times. Blend in the sugar or honey, sultanas and chopped walnuts. Spread the mixture over the pastry and roll up as for a Swiss roll. This quantity will make two rolls. Leave to rise for a further half an hour on a greased baking-tray before putting in the oven. Bake in a moderate oven 180°C (350°F) Mark 4 for 20-30 minutes. When ready, cool on a wooden board. Dust with sifted icing sugar.

Make this early in the morning when you are expecting guests as it is a fairly large quantity. It will go in no time but any left over can be stored in a tin.

Breakfast buns

15 g (½ oz) fresh yeast or
1 packet dried yeast
1 tablespoon sugar
150 ml (¼ pt) ⅔ cup milk
225 g (8 oz) 1¾ cups
plain flour
50 g (2 oz) 4 tablespoons
butter
2 eggs
pinch of salt

Mix the yeast with a teaspoon of sugar and a little warm water to a smooth paste. Add the warm milk and half the sifted flour and beat well with a wooden spoon. Cover with a cloth and leave in a warm place to rise. When it has doubled its bulk and there are bubbles on top add the melted butter, sugar, eggs, salt and the rest of the flour. Beat with a wooden spoon for 5-10 minutes until thoroughly mixed. Cover with a cloth and leave to rise a second time. When it has doubled its bulk again beat with a wooden spoon and put the mixture into small buttered cake-tins allowing enough room in each tin for the mixture to double its volume. Leave to rise again and then bake in a moderate oven 180°C (350°F) Mark 4 for about 20 minutes.

This quantity will make twelve buns.

These are fairly quick to make compared with most yeast baking. Try them if you have a bit of yeast left over and do not know what to do with it.

When young I used to get up early and had them ready to eat with coffee for breakfast.

Kulich *(Easter cake)*

25 g (1 oz) fresh yeast or
2 packets dried yeast
1 teaspoon sugar
275 ml (½ pt) 1¼ cups milk
600 g (1 lb 5 oz) 4¾ cups
plain flour
225 g (8 oz) 1 cup butter
3 eggs and 2 yolks
225 g (8 oz) 1 cup vanilla
sugar
100 g (4 oz) 1 cup candied
peel
100 g (4 oz) 1 cup sultanas
50 g (2 oz) ½ cup blanched
almonds
1 or 2 powdered
cardamom seeds
pinch of salt

This quantity makes one large kulich. Mix the yeast with a teaspoonful of sugar and a little warm water to a smooth paste. Add the warm milk and about 225 g (8 oz) 1¾ cups of sifted flour and beat till the consistency resembles a batter. Cover and leave in a warm place for about half an hour to rise. When it has doubled its bulk and there are bubbles on top, add the melted butter, eggs, vanilla sugar, peel, sultanas, chopped almonds, cardamom, salt and the rest of the sifted flour. Knead well until the dough comes away from the sides of the bowl without sticking. Cover and leave in warm place to rise a second time. Line a deep tin (20.5 cm deep x 15 cm wide) (8 in. deep x 6 in. wide) with buttered grease-proof paper. When the mixture has doubled its bulk again, flatten with the hand and transfer it to the tin. Leave to rise again in the oven. Bake on the bottom shelf in a moderate oven 180°C (350°F)

Mark 4 for one, to one and a quarter hours. When ready, turn out and cover with a clean towel. Cool and ice the top with pink or white icing (opposite page) or sour cream icing (page 118). Sprinkle the icing with hundreds and thousands or decorate with confectioner's roses.

Cut in slices about 30 mm (1¼ in.) thick and eat at Easter with Paskha (page 136).

This is the famous Russian Easter cake and there are many recipes for it. This cake is rather rich and takes time to rise. If you prefer a light cake use 175 g (6 oz) ¾ cup butter and 140 g (6 oz) ⅔ cup sugar. It will take less time and be much lighter. The heavy Kulich however, keeps better and should be kept in a tin after you have started eating it. You can cover it with a cloth before you start to eat it to prevent it going dry. Kulich should be cut across and not down owing to its height. If you do not make a tall kulich it will alter the flavour and it will no longer be a kulich. In Russia in the old days the housewives tried to outdo each other at Easter and make the tallest kulich in the community.

Remember to buy the cardamom seeds in the chemists. These are sold in small quantities and you can grind them. They will be fresh if you do your own. First remove outer husk. I keep two mills one for pepper and one for cardamom. They should be different sizes or you will mix them up.

The distinctive flavour of kulich is the cardamom. If you cannot get it, however, use nutmeg. This should also be freshly grated. Do not use the powder, the flavour evaporates.

Sponge

4 eggs
225 g (8 oz) 1 cup vanilla sugar
225 g (8 oz) 1¾ cups flour
rind of 1 lemon
icing or filling (page 117)

Beat the eggs for about five minutes. Gradually add the sugar and grated lemon rind, beating all the time. Beat for a further five minutes and fold in the flour. Put into a greased baking-tin 25 cm x 5 cm (10 in. x 2 in.) and bake on the middle shelf in a moderate oven 190°C (375°F) Mark 5 for 40-45 minutes. Cool on a rack. Use any of the fillings or icings in this chapter.

This is the basic sponge and can be made either round, square or oblong. If you wish to divide it the professional way is to put it into two tins of equal size and weigh each tin, then you will have two sponges of equal size.

Easter nut cake

5 large eggs
225 g (8 oz) 1 cup castor sugar
rind of 1 lemon
pinch of salt
few drops lemon juice or 1 teaspoon rum
200 g (8 oz) 1½ cups shelled hazel nuts

Grate the nuts in their skins. Beat the egg yolks with the sugar until they are white. Add the grated lemon rind and lemon juice or rum. Beat the egg-whites with a pinch of salt until they stand in peaks and fold them into the mixture. Add the grated nuts. Put the mixture into a greased cake-tin in a moderate oven 190°C (375°F) Mark 5 for about 40 minutes. It will shrink slightly when cooled. Ice when cool with mocha or chocolate butter icing (pages 117, 118) or use the fresh whipped cream filling in any flavour (see opposite) either as a filling or a topping.

This is a lovely cake and brings back memories of my childhood when we always had this for Easter. To decorate the cake if you are using the mocha or chocolate icing, cut a few glacé cherries in half and place round the cake. Almonds if roasted also make a difference. To roast almonds, either place them on a baking sheet and bake in a moderate oven 180°C (350°F) Mark 4 for 10 minutes or place them under a grill. They should be blanched of course. You can then cut them lengthwise and sprinkle on the top of the cake. Hazelnuts also make a good decoration. Do not do anything with these. They look good as they are.

Easter almond cake

4 egg whites
pinch of salt
75 g (3 oz) 6 tablespoons sugar
100 g (4 oz) ¾ cup shelled almonds
rind of ½ lemon
1 tablespoon rum or rose water
few drops almond essence

Grate the almonds. Beat the egg whites with a pinch of salt until they stand in peaks. Add the sugar gradually, beating all the time until the mixture becomes very thick. Fold in the rum or rose water, the grated lemon rind, nuts, and almond essence.

Line a 20.5 cm (8 in.) sandwich-tin with greaseproof paper. Brush with oil and transfer the mixture to the tin. Bake in a moderate oven 190°C (375°F) Mark 5 for about 30 minutes. Cool on a wire tray and ice the top with mocha or chocolate butter icing or sour cream icing (page 118).

This is another good recipe to use when you have left-over whites of egg. It makes quite a small cake but if you cover with mocha or chocolate butter icing it will appear a bit larger.

Coffee and chocolate nut cake

150 g (6 oz) 1¼ cups shelled walnuts
4 eggs
100 g (4 oz) 1 cup icing sugar
½ teaspoon powdered coffee
1 teaspoon cocoa
1 teaspoon dry breadcrumbs

Grate the nuts or chop them very finely. Beat the egg yolks and the sifted icing sugar until white. Add the coffee and cocoa and blend well. Beat the whites until they stand in peaks and fold them into the mixture. Add the grated nuts and breadcrumbs. Grease and line a 23 cm (9 in.) cake-tin and transfer the mixture. Bake for about 30 minutes in a moderate oven 180°C (350°F) Mark 4.

Cool on a wire tray and ice the top of the cake with mocha or chocolate butter icing, whipped cream topping (this page) or sour cream icing (page 118).

This is another version of the nut cake using coffee which gives it a distinctive flavour. The only way I can describe it, is expensive! This cake is larger than the previous one as it uses all the eggs. This recipe was given to me by a Polish lady who specialized in nut cakes. She always had one for birthdays and they were very large too. A good party cake in fact and let your guests guess the ingredients!

Pink or white icing

1 egg white
200 g (8 oz) 2 cups icing sugar
1 dessertspoon red wine
or 2 teaspoons lemon juice and grated rind 1 lemon

Beat the egg white until it begins to stiffen. Add the sieved icing sugar gradually, beating all the time. Add the wine for pink icing or the lemon juice and rind for white. Continue beating until the mixture is thick and smooth.

Half this quantity of icing is enough for the top of one kulich (page 115). The full quantity will very generously cover the sponge (page 116).

You can make this icing very well in a mixer. It is a very old recipe taken from the famous *Molohovetz* which has been in the family for upwards of 50 years. It is now out of print and a very valued possession. When we left Russia this cook book was one of the very few things we managed to bring to England.

Whipped cream topping or filling

165 ml ($\frac{1}{3}$ pt) ¾ cup double cream
2 teaspoons sugar
2 teaspoons rum
1 small egg white (optional)

Whip the cream until stiff. Fold in the sugar and rum. If you prefer a lighter consistency, beat an egg white until it stands in peaks and fold it in to the cream.

COFFEE FLAVOUR

Add 2 teaspoons of strong black coffee to the above mixture.

CHOCOLATE FLAVOUR

Add a few drops of vanilla essence and a teaspoon of cocoa to the above mixture. Mix the cocoa with the sugar and dissolve them in a little warm water.

The above quantities are sufficient to cover or fill a 23 cm (9 in.) cake. This cream will not keep unless it is left in the fridge overnight.

To whip cream, bowl and beater should all be chilled. You will find it easier. Do not overwhip. With very heavy cream you can add a little thin cream and it will still whip up.

Mocha icing

100 g (4 oz) ½ cup unsalted butter
100 g (4 oz) 1 cup icing sugar
1 small egg yolk
a few drops vanilla essence
2 teaspoons strong black coffee

Cream the butter with a wooden spoon until white.

Add the egg yolk and continue beating until well blended. Beat in the sifted icing sugar gradually. Add the vanilla essence and coffee and mix thoroughly.

The above quantity will ice or fill the sponge or ice the top of any of the nut cakes.

If you make this icing, it will not keep owing to the fact there is a raw egg in it. Keep the cake when you have finished with it in the fridge till you need it again. I think the icing tastes even better if chilled.

Chocolate butter icing

Use the same proportions of ingredients as above, substituting 2 teaspoonfuls of cocoa mixed with a little sugar and warm water for the black coffee. Use for the same cakes.

Sour cream icing

200 g (8 oz) 2 cups icing sugar
1 teaspoon orange or lemon juice
3 teaspoons sour cream
1 small egg white
a few drops lemon or orange essence or grated rind of lemon or small orange

Sift the icing sugar into a basin. Add the lemon or orange juice, the rind or essence and the sour cream. Beat the egg white until it stands in peaks and fold it in to the mixture. Beat with a wooden spoon until it is smooth and thick.

This quantity is enough to ice the tops of two 15-20.5 cm (6-8 in.) cakes.

This icing is softer than that made with the white of egg and has a slightly sour taste. The cake with this icing will keep quite a while in a tin.

Krendelki

makes 16 buns

500 g (1 lb 2 oz) 4 cups flour
2 eggs
200 ml ($\frac{1}{3}$ pt) scant 1 cup milk
50 g (2 oz) 4 tablespoons butter
115 g (4 oz) ½ cup sugar
rind of 1 lemon
a little vanilla essence
15 g (½ oz) fresh yeast or 1 packet dried yeast

Heat the milk to blood temperature. Put into a mixing bowl. Mix the yeast with 1 teaspoon sugar and allow to stand. Grate the rind of the lemon. When the yeast has dissolved add to the milk together with the rind and a few drops of vanilla essence. Add enough flour to make a thin batter. Cover with a cloth and allow to stand for 30 minutes in a warm place till it is full of bubbles and double in bulk. Add the melted butter which should not be too hot, the whisked eggs, the sugar and the remainder of the flour. Knead the dough by hand or put into the electric mixer using the dough hook till it leaves the sides of the bowl or leaves the hands clean. Put into a warm place to prove a second time covered with a cloth. This will take about 1 hour depending on the heat of the room. When it has risen put on floured board and divide the dough into two. Then divide into 8 equal parts and roll each into a sausage thinner at each end. Tie a knot. Butter two large baking-tins and put the buns on it. Allow to prove for 15 minutes whilst the oven is heating. Brush with melted butter and dust with castor sugar if you like or leave and put the thin icing on when the buns are still hot. Cook for 15 minutes at 220°C (425° F) Mark 7.

You can brush the buns when they come out of the oven with melted butter with a pastry brush if you prefer.

Cherry and almond cake

8 slices

75 g (3 oz) ¾ cup dry breadcrumbs
4 eggs
115 g (4 oz) ½ cup sugar
115 g (4 oz) ½ cup butter
75 g (3 oz) $\frac{1}{3}$ cup glacé cherries
75 g (3 oz) ¾ cup ground almonds
rind of ½ lemon
½ teaspoon cinnamon
a few drops of almond essence
butter to grease tin

Use an electric mixer if you have one or otherwise do by hand. Whip the butter and sugar till white. Separate the eggs. Whisk yolks and add gradually beating between each addition. Add the dry breadcrumbs, ground almonds, cinnamon, lemon rind, almond essence and cherries cut in half. Combine all ingredients thoroughly. Line and grease a 18 cm (7 in.) cake tin. Whip the whites till they stand in peaks and fold into the mixture. Put into the prepared cake tin and bake at 180°C (350°F) Mark 4, for 40-45 minutes. When ready turn out on wire rack to cool.

You can if you wish chop the almonds very

finely instead of using the ground almonds. Do not use shop breadcrumbs. Below is a recipe for making rusks and breadcrumbs.

To make rusks or breadcrumbs
Take a sliced white loaf and put slices of bread in single rows on trays and dry in the oven at 140°C (275°F) Mark 1-2 for 1½ hours. When ready either put in blender, grind with a rolling pin or mince. Put into airtight tins and keep if not needed at once. These rusks are quite nice with butter.

Fruit loaf Razumovsky

175 g (6 oz) 1 cup mixed dried fruit
225 g (8 oz) 1 cup soft brown sugar
225 g (8 oz) 1¾ cups self-raising flour
1 egg
1 cup of tea (no sugar or milk)

Put the fruit and sugar into a bowl. Pour the tea on top and leave for at least 6 hours. Then add the sieved flour and beaten egg and mix all ingredients. Put into a greased loaf tin and cook for 1 hour or until springy to the touch at 180°C (350°F) Mark 4.

This is quick and easy.

Apple doughnuts

serves 4-6

4-6 eating apples
3 eggs
3 teaspoons sugar
3 teaspoons flour
1 tablespoon castor sugar
1 tablespoon cinnamon
4-6 teaspoons jam
mixture of oil and fat for frying
250 ml (½ pt) 1¼ cups sabayon sauce (page 131)

Peel and core apples and put jam inside. Separate eggs. Whip yolks with 3 teaspoons sugar till white. Add 3 teaspoons flour. Heat the oil and fat in a large pan. Whip the whites till they stand in peaks and fold into the mixture. Coat the apples and put them into boiling fat at once. When honey coloured they are ready. Transfer with a perforated spoon on to kitchen paper to drain. When all are cooked put into individual dishes, dust with a mixture of castor sugar and cinnamon and serve with a jug of sabayon sauce.

This is rather an exotic pudding worthy of a party.

Sour cream sponge

8 slices

200 ml ($\frac{1}{3}$ pt) scant 1 cup sour cream
175 g (6 oz) 1 $\frac{1}{3}$ cups self-raising flour
115 g (4 oz) ½ cup sugar
3 eggs
vanilla essence
grated orange or lemon rind
1 tablespoon icing sugar

Whip the yolks with the sugar till white. Combine with the vanilla essence, grated orange or lemon rind and sour cream. Then add the flour. Whip the whites till they stand in peaks and fold into the mixture. Butter a tin 15 cm x 25.5 cm (6 in. x 10 in.) and cook in an oven at 180°C (350°F) Mark 4, for 25-30 minutes.

This mixture can also make 12 small cakes. Grease tart tins with butter allowing space for the cakes to rise and cook for 10-15 minutes.

Dust the cake or cakes with icing sugar when cool.

Yeast cheese buns

makes 18 small buns

200 g (8 oz) 1 cup curd cheese
1 yolk
50 g (2 oz) 4 tablespoons sugar
25 g (1 oz) 3 tablespoons currants
1 tablespoon melted butter or sour cream
sweet yeast pastry (page 107) (half quantity)
1 tablespoon castor sugar
1 teaspoon cinnamon (if liked)
butter to grease tins

Make yeast pastry as indicated on page 107 (half quantities are enough).

FILLING
Mix the curd cheese, yolk, sugar, currants and melted butter or sour cream together.

When the dough has risen twice roll out on floured board. Cut 7.5 cm (3 in.) squares approximately. Put a large teaspoon of the filling in the middle. Bring the ends together to form an envelope and put on a greased tin to rise for the third time. This takes about 20 minutes in a warm room.

Put into the oven for 10-15 minutes at 200°C (400°F) Mark 6 or till lightly brown. When ready transfer to wooden board and cover with a cloth.

When cool you can either dust them with icing sugar or combine castor sugar with the cinnamon and dust with this.

It is suggested to serve this with sour cream but this makes it almost into a pudding. Should be eaten the same day for best results. Start to bake in the morning.

Yeast swiss roll

half quantity sweet yeast dough (page 107) or left-over dough
100 g (4 oz) 1 cup mixed dried fruit or raisins
25 g (1 oz) 3 tablespoons candied peel
1 tablespoon oil
1 tablespoon sugar
1 teaspoon cinnamon

Make the yeast dough as indicated on page 107 or you can use left-over dough if you make the full quantity and have some left over. When the dough has risen twice roll on floured board. Brush with oil. Mix the sugar and cinnamon and sprinkle over the dough. Also the peel and the dried fruit. Roll up as if a swiss roll (jelly roll). Pinch the edges so it will not fall apart. Allow to rise a third time. Put into the oven at 180°C (350°F) Mark 4, for 45 minutes or till light brown. If you want to glaze: 5 minutes before the end of cooking brush the roll with a mixture of sugar and milk. When well cooked turn out on to a wooden board and cover with a cloth.

When cool you can either dust with icing sugar or ice if you wish. I always use left-over dough like this. You can also use up scraps of plain dough, ie use for pirogi but use more sugar for the filling.

Choux pastry *(basic recipe)*

115 g (4½ oz) 1 cup plain flour
150 ml (¼ pt) ⅔ cup water
pinch of salt
50 g (2 oz) 4 tablespoons butter
½ teaspoon vanilla essence
3 eggs

Heat the water and butter with the salt in a small pan. Bring to the boil. Stir in the flour till it forms a ball and beat for a few seconds only. Allow to cool slightly and add the vanilla and one egg at a time beating all the time till the mixture is well blended and glossy.

This can be used for cream buns, éclairs, etc. Oven temperature 200°C (400°F) Mark 6-7.

Mazurka with almonds *8-10 slices*

100 g (4 oz) 1 cup blanched almonds
140 g (5 oz) 1 cup plus 2 tablespoons plain flour
1 large egg
115 g (4 oz) ½ cup butter
115 g (4 oz) ¾ cup sugar
1 tablespoon cream

Chop almonds. Whip butter till white. Add the sugar and continue beating until well mixed. Combine with egg and cream. Add the nuts and flour gradually. Line and grease a 23 cm (9 in.) cake tin. Roll out the pastry to about the same size. Put into the tin and even out with your fingers.

Cook in the oven at 180°C (350°F) Mark 4, for 30 minutes. When ready take out and remove paper. Put on plate and dust with icing sugar if you like.

This is a high-class cake. It is something between a biscuit and a cake.

Vanilla filling for cakes

50 g (2 oz) 4 tablespoons sugar
1 egg
1 yolk
275-425 ml (½-¾ pt) 1¼ -2 cups milk
knob of butter
20 g (¾ oz) 3 tablespoons flour
15 g (½ oz) 2 tablespoons cornflour
vanilla flavouring

Break the egg and 1 yolk into a bowl. Beat with the sugar till white. Blend in the flour and cornflour. Dilute with milk. Bring the remainder of the milk to the boil and pour on the eggs stirring all the time. Transfer to saucepan or double boiler and cook slowly till the custard thickens. It should be stirred all the time. When ready add a few drops of vanilla flavouring and a knob of butter. Stir and cool ready for use.

Use for sponges, cream buns, sand layer cake in place of cream filling.

Sand layer cake *(3 layers)* *10 slices*

350 g (12 oz) 2⅔ cups plain flour
115 g (4 oz) ½ cup butter
115 g (4 oz) ½ cup sugar
2 eggs
vanilla flavouring
1 tablespoon icing sugar
1 egg to brush top
25 g (1 oz) ¼ cup blanched almonds (optional)
filling, jam, whipped cream or vanilla custard

Cut the butter into small pieces and rub into the flour till it resembles breadcrumbs. Add the sugar and eggs gradually to make a fairly stiff dough. Knead by hand on a floured board. Divide into three. Roll each into a round about 23 cm (9 in.). Prepare three 23 cm (9 in.) tins. Line and brush with oil. Put the rounds into them and even out with your fingers. Cook in the oven at 220°C

(425°F) Mark 7, for 15 minutes or till lightly honey coloured.

SECOND METHOD

Brush the last layer with egg. You can reserve some white of egg from the eggs used if you wish since you need a very small amount. Chop 25 g (1 oz) ¼ cup blanched almonds and sprinkle on top. Cook as above. When the rounds are cool put on a wooden board and decorate, ie you can either put whipped cream on one layer (half thin cream, half double) or vanilla custard, see recipe below. Jam on the second layer and sprinkle the top with icing sugar. This cake is similar in texture to the Mazurka, half cake, half biscuit.

This is a flat cake which should be baked in an oblong tin and cut into fingers. For the purposes of this book I have had to half the quantities and use round tins in some recipes. The thickness of the dough should not be more than the thickness of a finger. Some Mazurkas are similar to a light sponge whilst others are rolled out but not as stiff as pastry dough. For successful results either use an electric mixer or take your time whipping the eggs and sugar. These cakes come under the heading of La Pâtisserie Fine as do most Russian cakes. Improves with keeping.

Ukrainian lemon mazurka

8 slices

½ large lemon
75 g (3 oz) ½ cup sugar
2 large eggs
60 g (2½ oz) ⅔ cup cornflour
butter to grease tin

Grate the rind of the lemon. Cut in half and extract the juice from one half.

Separate the eggs. Whip the yolks with the sugar till white. Add the lemon juice and rind. Fold in the cornflour. Line and grease a 23 cm (9 in.) sandwich tin. Whip the whites till they stand in peaks and fold into the egg mixture. Pour into the prepared tin and bake at 180°C (350°F) Mark 4, for 25 minutes. When ready slice and turn out on wire tray to cool.

This is a very light lemon sponge. You can dust with icing sugar before serving if you wish. Will keep in a tin.

Raisin and almond mazurka

115 g (4 oz) ½ cup butter
150 g (6 oz) ¾ cup sugar
150 g (6 oz) 1 cup raisins
50 g (2 oz) ½ cup blanched almonds
50 g (2 oz) ½ cup mixed peel
225 g (8 oz) 1¾ cups plain flour
2 eggs

Melt the butter. Set aside. Mince the raisins. Chop the almonds. Use an electric mixer if you have one for this recipe. Combine all ingredients except the butter adding this gradually mixing between each addition. Mix till all ingredients are well blended. Line and grease an oblong tin about 20.5 cm x 25.5 cm (8 in. x 10 in.). Roll out the dough on floured board and put into the prepared tin. Level out with your fingers. Cook in the oven at 180°C (350°F) Mark 4, for 30 minutes. When ready take out of the oven and cut into slices. Cool on wire rack.

Although it says plain flour, this recipe can be done with self-raising. The dough should not be thicker than a finger when it is rolled out. Serve with afternoon tea or morning coffee. This cake will keep well in a tin. If you have no peel, grate the rind of an orange or lemon.

Chocolate cake

12 slices

175 g (6 oz) 1⅓ cups plain flour
¼ teaspoon baking powder
1 teaspoon bicarbonate of soda
pinch of salt
2 eggs
50 g (2 oz) ½ cup cocoa
275 ml (½ pt) 1¼ cups water
115 g (4 oz) ½ cup butter
275 g (10 oz) 1¼ cups castor sugar

Sift flour, salt, baking powder and bicarbonate of soda together. Blend the cocoa with the water, set aside. Beat butter and sugar till white. Whisk eggs and add to the creamed mixture. Combine all ingredients stirring in the sifted flour and cocoa with water alternately. Line and grease two cake tins 20.5 cm - 23 cm (8-9 in) in diameter. Divide the mixture between the tins and cook for 30-35 minutes at 180°C (350°F) Mark 4. Put on wire tray to cool when ready.

You can use the following toppings and fillings for this cake. Spread the bottom layer with jam, ie apricot or strawberry. Sprinkle with rum. Cover with whipped cream, 1 small carton is enough for this size (page 117) coat the top with sifted icing sugar or white icing flavoured with vanilla (page

117). Just before the icing sets, decorate with grated bitter chocolate. Use the coarse grater. You can also use chocolate butter icing (page 118). If you want to cover the cake and have some left over for the filling use double the quantity.

This cake is rather large and a great favourite with the family. It is not very sweet so needs either a sweet topping or centre.

Fruit tart with sour cream

200 g (8 oz) plums or cherries	150 ml (¼ pt) ⅔ cup sour cream
75 g (3 oz) 6 tablespoons sugar	short pastry using 115 g (4 oz) ½ cup fat

Roll out the pastry and use a 20.5 cm (8 in.) flan ring. Press to the sides of the flan ring and see that the pastry is well above the edge or the fruit juices may go over the top. Remove stones, if any, from fruit and mix fruit with sugar. Cover surface of pastry. Pour the sour cream over. Bake in an oven at 200°C (400°F) Mark 5-6, for approx. 30 minutes or till the pastry is golden.

This can also be done with yeast pastry. Try it when you have some yeast pastry left over. It is excellent for tea but should be eaten the same day since yeast pastry does not keep as well as puff or short pastry.

Pampushnik *(yeast cake)*

725 g (1 lb 10 oz) 5¾ cups flour	FLAVOURING
200 ml (⅜pt) 1 cup milk	vanilla essence or 2 teaspoons rum
15 g (½ oz) fresh yeast or 1 packet dried yeast	few drops almond essence
115 g (4 oz) ½ cup butter	50 g (2 oz) ½ cup raisins or sultanas
4 egg yolks	25 g (1 oz) 3 tablespoons peel or rind of lemon
pinch of salt	
25 g (1 oz) ¼ cup blanched almonds	

Mix the yeast with 1 teaspoon sugar in a cup and wait till it dissolves. Warm the milk to blood temperature and put into mixing bowl. Add the yeast and a little flour to make a thin batter. Put in a warm place. Cover with a cloth till it is full of bubbles and has risen to double its size. This should take about 30 minutes. Add the melted butter which should not be too hot, the remainder of the flour, sugar, whisked eggs, rum or vanilla flavours, almond essence if liked, raisins, rind of lemon and chopped blanched almonds.

Either knead by hand till the dough leaves the hands clean or put in electric mixer and using dough hook wait till it leaves the sides of the bowl. The dough should not be too stiff and not too soft, similar to cake dough but elastic. Cover with cloth and leave to rise a second time in a warm place. This will take 1-2 hours depending on the temperature of the room. Wait till it increases to double in size. Line a 23 cm (9 in.) cake tin and grease with butter. See that the paper goes over the edge of the tin to allow dough to rise. Put the dough on a floured board and knead lightly. Transfer to prepared tin and allow it to rise a third time. About 20-30 minutes.

Meanwhile heat the oven. Put in oven at 180°C (350°F) Mark 4, for 45 minutes. When ready it should be well browned. Take out of tin when it has cooled a little and put on wire rack to cool. When cold you can dust with icing sugar or if you have a sweet tooth use any of the icing on pages 117, 118.

This is a large cake for a festive occasion.

Shanezki *(yeast buns)* *makes 16 large buns*

450 g (1 lb 2 oz) 3½ cups flour	275 ml (½ pt) 1¼ cups milk
75 g (3 oz) 6 tablespoons sugar	2 egg yolks
15 g (½ oz) fresh yeast or 1 packet dried yeast	4 cardamom seeds
1 small egg for glazing	50 g (2 oz) ½ cup currants or 50 g (2 oz) ½ cup sultanas and 25 g (1 oz) 3 tablespoons candied peel
½ teaspoon cooking salt	
few drops vanilla essence	

Warm the milk to blood heat and put into mixing bowl. Mix the yeast with a little sugar. Allow to stand. Either grind the cardamom seeds in a pepper mill (use a special mill without pepper) or crush with a rolling pin on a board. Add these to the milk. The yeast will have dissolved by now so add to the milk and about 115 g (4 oz) scant 1 cup flour sifted with the salt. Blend to a smooth batter and leave in a warm place to rise covered with a clean tea towel. This takes about 30 minutes. Separate the eggs. Melt the butter. Add the yolks, the sugar, melted butter which should not be too hot. Add the rest of the flour and knead either by hand or by electric mixer using the dough blade. Wait till the dough leaves the hands or the sides of the bowl clean. Roll out on floured board. If you find the dough too soft, knead a little more flour into it. Roll out into a fat sausage. Cut into 16 equal portions. Roll each into a ball. Grease two large baking tins and put the buns on it. Brush with egg. Allow to prove a third time. Meanwhile heat the oven. This takes about 15 minutes. Cook 1 tin at a time in a hot oven at 200°C (400°F) Mark 6, for 15 minutes. Turn the tin when the buns start to brown so that they are evenly cooked.

When ready take out and put on a large wooden board or wire rack to cool, and decorate as below.

These buns have better keeping qualities since they contain more butter and will keep overnight. Start to bake in the morning however, and allow yourself plenty of time. It is well worth spending a few extra minutes on decoration and getting the reputation of a pâtissier. See below for instructions.

DECORATION FOR YEAST BUNS

1 tablespoon icing sugar or
25 g (1 oz) ¼ cup blanched almonds
or
25 g (1 oz) 6 lumps cube sugar
75 g (3 oz) ¾ cup icing sugar
1½ tablespoons water
3 drops vanilla essence

GLAZE

1 tablespoon sugar
1 tablespoon water

Brush the buns with egg before putting them in the oven if you do not intend to glaze or ice them. Sprinkle with either chopped almonds or crushed cube sugar (crush with rolling pin on wooden board) or both.

ICING

Ice with 75 g (3 oz) ¾ cup icing sugar, 1½ tablespoons water and a few drops of vanilla essence. They should be iced whilst still hot. Use a pastry brush.

GLAZE

Use 1 tablespoon sugar to 1 tablespoon water and boil to a slight syrup. Brush the buns with this when they start to brown after 10 minutes and turn the tin to cook evenly.

You can also dust the buns with icing sugar if you use the almonds or crushed cube sugar for decoration.

Wine mazurka

8-10 slices

150 ml (¼ pt) ⅔ cup sour cream
75 g (3 oz) ⅓ cup sugar
½ egg
225 g (8 oz) 1¾ cups plain flour
25 g (1 oz) blanched almonds
25 g (1 oz) 2 tablespoons cube sugar
25 g (1 oz) ¼ cup icing sugar
60 ml (⅛ pt) ⅓ cup sweet wine
butter to grease tin
juice and rind of ¼ lemon

Combine the sour cream, sugar, wine, half an egg, squeeze of lemon-juice and rind with the flour. The dough should be fairly soft but stiff enough to roll out. Put the pastry in the fridge for 1 hour to cool. Line a 23 cm (9-in.) tin with buttered greaseproof paper. Roll out the pastry on a floured board and put into the prepared tin. Even out with your fingers. Brush with wine. Chop the almonds and crush the sugar and sprinkle on the top of the cake. It is important not to crush the sugar too much or it will be exactly like granulated. It should have little lumps left which give the cake flavour. Cook at 180°C (350°F) Mark 4, for at least 40 minutes or till the cake begins to brown. Should be dry on top. When ready cool on wire rack.

This is rather a difficult cake to make and should be flat and crusty so bake long enough. Dust with icing sugar when cool. This cake should really be square shaped but this recipe uses half-quantities and just fits into a 23 cm (9 in.) tin. The pastry should be about 15 mm (½ in.) thick. In the Russian book this is described as 'finger thickness'.

Home-made Halva from Uzbek

225 g (8 oz) 1¾ cups cornflour
200 g (8 oz) 2 cups shelled walnuts
½ cup honey
2 teaspoons salted butter
1 egg white
50 g (2 oz) ¼ cup sugar

Roast the walnuts. Put on a tin without fat at 180°C (350°F) Mark 4, for about 10 minutes. Turn with a fork so that the nuts do not burn or stick. Put through the mincer once or grate in electric blender. Put the honey into a stainless steel saucepan. Bring to the boil, then add the sugar, cornflour, walnuts and butter. Stir well. Set aside. Whip the white of the egg and fold into the honey mixture. Put into a shallow tin 23 cm x 23 cm (9 in. x 9 in.), lined with greaseproof paper. Level out with your fingers. The halva is too sticky to roll out. Put into fridge to cool. Cut into portions before serving.

Serve with black coffee or Russian tea. This is very sweet but good.

Upside-down-cake *12 slices*

2 eggs
350 g (12 oz) $2\frac{2}{3}$ cups flour
150 ml (¼ pt) $\frac{2}{3}$ cup oil
1 small orange
250-300 g (10-12 oz) 1-1¼ cups jam
225 g (8 oz) 1 cup sugar
a little rum if liked
butter to grease tin

Use a 20.5 cm (8 in.) rum baba tin for this and grease well particularly at the bottom since the jam tends to stick. Whip the egg with the sugar till white. Add the juice and rind of the orange and then the oil. Continue to whip till well blended. Føld in the flour and add a little rum if liked.

Put the jam at the bottom of the tin so that it is well covered. If the jam is too thick you just add a little water. It will dry off in the oven so do not use thick jam. Pour the mixture on top and bake at 180°C (350°F) Mark 4, for 35-40 minutes. When it has cooked put on wire rack to cool.

This cake is very good made with home-made jam or marmalade on top. It should be well baked as it tends to be soggy if not brown on the outside. Will keep in tin. Good party cake and has a festive air.

Ukrainian tarts

200 g (8 oz) 1¾ cups plain flour
40-50 g (1½-2 oz) 3-4 tablespoons sugar
175 g (6 oz) ¾ cup butter or lard
1 egg
200 g (8 oz) strawberries
275 ml (½ pt) 1¼ cups whipping cream

Put the butter and sugar in a mixer if you have one otherwise do by hand. Blend till white and fluffy, add the egg and the flour. The dough should be fairly soft but suitable for rolling out.

Put onto floured board and knead lightly. Roll out. Cut into rounds with glass or something which is the exact size of the tart tins. Put the round of pastry into each tin and press with the fingers so that it touches the sides and bottom of the tin. Prick base with fork. Bake at 200°C (400°F) Mark 6, for 15 minutes or till the pastry turns golden. When ready turn onto cake rack to cool.

DECORATION
Whip the cream and hull the strawberries. Put a little whipped cream into each tart and a strawberry on top. You can put jam at the bottom of the tarts and whipped cream on top or use vanilla custard instead of cream (page 120). If you wish to, have more strawberries in the tarts. Wash and hull and cover with icing sugar. Leave in the fridge for at least half a day for the juices to come out.

GLAZE
Remove strawberries and measure the juice. Make up to 150 ml (¼ pt) $\frac{2}{3}$ cup. Add food colouring or a little redcurrant jelly if you like, to improve the colour. Add 1 teaspoon arrowroot or potato flour to a little of the syrup. Boil the remainder of the syrup and add the arrowroot mixture. Stir quickly to combine all ingredients till the glaze thickens. Allow to cool a little and pour spoonfuls of the glaze on to the strawberries in the tart cases. Decorate with whipped cream. This can be done with raspberries or redcurrants. Use drained tinned fruit in the winter if you like.

This pastry can be used for any tarts, ie jam tart, apple tart, plum or cherry tart. Do not use for vatrushka since this is a rich short pastry and it is better done with yeast pastry. This quantity will make a tart approximately 30 cm x 20.5 cm (12 in. x 8 in.).

Kitty's cake *(cinnamon cake)*

225 g (8 oz) 1¾ cups self-raising flour
75 g (3 oz) 6 tablespoons sugar
50 g (2 oz) 4 tablespoons margarine
50 g (2 oz) 4 tablespoons lard
1 tablespoon icing sugar
1 teaspoon cinnamon
1 teaspoon mixed spice
1 egg
175 g (6 oz) ½ cup jam or apple purée

Cut fat into small pieces with a knife. Rub the fat into the flour to resemble breadcrumbs. (Use mixer if you have one.) Combine with the sugar, spices and egg.

Butter a 20.5 cm (8 in.) sandwich tin. Divide pastry into two. Roll out half into a round so that it fits the tin. Even out with your fingers. Cover with jam or apple purée. Roll out rest of pastry and cover. Cook for 35-40 minutes at 180°C (350°F) Mark 4. When ready cool on wire rack. Dust with icing sugar when cold.

This recipe was given me by an excellent cook and has been a family favourite ever since. If you do double quantities you can bake cookies. Use oblong tin and cut into portions when cold.

Coffee walnuts

100 g (4 oz) ⅔ cup ground walnuts
3-4 tablespoons strong coffee
1 teaspoon rose water or rum
extra walnuts or glacé cherries for decoration
225 g (8 oz) 1¾ cups icing sugar
a few drops of vanilla essence
1 tablespoon granulated sugar

Grind the walnuts by either putting through a mincer or with a nut grinder or blender. Sift the icing sugar. Mix all the ingredients and form into small balls. Press the top to flatten slightly and roll in granulated sugar.

CHOCOLATE FLAVOUR
Divide the mixture into two and add 1 tablespoon cocoa to one half and a little rum to moisten. Proceed as above.

TO DECORATE
Put either a small piece of glacé cherry or walnut on the top. If you do this roll in sugar afterwards as the decoration will not stick if it is already rolled in sugar. Put into sweet papers.

Sweet papers can be bought from department stores particularly at Christmas time. When making the sweets first ensure that they will fit the papers. These make a welcome gift at Christmas if put into a box and wrapped in pretty paper and tied with ribbon.

Chocolate glacé icing

50 g (2 oz) 2 squares plain chocolate
115 g (4 oz) 1 cup icing sugar
1 tablespoon water
2-3 drops oil

Melt the chocolate in a small bowl over a pan of boiling water. Blend in 115 g (4 oz) 1 cup sieved icing sugar and 1 tablespoon water. Add a few drops oil for extra gloss if liked.

This can be used for cream buns, éclairs, or sponge cakes.

Short crust pastry *(for pies, tarts, etc)*

225 g (8 oz) 1¾ cups plain flour
115 g (4 oz) ½ cup fat, ie butter, or a mixture of butter and lard
pinch of salt
water to mix

Sift the flour and salt. Rub the fat lightly into the flour till it resembles breadcrumbs. Mix to a stiff paste with cold water suitable for rolling out.

You can of course use margarine for the above or a mixture of margarine and lard to make the pastry lighter. For sweet short pastry add 25 g (1 oz) 2 tablespoons sugar to the above. For a richer pastry use 175 g (6 oz) ¾ cup butter to 225 g (8 oz) 1¾ cups flour.

Bake at 220°C (425°F) Mark 7 for about 20 minutes or till well browned.

Kaimak *(Russian cream)*

150 ml (¼ pt) ⅔ cup double cream
150 ml (¼ pt) ⅔ cup single cream
1 vanilla pod or essence
squeeze of lemon juice
25 g (1 oz) 2 tablespoons sugar

Put the single cream into a small stainless steel saucepan. Slit the pod and remove the seeds. Put the pod together with the seeds and sugar into the single cream and boil slowly for a few minutes stirring all the time to reduce the quantity. Set aside to cool. Take out the pod. Add the vanilla essence if you are using it. When cool add a squeeze of lemon juice and put in fridge to get cold. Whip the double cream and add the boiled cream gradually so that both creams are mixed and whipped together. Return to fridge.

Use the cream whenever you would whipped cream, ie in sponges, meringues, fruit, ice cream.

Coffee Kaimak

2 teaspoons strong coffee
150 ml (¼ pt) ⅔ cup thin cream
150 ml (¼ pt) ⅔ cup double cream
25 g (1 oz) 2 tablespoons sugar
1 vanilla pod or essence

Use the same method as above but omit the lemon. Use with meringues, sponges, ice cream.

Chocolate kaimak

25 g (1 oz) 1 square finely chopped bitter chocolate
150 ml (¼ pt) $\frac{2}{3}$ cup thin cream
150 ml (¼ pt) $\frac{2}{3}$ cup thick cream
25 g (1 oz) 2 tablespoons sugar
1 vanilla pod or essence

Use the same method as above but omit the lemon. Use for ice cream, sponges, meringues.

Desserts

Berry kissel

serves 4-6

400 g (1 lb) strawberries or raspberries
500 ml (1 pt) 2½ cups water
100 g (4 oz) ½ cup sugar (approx)
2 tablespoons potato flour or arrowroot

Stalk and clean the fruit and put it in a saucepan with the water. Bring to the boil, reduce heat and simmer for at least 15 minutes. The softer the fruit the more juice can be extracted. Strain through a fine wire sieve or muslin. Avoid pressing it too much as this makes the kissel cloudy. Return the juice to the saucepan, keeping back a little of the liquid to blend with the flour. Add the sugar to the saucepan and bring to the boil. Add the blended flour and liquid and simmer for a few minutes stirring briskly all the time. Serve hot or cold with castor (verifine) sugar and cream or milk.

This kissel can also be made from gooseberries, blackcurrants or morello cherries. Adjust the amount of sugar to the type of fruit.

To make a thinner kissel or a fruit sauce use half the amount of flour.

If making the kissel from cherries hold back the fruit and thicken the fruit juice only. The cherries are best left whole in a thickened fruit sauce.

This pudding is very popular in the summer. Now however, one can change the seasons and make it from frozen berries in the winter as well.

Apple kissel

serves 4-5

4 medium cooking apples
500 ml (1 pt) 2½ cups water
1 slice lemon rind
juice ½ lemon
100 g (4 oz) ½ cup sugar
1 tablespoon potato flour or arrowroot

Peel, core and slice the apples. Cook them in the water with the lemon rind for about 20 minutes until tender. Sieve. Add the lemon juice and sugar and return to the saucepan. Bring to the boil. Mix the flour with a little water and stir it into the purée. Cook for a few minutes, stirring all the time until it thickens. Serve hot or cold, with or without cream.

If you wish you can flavour the apple with orange instead of lemon, in which case grate a little orange rind finely and add to the apples when cooking together with the juice from the orange.

If the apples are tart you may need more sugar and they take longer to cook.

Milk kissel

serves 4

500 ml (1 pt) 2½ cups milk
40 g (1½ oz) 3 tablespoons sugar
flavouring (optional)
2 level tablespoons potato flour or arrowroot

Put the sugar and most of the milk into a saucepan

and bring to the boil. Mix the flour with the remaining milk and add to the boiling kissel, stirring all the time until it thickens. Flavour with vanilla or almond essence or grated lemon or orange rind. Serve with fruit.

This kissel is a favourite with small children and can of course be served on its own. A good quick pudding for those on a diet or invalids.

Kissel with wine

serves 6

400 g (1 lb) berries (cranberries, blackberries, redcurrants, etc)
500 ml (1 pt) 2½ cups water
100 g (4 oz) ½ cup sugar
125 ml (¼ pt) ⅔ cup dry red wine
3 dessertspoons potato flour or arrowroot

Clean the fruit, remove the stalks and put it into a saucepan with the water. Bring to the boil, reduce heat and simmer for about 15 minutes. Put the fruit through a fine wire sieve or muslin. Return the juice to the saucepan, add the sugar and bring to the boil. Mix the wine with the flour and add to the juice. Stir until it thickens. Serve hot or cold with cream and castor sugar. Cold kissel can be decorated with whipped cream and chopped blanched almonds.

Kissel is a Russian national dish and very popular especially in summer when the fruit is in season. Nowadays you can of course use frozen fruit equally well or even canned.

Compôte of fresh fruit

serves 6

4 medium cooking apples
200 g (8 oz) morello cherries
3-4 medium yellow plums
3-4 apricots
300 g (12 oz) 1½ cups sugar
500 ml (1 pt) 2½ cups water

Peel, core and slice the apples. Stalk and wash the other fruit. Stone the cherries very carefully so that the cherries remain whole. Boil the cherry stones in the sugar and water for a few minutes. Strain and add the apples. Simmer gently for about 10 minutes. Add the whole apricots, plums and cherries. Simmer for a further 10 minutes or until the fruit is tender.

You can cheat here and use frozen fruit. Canned is not recommended because it does not give the fresh flavour. The secret of a good compôte is that each fruit should be separate. For this reason it is really better if you have time to cook each fruit separately and watch over it. Then mix the fruits together when cooked. You can add berries, say, raspberries or redcurrants to this if you wish. This is of course very popular in the summer when the fruits are in season. Best eaten chilled on a hot summer's day. It is very refreshing and light.

Fresh berries with sugar and wine

serves 6

600 g (1½ lb) mixed fruit (blackcurrants, redcurrants, strawberries, raspberries, cherries, gooseberries or grapes)
200 g (8 oz) 1 cup castor (verifine) sugar
4 wineglasses sherry, madeira or muscatel

Use a mixture of any three fruits available. Remove stalks and wash the fruit, removing the stones from the cherries and pips from the grapes. Put the fruit into a glass dish. Cover with sugar and pour the wine or sherry over. Leave to stand for 2-3 hours before serving.

This is a good party sweet. You can of course use frozen berries and have it in the winter. It is best, however, in the summer when the fresh fruit is available, eaten chilled.

Vozdushni pirog
(Air pudding with apples)

serves 6

6 medium cooking apples
150 g (6 oz) ¾ cup castor (verifine) sugar
6 egg whites
pinch of salt

Peel and core the apples and cook them with the sugar in a very little water until tender. Sieve to make a purée. Cool. Beat the egg-whites with a pinch of salt until they stand in peaks. Fold the apple purée into the egg whites and put the mixture into a greased soufflé-dish. Bake in a fairly hot oven 200°C (400°F) Mark 6 for about 15 minutes until brown and risen. Serve immediately.

This is another very popular Russian pudding and easy and quick to make. Be careful that the whites of the eggs have no yolk in them or you will not be able to whip them.

Instead of the apples, strawberry or raspberry jam 100 - 150 g (4-6 oz) ½ cup can be used. Use same method as for Vozdushni with apples, but use less sugar – 50 g (2 oz) 4 tablespoons castor sugar and serve with single (light) cream.

Cream of sour milk or yoghurt mould

serves 4

575 ml (1 pt) 2½ cups sour milk or yoghurt
2 tablespoons cream or sour cream
50 g (2 oz) 4 tablespoons sugar
15 g (½ oz) 2 envelopes gelatine
1 yolk of egg
½ teaspoon cinnamon

Blend yolk with sugar till it turns white, add the cinnamon. Dissolve the gelatine in a cup of hot water and place the cup in a pan of boiling water for a few minutes stirring all the time to make sure it has dissolved properly. Remove from stove and cool slightly.

Whip or put into mixer the yolk mixture together with the cream and sour milk or yoghurt till it is frothy. Add the gelatine gradually. Test for sweetness. Put into wetted mould and chill.

Use only real sour cream, ie sour cream you have made yourself or real cream. This gives a better flavour. Shop yoghurt will make this dish too sour, see instructions for making yoghurt at home (page 147).

Cherry charlotte

serves 6

6 eggs
150 g (6 oz) ¾ cup sugar
250 ml (½ pt) 1¼ cups milk
1 teaspoon cinnamon
75 g (3 oz) 1½ cups fresh breadcrumbs
100 g (4 oz) ½ cup melted butter
400 g (1 lb) stoned morello cherries
1 teaspoon mixed peel (optional)

Separate the eggs and beat the yolks with the sugar until white. Add the milk, cinnamon and breadcrumbs. Stir in the melted butter, when it has cooled slightly, and mix well. Add the cherries and the peel. Beat the whites until very stiff and fold them into the mixture. Put the mixture in a greased soufflé-dish which has been dusted with breadcrumbs and bake for about half an hour in a moderate oven 180-200°C (350-400°F) Mark 4-6 until brown and risen. Serve with cherry sauce (page 92).

Since the cherry season is so short you will most probably have to use frozen or canned cherries for this. However, cherry plums are a good substitute for cherries if you want to try this dish. They are available for a short season in July. The flavour will not, however, be the same.

Apricot soufflé

serves 6

400 g (1 lb) apricots
165 ml ($\frac{1}{3}$ pt) ¾ cup water (approx)
100 g (4 oz) ½ cup sugar
1 dessertspoon flour
25 g (1 oz) 2 tablespoons butter
4 eggs
1 tablespoon rum or sherry

Wash and stone the apricots and cut them in small pieces. Put them in a saucepan with the water, cover and simmer for about 15 minutes or until tender. Put through a coarse sieve and return to the saucepan. Add the sugar and cook slowly for about five minutes until the mixture turns a deeper colour. Do not let it thicken too much at this stage. Mix the flour to a smooth paste with a tablespoon of water and add it to the purée, stirring all the time until it has heated through. The mixture should thicken further. Stir in the butter and put aside to cool slightly. Separate the eggs and add the beaten egg yolks and the rum or sherry. Beat the egg whites until they stand in peaks and fold them into the mixture. Transfer the mixture to a greased soufflé dish, sprinkle with a little castor sugar and bake at 200°C (400°F) Mark 6 for about 30 minutes or until brown and risen. Serve by itself or with egg custard (page 131).

This soufflé can also be made from morello cherries or damsons. Adjust the amount of sugar to the type of fruit used.

You can use dried apricots for this recipe or frozen fruit if you wish. Best flavour of course is made with fresh fruit.

Soufflé with wine or rum

serves 4-6

50 g (2 oz) 4 tablespoons butter
65 g (2½ oz) 1¼ cups fresh white breadcrumbs
125 ml (¼ pt) $\frac{2}{3}$ cup white wine or 60 ml ($\frac{1}{8}$ pt) ¼ cup wine and 60 ml ($\frac{1}{8}$ pt) ¼ cup rum
65 g (2½ oz) $\frac{1}{3}$ cup castor (very fine) sugar
3 large eggs
pinch cinnamon

Melt half of the butter and fry the breadcrumbs lightly. Add the wine or wine and rum and withdraw the pan from the heat. Transfer the contents to a bowl and whisk. Leave to cool a little. Beat the remainder of the butter with the sugar and blend with the egg yolks. Add to the wine and breadcrumbs and stir. Beat the whites until very stiff and fold them into the mixture. Transfer to a buttered soufflé-dish and cook for about 30 minutes 200°C (400°F) Mark 6 until well browned and risen. Serve with rum sauce (page 94) or cream.

This is a winter pudding. A good party dish.

Sweet omelette with fruit sauce

serves 4

SAUCE
200 g (8 oz) morello cherries or berries in season.
250 ml (½ pt) 1¼ cups water
sugar to taste – about 50 g (2 oz) 4 tablespoons
1 dessertspoon potato flour, cornflour or arrowroot
1 egg white

OMELETTE
3 eggs
1 tablespoon plain flour
1 heaped tablespoon sugar
rind of ½ lemon
butter for frying

The sauce should be half ready before you start the omelette.

CHERRY SAUCE
Remove stalks and wash and carefully stone the cherries. Boil them in the water with sugar for about ten minutes until tender. Lift them out of the water with a perforated spoon and keep them warm. When the omelette is nearly ready bring the liquid back to the boil and thicken it with the potato flour mixed with a little water. Stir and allow to simmer for a few minutes. Beat the egg white till it is very stiff. Remove the liquid from the heat and fold in the egg white.

This is another recipe which is strictly a summer pudding. You can of course substitute frozen berries. This is rather filling so have it when the rest of the meal is light.

Remember to have a frying pan with a thick base and do not attempt to pour the omelette into the pan before it is quite hot.

BERRY SAUCE
Remove stalks, wash the fruit and cook it in water with the sugar for about 20 minutes until tender. Put through a sieve. When the omelette is almost ready thicken the sauce with a dessertspoon of potato flour mixed with a little water. Stir until the mixture thickens. Beat the white of the egg until stiff. Remove the liquid from the heat and fold in the egg white. Serve with the omelette.

OMELETTE
Beat the yolks with the sugar and sifted flour until white. Add the grated lemon rind. Beat the whites until they stand in peaks and fold them into the mixture. Heat a large omelette pan, melt the butter and pour in the mixture. This will take longer to cook than an ordinary omelette. If it is to be served with cherry sauce put the whole cherries across it before folding over.

Zephyr

serves 6

500 ml (1 pt) 2½ cups double (heavy) cream
75 g (3 oz) 6 tablespoons castor (verifine) sugar
grated rind of 1 lemon
200 g (8 oz) either strawberries, raspberries or 6 stoned plums
6 meringues (optional)

Beat the cream until it is thick. Remove stalks and wash the fruit. If you use large strawberries or dessert plums cut them in quarters. Mix the fruit, sugar and lemon rind with the cream. Put it into a suitable serving-dish and chill. Decorate with meringues if you wish and serve with sweet biscuits or sponge fingers.

This is another good party pudding best eaten in the summer when the fruit is in season. Can of course be made with frozen fruit. Eat chilled on a hot summer's day on the patio.

Snowballs

serves 6

750 ml (1¼ pt) 3¾ cups milk
1 vanilla pod or grated rind of 1 lemon
6 eggs
100-150 g (4-6 oz) ½-¾ cup sugar (according to taste)

Slit the vanilla pod and put it in a saucepan with the milk. Bring to the boil. Meanwhile, beat the egg whites until they stand in peaks. Put tablespoons of the beaten egg whites into the boiling milk to cook. When they rise to the surface they are ready. Lift out with a perforated spoon and put on a large plate to cool.

Beat the egg yolks with the sugar until white. Remove the vanilla pod, cool the milk slightly; add yolks and sugar. Mix well; cook over low heat, stirring all the time until the mixture resembles a thick cream. On no account allow it to boil. Add the grated lemon rind at this stage if you are using it instead of the vanilla pod. Pour the custard into a shallow dish and float the snowballs on top. Chill and serve.

This was always a great favourite with us as children. It is also a good party dish and best served in the winter months. Be careful not to overcook the custard. It is safer to make in a double saucepan.

Egg custard

serves 4

4 egg yolks
50 g (2 oz) 4 tablespoons sugar
500 ml (1 pt) 2½ cups milk
1 vanilla pod

Beat the egg yolks with the sugar until white. Heat the milk in a saucepan with the slit vanilla pod. Bring to the boil and put aside to cool slightly. Pour the milk with the vanilla pod over the egg and sugar mixture. Stir and transfer the custard to the saucepan. Cook on a very low heat, stirring all the time, till the mixture resembles a thick cream. Do not let it boil. Remove the vanilla pod and serve hot or cold.

To get the maximum flavour out of the pod, slit it lengthways and remove the seeds, ie put them in the milk. Cook the milk with the seeds and remove them when the custard is finished. This is another recipe where it is safer to use a double boiler in case the egg curdles.

You can flavour the custard with grated lemon rind if you wish or with cinnamon instead of the vanilla pod.

Sabayon

serves 4

5 egg yolks
65 g (2½ oz) $\frac{1}{3}$ cup vanilla sugar
grated rind of 1 lemon
2 wineglasses sherry (port or madeira)

Beat the vanilla sugar with the egg yolks until white and fluffy. Add the sherry and lemon rind and cook over a low heat, stirring all the time, until it resembles a thick cream. Do not let it boil. Serve alone, hot or cold, or with fruit salad.

This is a very popular sauce in Russia. A suggestion from my old Russian cook book is to whisk the custard whilst you are cooking it till it foams. It is safer for all custards to be made in a double boiler however. This sauce can be eaten with any type of stewed fruit or cold rice pudding, etc.

Gogol mogol

PER PERSON
1 egg yolk
1 level tablespoon castor (verifine) sugar
1 teaspoon rum or brandy (optional)
2 wafers

Beat the sugar with the egg yolk until white. Stir in a teaspoon of rum or brandy. Pour into an individual dish. Chill and serve with wafers.

This is a children's favourite, without the rum of course. You can flavour it with a little finely grated lemon or orange rind if you wish. It is quick and easy to prepare. Use the egg white for vozdushni pirog.

It is rather sweet for some tastes, however, so go easy on the sugar if you have not got a sweet tooth.

Lemon water ice

serves 4

375 ml (¾ pt) 2 cups water
150 g (6 oz) ¾ cup sugar
slice of lemon rind
juice of 1 large lemon
handful redcurrants (optional)
1 egg white

Boil the sugar and water with a thin strip of lemon rind for a few minutes. Cool. Add the lemon juice. Strain the liquid into a container and freeze. Remove from freezer when it is mushy – after about an hour. Whip the egg white until stiff, beat the ice a bit, fold the white into the ice and return it to the freezer. Decorate with redcurrants before serving.

Ice cream of all types is very popular in Russia even in winter. If you wish to serve lemon ice have a substantial meal beforehand as it is very light. You can give this a mint flavour by adding a sprig of fresh mint from the garden to the lemon syrup and leave it to infuse. You can decorate the ice with a few mint leaves. Wash and dry each leaf, brush leaves in egg white and roll in castor sugar. Dry. Mint if done this way will keep for 2-3 days.

Vanilla ice cream

serves 6

6 egg yolks
150 g (6 oz) ¾ cup sugar
750 ml (1½ pt) 3¾ cups milk or single (light) cream
1 vanilla pod or grated rind of 1 lemon

Beat the egg yolks and sugar with a wooden spoon

until white. Put the milk or cream in a saucepan with the slit vanilla pod and bring it to the boil. Remove from the heat and leave for a few minutes. Add the eggs and sugar and stir. Return to the saucepan and cook very slowly over a low heat for about 5-10 minutes, stirring all the time until the mixture resembles a thick cream. Don't let it boil. If lemon rind is used instead of a vanilla pod it should be added now. Cool. When the custard is quite cold transfer it to a bowl. Stand this bowl in a larger bowl containing as many ice cubes as possible. Add a little cooking salt to the ice and whip the custard with a whisk or rotary beater until it thickens. Transfer it to the ice tray in the fridge to use when required.

Vanilla ice cream can be eaten any time of course but is particularly good for a party or a wedding. You will find this recipe much sweeter than the shop variety and I hope much better. Set the refrigerator to the coldest setting before starting. Whisk the ice cream in freezing tray with a fork every half an hour till half frozen. This is to let the air in otherwise it will be too solid.

One hour before serving transfer the ice cream to the main part of the fridge so it is not too hard. Ice cream should be over-sweetened and over-flavoured as much is lost when it freezes.

COFFEE ICE CREAM

Follow the recipe for vanilla ice cream adding 3 teaspoons of instant coffee dissolved in a table-spoon of water to the milk instead of the vanilla pod.

CHOCOLATE ICE CREAM

Follow the recipe for vanilla ice cream adding 3 heaped teaspoons of cocoa mixed with a little water to the milk instead of the vanilla pod.

Strawberry ice cream

serves 6

4 egg yolks
200 g (8 oz) 1 cup sugar
500 ml (1 pt) 2½ cups double cream
3 tablespoons rose water
400 g (1 lb) strawberries

Beat the egg yolks and sugar with a wooden spoon until white. Add the cream and transfer to a sauce-pan. Cook very slowly over a low heat, stirring all the time until the mixture resembles a thick cream. On no account allow it to boil. Add the rose water and cool.

Remove stalks and wash the fruit. Put it through a sieve. There should be about 250 ml (½ pt) 1¼ cups of purée. Add the sieved berries to the cream and blend well. Transfer the mixture to a bowl and stand the bowl in a larger bowl containing as many ice cubes as possible. Add a little cooking salt to the ice and whip the custard with a whisk or rotary beater until it thickens. Transfer to the ice tray in the fridge.

This can also be made with raspberries.

Orange rice

serves 4-6

100 g (4 oz) $\frac{2}{3}$ cup rice
125 g (5 oz) $\frac{2}{3}$ cup sugar
2 large oranges or 4 small
2 cloves
750 ml ($\frac{2}{3}$ pt) 1½ cups water

Boil the rice in plenty of salted water until ready but not overdone. Take care not to overcook it as this will spoil the pudding. It should take about 20 minutes.

Transfer the rice to a colander when ready and run cold water through to get rid of the starch and to separate the grains. Drain completely and put into a bowl to cool.

While the rice is cooking, make a syrup by boiling 65 g (2½ oz) $\frac{1}{3}$ cup sugar with 165 ml ($\frac{1}{3}$ pt) ¾ cup water for a few minutes. Allow to cool. When cold pour over the rice.

Remove the rind from the oranges with a sharp knife and using half the peel only cut up small as for marmalade. Remove the pith and any pips from the oranges, and cut into thin slices. Place the orange slices in a large serving-dish.

Now boil the rest of the sugar and water briskly with the orange peel and cloves for 5 minutes. Allow to cool.

When the rice is quite cold spread it over the oranges. Pour over the cold syrup with the peel and allow to drain to the bottom of the dish, making the orange slices moist. This is a most refreshing pudding. It is also easy to prepare and the ingred-ients are always handy.

This is an excellent cold winter pudding. In Russia in the old days, and even now, oranges were scarce and expensive so it was rather a treat.

Rice layer pudding *serves 6*

500 ml (1 pt) 2½ cups milk
50 g (2 oz) $\frac{1}{3}$ cup rice
pinch of salt
½ vanilla pod
2 egg yolks
25 g (1 oz) 2 tablespoons sugar
150 g (6 oz) ½ cup approx jam or apple purée
butter for cooking

Put the rice, milk, salt and half a vanilla pod in a saucepan and bring to the boil. Simmer slowly for 15-20 minutes, stirring frequently until it thickens. Cool slightly and remove the vanilla pod.

Beat the egg yolks with the sugar until white and add to the rice. Butter a fireproof dish and put in layers of rice and layers of jam or apple purée, ending in a rice layer. Brown in a moderate oven 170°C (325°F) Mark 3 for about 20 minutes. Serve hot or cold with egg custard (page 131).

It is safer to do the rice pudding in a double boiler in which case it will take longer. Milk burns quite easily in thin based pans. Use the best milk or add a little cream or butter to the pudding when you are cooking it. This is also good with cream if cold.

Rice pudding with pumpkin *serves 6*

400 g (1 lb) pumpkin
25 g (1 oz) 2 tablespoons sugar
50 g (2 oz) $\frac{1}{3}$ cup rice
500 ml (1 pt) 2½ cups milk
pinch of salt

Peel the piece of pumpkin and remove any seeds. Chop into cubes. Cook with the sugar in a little water for about 10-15 minutes. Put the rice, milk and salt in another saucepan and simmer slowly for 15-20 minutes, stirring frequently, until it thickens. When it is ready, add the cooked pumpkin which can be mashed if you wish. Put the mixture in a fireproof dish and bake for 20-30 minutes 170°C (325°F) Mark 3 in the oven. Serve with sugar. Millet can be substituted for rice in this recipe.

This is a lovely summer pudding. For a change add sultanas, candied peel and chopped walnuts instead of the pumpkin for a winter pudding. All milk puddings are greatly improved if the very best milk is used, ie with plenty of cream. Milk puddings have a touch of *haute cuisine* if you add 1 or 2 yolks. If you like, use the whole egg but whip the white separately and fold in before you put into the oven. The yolk should of course be blended with the sugar.

Rice with fruit sauce *serves 4-5*

100 g (4 oz) ½ cup rice
25 g (1 oz) ¼ cup currants
25 g (1 oz) ¼ cup sultanas
rind of ½ lemon grated
juice of ¼ lemon
2 tablespoons vanilla sugar
250 ml (½ pt) 1¼ cups Berry Kissel (page 127)
pinch of salt

Put the rice, currants, sultanas and salt in a muslin bag, leaving room for it to expand and boil for about 20 minutes. Meanwhile, squeeze the juice from the lemon and stir into it the grated rind and 1 tablespoon sugar. Mix thoroughly.

When the rice is ready, transfer to a colander, remove the muslin and pour cold water through to remove starch and separate the grains. Drain thoroughly. Mix with the sugar and lemon juice. Transfer to a suitable mould which has been rinsed in water and dusted with 1 tablespoon sugar. Press down with a spoon to make the top even. Cool. When cold turn out on to a serving-dish and pour over the Kissel which should be made as a sauce with half the quantity of flour.

This is another summer pudding but you can have it all the year round if you use frozen berries. We used to love it as children. For a touch of glamour add chopped blanched almonds to the rice and use wine instead of lemon juice.

ALTERNATIVE SAUCE
200 g (8 oz) raspberries, strawberries or redcurrants
50-75 g (2-3 oz) 4-6 tablespoons sugar
60 ml ($\frac{1}{8}$ pt) ¼ cup water
60 ml ($\frac{1}{8}$ pt) ¼ cup red or white wine

Remove stalks and wash the fruit and rub it through a sieve. Put 50-75 g (2-3 oz) $\frac{1}{4}$-$\frac{1}{3}$ cup sugar, depending on the type or fruit, in a saucepan with the water and bring to the boil. Add the wine and the sieved fruit. Bring to the boil again, stir and remove any scum which has formed. Serve the sauce either hot or cold with the hot rice.

Chocolate and vanilla rice pudding

serves 6

50 g (2 oz) $\frac{1}{3}$ cup rice
500 ml (1 pt) 2½ cups Jersey milk
50 g (2 oz) 4 tablespoons sugar
½ vanilla pod
2 egg yolks
50 g (2 oz) 2 squares grated chocolate

Put the rice, milk, half a vanilla pod and 1 tablespoon of sugar into a saucepan and cook very slowly for about 20 minutes, stirring frequently. Cool and remove the vanilla pod.

Beat the egg yolks with the remaining sugar and mix with half the rice. Mix the grated chocolate with the other half. Put layers of chocolate and vanilla rice into a buttered fireproof dish, ending with a vanilla layer. Brown in a moderate oven 170°C (325°F) Mark 3 for about 20-30 minutes. Cool and turn out on to a dish. This pudding can be decorated with whipped cream and glacé cherries. Serve with chilled egg custard (page 131).

This is a neglected winter pudding and extremely tasty. Suitable for a party either for children or grown-ups. Be careful not to burn the rice. A tip from the Russian book: grease sides of pan with butter or oil. Sprinkle with dry breadcrumbs and then cook the rice with the milk. This should prevent burning.

Kutia

serves 6

200 g (8 oz) 1¼ cups poppy seeds
25 g (1 oz) 2 tablespoons sugar
50 g (2 oz) ½ cup shelled walnuts (optional)
2 tablespoons honey
50 g (2 oz) ½ cup sultanas
200 g (8 oz) 1 $\frac{1}{3}$ cups rice

Pour boiling water over the poppy seeds and allow them to stand for two to three hours. Put the seeds through a mincer two or three times, adding the sugar the last time. Dry the walnuts for about 10 minutes in the oven. Mix the seeds and sugar with the honey, sultanas and chopped walnuts.

Boil the rice until cooked and strain. Mix all the ingredients together and leave to stand for about two hours before serving.

Kutia can also be made from wheat grain instead of rice, if this is available.

This is traditionally eaten at 'Wakes' or 'pominka' which means 'Memory of the dead' in Russian. After the service relatives and friends gather in the house of the departed and a close relative makes pirogi or piroshki and Kutia. They also have quite a few drinks and by the end of the Pominka memories of the departed are not so sad and people are in a good mood.

This is also eaten on Christmas Eve in some parts of Russia.

Gurevskaya kasha (1)
(Semolina pudding with nuts)

serves 6

100 g (4 oz) $\frac{2}{3}$ cup shelled almonds or walnuts
500 ml (1 pt) 2½ cups Jersey milk
25 g (1 oz) ¼ cup semolina
few drops almond essence
40 g (1½ oz) 2½ tablespoons vanilla sugar
1 large egg
1 tablespoon granulated sugar
100 g (4 oz) ½ cup jam or 200 g (8 oz) fresh fruit (optional)

Grate half the nuts and chop the other half. Heat the milk in a saucepan and add the semolina just before it boils. Bring to the boil and simmer for several minutes until it is cooked, stirring all the time. It should have a thin consistency. Remove from the heat and add the nuts and almond flavouring. Beat the egg yolk with the vanilla sugar until white and add to the semolina mixture. Beat the egg-white until very stiff and fold it in. Transfer to a buttered pie-dish and sprinkle with the granulated sugar. Put the dish under a hot grill to caramelize the sugar. When golden brown put in a fairly hot oven 200°C (400°F) Mark 6 for 15-20 minutes. It will rise slightly. Eat hot with fruit compôte or jam, or cold with fruit compôte and cream.

An alternative method is to put a layer of fresh fruit or jam between two layers of semolina mixture in the pie-dish and cook in the same way. The fruit must, of course, be suitably prepared; peeled, sliced and stoned as necessary.

To get good results it is best to add some thin cream to the pudding instead of the milk. The second version is a much richer one. This is an everyday winter pudding.

Gurevskaya kasha (2)
(Semolina pudding with nuts and cream)

serves 8-10

250 ml (½ pt) 1¼ cups double cream
100 g (4 oz) $\frac{2}{3}$ cup shelled almonds or walnuts
500 ml (1 pt) 2½ cups single cream
25 g (1 oz) ¼ cup semolina
few drops of almond essence
50 g (2 oz) 4 tablespoons vanilla sugar
1 tablespoon granulated sugar
100 g (4 oz) ½ cup jam or 350 g (12 oz) fresh fruit (optional

Grate half the nuts and chop the other half. Put the cream in a fairly shallow basin and place under the grill or in a fairly hot oven 200°C (400°F) Mark 6. Skim off the brown skins as they form and put them in a dish, until half the cream has been used up. Warm the single cream in a saucepan and add the semolina. Stir quickly to prevent any lumps forming and boil for a few minutes until cooked. It should have a thin consistency. If it has thickened too much add a little milk. Add all the nuts, almond essence and vanilla sugar. Put half the cream skins on the bottom of a buttered pie-dish. Cover with half the semolina. Put the rest of the skins on top and end with a semolina layer. Sprinkle with granulated sugar and put under a hot grill to caramelize the sugar. When golden brown put in a fairly hot oven 200°C (400°F) Mark 6 for about 15 minutes to heat through. Serve with fruit compôte or jam, or put a layer of either fresh fruit or jam between layers of cream and semolina, and cook in the same way. The fruit should be prepared, ie stoned if necessary.

This is a famous and lovely pudding. Forget about the semolina pudding you had at school. This has no connection with it and your guests will never guess what it is made of if they try it. It is rather rich and expensive therefore suitable for a party. It will go down very well.

Olady

serves 8

25 g (1 oz) fresh yeast or 2 packets dried yeast
1 tablespoon sugar
500 ml (1 pt) 2½ cups milk
400 g (1 lb) 4 cups plain flour
2 eggs
1 teaspoon salt
4 medium cooking apples
butter for frying

Mix the yeast in a little warm water with the sugar. Add the warm milk and sifted flour. Cover and leave to rise in a warm place for about half an hour. Add the beaten eggs and salt. Beat the mixture with a wooden spoon until it is smooth. Allow it to rise a second time. The batter is now ready.

Peel and core the apples and cut them in slices. Cut the slices in half if they are large. Coat the slices in batter and fry them in hot butter in a thick frying-pan, turning them when they are brown on one side. Serve with sugar or jam.

Olady can also be made as small pancakes without the apple and eaten with jam.

This is similar to apple fritters but lighter since the batter is made with yeast. Eaten best in the fall when the apples are just ripe.

Tvorozhniky

serves 6

400 g (1 lb) 2½ cups curd cheese
40 g (1½ oz) $\frac{1}{3}$ cup flour
25 g (1 oz) 2 tablespoons vanilla sugar
1 tablespoon sultanas (optional)
pinch of salt
rind of 1 lemon
1 egg
flour for coating
butter or oil for frying

Sieve the cheese to remove any lumps. Add the flour, vanilla sugar, sultanas, salt, grated lemon rind and egg. Mix well. Turn on to a floured board. Taking a tablespoonful of the mixture at a time form into small rissole shapes. Coat in flour and fry in butter or oil until golden brown. Sprinkle with sugar and serve with jam or a thin berry kissel (page 127).

These are quite easy and simple to make. Be careful that the mixture is stiff enough. Curd cheese or cottage cheese can be rather moist. Add a little more flour if necessary. You should make the first rissole for a test. These are also delicious with sour cream served with cinnamon mixed with castor (verifine) sugar.

Zapekanka of cream cheese

serves 6

400 g (1 lb) 2½ cups curd cheese
4 eggs
40 g (1½ oz) 3 tablespoons melted butter
100 g (4 oz) ½ cup sugar
50 g (2 oz) ½ cup semolina
1 tablespoon sultanas
rind of lemon or orange
50 g (2 oz) ½ cup candied peel
1 tablespoon dry bread-crumbs

Sieve the cheese and add the beaten egg yolks, melted butter, sugar and semolina and mix well with a wooden spoon until smooth. Add the washed sultanas, grated lemon or orange rind and chopped peel. Beat the egg whites until very stiff and fold them into the mixture. Butter a fireproof dish and dust it with breadcrumbs. Transfer the mixture and bake it in a moderate oven 200°C (400°F) Mark 6 for half an hour or until brown. Serve hot or cold with sour cream.

This is a winter pudding and a great favourite with friends. 'Zapekanka' means something cooked in the oven so one can translate this pudding as 'cream cheese bake'.

Cheese baba

serves 4

300 g (12 oz) 1½ cups curd cheese
50 g (2 oz) 4 tablespoons sugar
1 tablespoon sultanas
lemon rind (optional)
1 tablespoon cream
1 egg
vanilla flavouring

Sieve the cheese and add the sugar. Bought cheese will need more than home-made. Add the washed sultanas, grated lemon rind, cream, beaten egg, and vanilla flavouring. Mix well and put into a greased baking-dish. Sprinkle with sugar and dot with butter. Bake in a moderate oven 190-200°C (375-400°F) Mark 5-6 for half an hour or till brown. Serve hot or cold with cream or sour cream.

This is another winter favourite for parties as it is so quick and easy to prepare.

PASKHA

The word 'paskha' means 'Easter' in Russian and paskha is traditionally eaten at Easter together with kulich (page 115) and coloured eggs to break the long Lenten fast.

The paskha is made in a special mould made from five pieces of wood slotted together. It is in the shape of a pyramid with the letters 'XB' and 'BB' which means 'Christ is risen and truly he has risen'. The mould often has a cross on it as well.

Fresh paskha

serves 12-14

400 g (1 lb) 2 cups sugar
5 egg yolks
250 ml (½ pt) 1¼ cups milk
1 vanilla pod
200 g (8 oz) 1 cup fresh butter
1.6 kg (3½ lb) 7 cups curd cheese
1 tablespoon currants (optional)
grated lemon rind (optional)
50 g (2 oz) ½ cup finely chopped blanched almonds
125 ml (¼ pt) ⅔ cup double cream

Beat the yolks with 100 g (½ lb) 1 cup of sugar until white. Add the milk and the vanilla pod and cook in a double boiler until the mixture thickens. Add the butter in very small pieces and allow it to melt. Cool.

Sieve the cheese into a large bowl to remove any lumps. Add the cooled custard and the remainder of the sugar. The mixture should be very sweet as a lot of the sugar will drain away. Add the lemon rind, cleaned currants and almonds. Whip the cream and add. Mix well.

Although Russians have a special wooden shape for making paskha it can equally well be made in a large flower-pot or colander lined with a piece of wet muslin folded double. Fill the receptacle with the paskha and fold the muslin over at the top. Stand it over a dish to catch the liquid that drains away and put a plate with a small weight on top of the muslin. Leave overnight in a cool place to drain. Turn out on to a large dish the following day. Cover with a damp napkin and keep in the fridge. The paskha should keep for about a week if the napkin is renewed every day. Serve with a slice of kulich.

Paskha is traditionally only eaten at Easter and Whitsun. It is much easier to prepare than the cooked paskha and quick if you use an electric mixer. At Easter all the guests go from house to house to decide which housewife makes the best paskha and kulich. It can be difficult to judge the right amount of sugar, however, since most of it drains away so it must be over sweetened to start with. Cheese varies so much. If kept it goes sour. If fresh it is hardly sour at all. In fact, the best paskha should be slightly sour or it will be too rich.

Cooked paskha

serves 10

1 kg (2½ lb) 5 cups curd cheese
500 ml (1 pt) 2½ cups sour cream
5 eggs
100-200 g (4-8 oz) ½-1 cup butter
1 vanilla pod
1 tablespoon cleaned currants
grated lemon rind
400 g (1 lb) 2 cups sugar
25 g (1 oz) ¼ cup finely chopped blanched almonds

Sieve the cheese into a large bowl to remove any lumps. Add the sour cream, beaten eggs and butter. You will need about 200 g (8 oz) 1 cup butter if you are using bought cheese; 100 g (4 oz) ½ cup should be enough for home-made. Transfer the mixture to a large saucepan and cook over a low heat, stirring all the time. Do not let it boil. When cooked, the mixture will steam. This may take a fairly long time but it is most important to cook it properly. When ready, stand the saucepan in a large bowl of ice. Add a slit vanilla pod and seeds and a little grated lemon rind. When the mixture is quite cold add the sugar, almonds and currants. The amount of sugar will depend on whether the cheese is home-made or bought. (Bought cheese needs more.)

Drain and serve in the same way as fresh paskha (see above).

Cooked paskha is considered to be difficult

to prepare mainly because it is cooked. This requires experience. It is similar to cooking eggs for a custard and making sure that they do not curdle. However, it has a delicious taste and keeps better. We always have two paskhas at Easter, one fresh and one cooked, and guests tell me which they prefer.

If you make some cheese at home mix it with the shop variety which is quite sour by comparison then you will get that slightly sour flavour which prevents it appearing too rich.

Raspberry paskha

serves 8

1 kg (2½ lb) 5 cups curd cheese
200 g (8 oz) ¾ cup raspberry jam (jelly)
150 g (6 oz) ¾ cup sugar
3 eggs
100 g (4 oz) ½ cup unsalted butter
250 ml (½ pt) 1¼ cups sour cream
a little raspberry flavouring (optional)

Sieve the cheese into a bowl to remove any lumps. Add the raspberry jam and the sugar and mix well. A few drops of raspberry flavouring may be added if desired. Beat the butter and add with the eggs and sour cream. Mix very well. A little more sugar may be necessary. Drain and serve in the same way as fresh paskha.

A NOTE ON CURD CHEESE

Curd cheese can vary considerably in quality and flavour so it is important to understand how to treat the different types. Home-made cheese is fresh and therefore mild in flavour and needs very little sugar. In England shop-bought curd cheese is often sour, particularly in warm weather. To counteract this use fresh cream instead of sour and add an extra egg in the paskha recipes. If necessary more sugar may be used: up to 200 g (8 oz) 1 cup sugar to 400 g (1 lb) 2 cups cheese. If you have a little home-made cheese mix this with the bought cheese to improve the flavour. Always keep cheese in the fridge if possible.

For chocolate flavour: melt 150 g (6 oz) 6 squares bitter chocolate in a saucepan with 1 tablespoon water. Quickly add the melted chocolate to the cheese mixture stirring all the time (an electric mixer is best). The chocolate goes hard very quickly so you have to do this in the shortest possible time. Test for sweetness. It should be over sweet as much of the sugar drains away. This is a very rich pudding and best eaten chilled.

You can of course try half quantities to see how far it goes.

Zapekanka of cheese and apple

serves 3-4

200 g (8 oz) 1 cup curd or cottage cheese
2 whites of egg
50 g (2 oz) 4 tablespoons sugar
2-3 slices white bread
sugar for top
1 dessertspoon sultanas
2 tablespoons sour or fresh cream
knob of butter
2 medium cooking apples
1 teaspoon semolina

Put the cheese through a sieve or in the mixer. Butter a fireproof dish. Remove crusts from bread and cover with milk to soak. Add cream to the cheese, semolina, sultanas and sugar. Whip the egg whites separately and fold into the mixture. Peel and core apple. Chop into small pieces. Blend with the rest of the ingredients. Put into the prepared dish. Cover with slices of bread. Sprinkle with sugar. Dot with butter. Put into the oven at 180°C (350°F) Mark 4, for 40 minutes or till the bread turns golden. Serve hot.

It you use very sharp apples these take longer to cook so chop more finely and add a few extra sultanas. If the cheese is dry add more cream. It is inclined to dry if kept in the fridge.

Melon water ice

serves 6

200 g (8 oz) melon
250 ml (½ pt) 1¼ cups water
100 g (4 oz) ½ cup sugar
a little grated lemon rind

Bring the sugar to the boil with the water. Allow to cool. Remove seeds from the melon and grate the melon flesh. Put into mixing bowl. Grate a little lemon rind and mix all ingredients. Put the basin into a freezer and when it is on the point of setting after about 1 hour whisk with a fork. Do this several times. Allow to set.

Half an hour before the meal put into fridge compartment to thaw. Divide into ice cream dishes and serve.

This is very refreshing and best eaten on a hot day or after a heavy meal. You can use up any left-over melon in this way but remember to use the correct proportions.

Noodles with honey and almonds

serves 6

100 g (4 oz) noodles
50 g (2 oz) ¼ cup butter
50 g (2 oz) 3 tablespoons honey
50 g (2 oz) ½ cup blanched almonds
1.25 l (2 pt) 5 cups water
1 teaspoon salt

Put the water into a large saucepan together with the salt. Bring to the boil. Add the noodles and cook briskly for about 20 minutes without a lid or till ready. Drain and rinse in cold water to prevent the noodles sticking. Heat the butter in a pan and add the noodles. Chop the almonds and put in to a separate pan together with the honey and bring to the boil. Mix in with the noodles and butter. Heat together gently for 5 minutes so that all flavours are mixed and serve.

This is an eastern pudding best eaten in winter.

Slav pudding

serves 6

75 g (3 oz) 6 tablespoons castor sugar
25 g (1 oz) ¼ cup blanched almonds
40 g (1½ oz) 1½ squares plain chocolate
4 eggs
2 tablespoons grated rye bread (dark)
375 ml (¾ pt) 2 cups single (light) cream
50 g (2 oz) ½ cup raisins
2 teaspoons butter

RUM SAUCE (page 94)

Combine the egg yolks and sugar till white. Chop the almonds. Grate the chocolate and the rye bread. Add to the yolks and sugar mixture. Dilute with cream. Add the raisins and blend all ingredients thoroughly. Butter a soufflé dish allowing room for it to rise. Whip the whites till they stand in peaks and fold into the mixture. Pour the pudding into it and bake at 190°C (375°F) Mark 5, for 15-20 minutes. If you wish you can steam the pudding. Use a pudding basin, cover with greaseproof paper and steam for 1 hour.

Make the rum sauce (page 94) 5 minutes before serving. Serve the pudding immediately it is ready with the rum sauce.

This is rather an extravagant pudding.

Caucasian sweet

400 g (1 lb) 4 cups almonds
600 g (1½ lb) 2 cups honey
75 g (3 oz) 6 tablespoons sugar

Put the almonds in a bowl and pour boiling water over them. Allow to stand till the skins come away freely. Peel almonds. Preheat oven to 180°C (350°F) Mark 4. Spread the nuts in an ungreased tin in a single layer and toast for 10 minutes. Turn with a fork from time to time to avoid burning. Put the sugar and honey into a heavy medium sized pan and bring gently to the boil stirring constantly. Continue to boil for 5 minutes still stirring. Then lower the heat and add the nuts. Stir constantly for 15 minutes. Brush the inside of a medium sized pie dish with cold water and pour in the mixture. Leave to cool and when firm, dip the pie tin in hot water for a second or two to loosen the sweet. Turn out on to a wooden board. Cut into portions with a very sharp knife.

Will stay fresh for 1 week. Good idea for Christmas.

Semolina pudding with wine

serves 6

50 g (2 oz) ½ cup semolina
50 g (2 oz) ¼ cup sugar
375 ml (¾ pt) 2 cups white wine (medium dry)
125 ml (¼ pt) $\frac{2}{3}$ cup water
2 eggs
few drops vanilla essence
200 g (8 oz) ¾ cup home-made jam (blackcurrant or cherry)
2 tablespoons water
1 teaspoon castor sugar
1 teaspoon butter

Put the wine and water into a stainless steel sauce-pan and bring to the boil. Gradually add the semolina stirring briskly to avoid lumps. Reduce heat and cook for a few more minutes till it thickens and becomes soft after about 5-10 minutes. Add sugar and vanilla essence. Stir thoroughly. Set aside. Separate eggs. Blend the semolina with the yolks. Butter a 500 ml (1 pt) dish and dust with castor sugar. Whip the whites till they stand in peaks and fold into the mixture. Put the pudding into the prepared dish. Put in a pan of water that reaches half way up the dish, and bake in the oven at 150°C (300°F) Mark 2, for 30-35 minutes. When ready take out of the oven and cool. Serve in the same dish. Add 2 tablespoons water to the jam to make a sauce. Put in sauceboat or separate dish on the table.

This is an eastern pudding which can be eaten any time.

Apple zephyr

serves 4-6

6 medium cooking apples
100 g (4 oz) ½ cup sugar
2 whites of egg
juice of ½ lemon and rind
180 ml (⅜ pt) 1 cup thick cream (optional)
glacé cherries for decoration

Core the apples and put in a greased dish to bake in the oven at 180°C (350°F) Mark 4, till quite soft. This will depend on the size of the apples. When ready put through a sieve and add the lemon juice and rind. If the colour is poor add a little pink colouring. Put into fridge and chill. Make the pudding only when all the ingredients are chilled properly. Add the sugar and put into an electric mixer. Whip the purée for a few minutes and then add the whites of egg and continue to whip till light and frothy. Or do by hand. For extra glamour add the whipped cream. Transfer to dish and decorate with glacé cherries. Put back in fridge to chill. You can of course cook the apples in the minimum of water in a saucepan. Peel and core and add the lemon juice before cooking to preserve colour.

Serve with sponge fingers. This pudding should be eaten the same day as it will not keep.

Dragli au vin
(Ukrainian wine aspic)

serves 4-6

500 ml (1 pt) 2½ cups dry white wine
200 g (8 oz) 1 cup sugar
¼ lemon juice and rind
½ teaspoon powdered cinnamon
1 clove
20 g (¾ oz) 3 envelopes gelatine

Put the wine in a stainless steel saucepan and add the sugar, cinnamon, clove and a little lemon rind and a squeeze of lemon. Check for sweetness. Boil for a few minutes. Remove froth. When the sugar dissolves stir in the powdered gelatine. Wait for it to dissolve stirring all the time. Strain. Cool. Prepare a metal mould. Scald and rinse with cold water. Put in the aspic when it is on the point of setting. Put into fridge to set. Before turning out mould, dip in hot water.

SECOND VERSION

250 ml (½ pt) 1¼ cups whipping cream
glacé cherries and angelica to decorate

Make the jelly as previous recipe. Scald and rinse a rum baba tin 20.5 cm (8 in.) in diameter. Pour the jelly in when quite cold and on the point of setting. Put in fridge. When ready dip the tin in hot water and turn out on a silver dish if possible. Whip the cream and put in the centre of the jelly ring. Decorate with glacé cherries and angelica.

This is a good party dish and should be enough for 8.

Macaroni pudding with cheese (1)

serves 4-6

200 g (8 oz) curd cheese
100 g (4 oz) 1 cup macaroni or noodles
1 egg yolk
40 g (1½ oz) 3 tablespoons sugar
180 ml (⅜ pt) 1 cup sour cream for table
1 tablespoon sour cream (for cheese)
1 tablespoon dry breadcrumbs
vanilla flavouring
50 g (2 oz) ¼ cup butter
1 tablespoon castor (verifine) sugar for top
water
salt to taste

Put plenty of water and salt into a medium sized pan. Bring to the boil. Add the macaroni or noodles and continue to boil briskly till it is cooked, ie 15-20 minutes. It should not be over cooked, better to be under cooked since it will be heated up in the oven. Mix the curd cheese with the sugar, egg yolk, vanilla and cream till well blended and there are no lumps. Combine with the macaroni. Butter a 500 ml (1 pt) dish and put the mixture into it. Sprinkle with breadcrumbs and dot with butter. Cook for 20 minutes at 180°C (350°F) Mark 4. When ready take out of the oven and sprinkle the top with castor sugar. Serve in same dish.

Serve with sour cream on the table and more sugar mixed with a little cinnamon if liked. Favourite pudding of mine when young.

Macaroni or noodle pudding with cheese (2)

serves 4-6

You can use either noodles or macaroni for this pudding. The quick macaroni (cut in small pieces) is very good for this. Instead of mixing the cheese with the macaroni put the macaroni or noodles when drained back in the saucepan. Add a knob of butter and mix well so that they do not stick

Put layers of macaroni or noodles and layers of cheese, ending with a macaroni layer. Finish as above. This is quite filling and a good substantial pudding to serve when there is little meat in the other courses.

Berry soufflé

serves 6

400 g (1 lb) raspberries or strawberries
75 g (3 oz) 6 tablespoons sugar
4 egg whites
butter to grease soufflé dish
1 tablespoon castor sugar (verifine) sugar

Remove stalks from the berries and wash. Rub through a fine nylon sieve. Add the sugar and beat till the sugar nearly dissolves. Whip the whites till they stand in peaks and fold into the fruit purée. Butter a soufflé dish. Allowing space to rise pour mixture into the dish and bake at 200°C (400°F) Mark 6 for 15-20 minutes or till well browned and risen. Serve at once.

Do not keep opening the oven door or the soufflé will fall.

Honey mousse

serves 4-6

300 g (12 oz) 1 cup honey
4 eggs

Separate eggs. Whip the yolks in a bowl and add the honey gradually till well blended. Put into a saucepan on a low heat and stir constantly until the mixture thickens. Set aside. Cool. Whisk the egg whites till they stand in peaks and fold into the yolk and honey mixture when cold. Pour into serving dish and chill.

This is rather a sweet pudding. You can use 165 ml ($\frac{1}{3}$ pt) ¾ cup whipped cream instead of the whipped white of egg if you wish.

Whipped cream au café *(Ukrainian version)*

serves 6

375 ml (¾ pt) 2 cups double cream
2-3 teaspoons very strong coffee
5 g (¼ oz) 1 envelope gelatine
4 yolks of egg
100 g (4 oz) ½ cup sugar
60 ml ($\frac{1}{8}$ pt) ¼ cup water
vanilla essence

Soak the gelatine in warm water in a small saucepan. Add the vanilla and boil through. Stir till it clears and the gelatine dissolves. Beat the sugar with the yolks till they turn white, or put into an electric mixer. Pour the mixture slowly into the hot gelatine which should be on the stove on low heat. Do not allow it to boil. When well blended set aside. Make some very strong coffee with instant coffee. Put into the mixture and allow it to cool. When on the point of setting, whip the double cream and fold into the coffee eggs and gelatine. Put into a wetted mould and allow to set in the fridge.

Use the whites of egg for Vozdushni pirog (page 129) or Easter almond cake (page 116).

Real lemon jelly *(jello)* (1)

serves 4

500 ml (1 pt) 2½ cups water
1 lemon
100 g (4 oz) ½ cup sugar
15 g (½ oz) 2 envelopes gelatine

Cut the lemon in half and squeeze out the juice. Soak the gelatine in a little water till it absorbs the liquid. Pour just under 500 ml (1 pt) 2½ cups of water into a saucepan, add the sugar and gelatine. Cut thin strips of the outer rind off half the lemon avoiding the pith and add to liquid. Boil through. Strain the lemon juice and add to the jelly. If the liquid is cloudy strain again through muslin. Add food colouring since the colour is poor, ie yellow, green or pink. Allow to cool and when on the point of setting wet a mould or moulds and pour the jelly in. When set dip the mould into hot water for a few seconds and turn out. Decorate with whipped cream and glacé cherries if you wish.

This is very refreshing and a favourite with children. Best on a hot day.

Fruit jelly *(jello)* (2)

Either 1 banana
a few black pitted grapes or
1 tangerine in sections

Make jelly as above. Wait till it is on the point of setting. Scald a metal mould and rinse with cold water. Cover the bottom with the setting jelly about 15 mm (½ in.) thick. To avoid bubbles in the jelly tilt the mould and place the jelly in spoonfuls on the bottom. Put back into fridge. Meanwhile keep the rest of the jelly in a warm room to avoid it setting too quickly. When the jelly is set in the fridge take out and place a layer of fruit on the bottom. Cover with the jelly which has been left in the warm room and put back in the fridge to set finally.

This is quite involved and many people just add a little fruit to the jelly when it is cold.

Whipped lemon jelly *(jello)* (3)

1 white of egg
jelly as above

Make jelly as opposite. Before the jelly sets whip the white of egg till it starts to foam. Mix with the lemon jelly and whip both together till they increase in bulk and are light and fluffy. Put quickly into a wetted mould or moulds and leave to set in the fridge.

This is very light and you can eat a great deal on a hot day. Could be served with whipped cream for those who like it.

Apple charlotte with wine

serves 6

1 small loaf white bread
8 medium cooking apples
100 g (4 oz) ½ cup sugar
2 glasses sherry or wine
cinnamon if liked
grated rind of lemon
50 g (2 oz) 4 tablespoons butter

Take a stale white loaf and remove all crusts. Cut into slices. Soak in wine and sugar and allow to drain. Sprinkle with cinnamon. Butter a pie dish and line with bread. Peel, core and grate the apples coarsely. Fill the pie dish. Add sugar mixed with wine (any left over) and the grated lemon rind and cinnamon if used. Cover with soaked bread, dot with butter. Bake at 180°C (350°F) Mark 4, for 40 minutes or till the apples are soft.

This is a Lenten dish. Serve with cream if you are not fasting.

Apple pudding

serves 4

2 medium grated cooking apples
2 eggs
125 ml (¼ pt) $\frac{2}{3}$ cup thick cream
100-150 g (4-5 oz) $\frac{1}{2}$-$\frac{2}{3}$ cup sugar
50 g (2 oz) ½ cup dry breadcrumbs
50 g (2 oz) ¼ cup melted butter

Butter a pie dish. Mix all ingredients thoroughly. Best done in a mixer if you have one. Pour into the prepared dish. Bake at 180°C (350°F) Mark 4, for 40 minutes or till well browned. Eat hot or cold.

If you like cinnamon serve cinnamon mixed with sugar on the table and some cream. Or thin kissel or cherry jam thinned down to make a sauce. Use 2 tablespoons of water to 200 g (8 oz) ¾ cup homemade jam.

Cheese and apricot juice dragli *(mould)*

serves 4

100 g (4 oz) ½ cup curd cheese
25 g (1 oz) 2 tablespoons sugar
1 tablespoon double (heavy) cream or sour cream
vanilla essence few drops
5 g (¼ oz) 1 envelope gelatine
60 ml ($\frac{1}{8}$ pt) ¾ cup apricot juice
water to make up to 250 ml (½ pt) 1¼ cups

Take the apricot juice and make up to just 250 ml (½ pt) 1 cup. Soak the gelatine in a little cold water in a cup. Put into a saucepan with boiling water to dissolve. Stir. Rub the cheese through a sieve if necessary. Add the sugar, cream and vanilla. Mix in the apricot juice with a whisk and keep on whisking till well blended and there are no lumps. Add the dissolved gelatine little by little. Blend well and allow to cool. When it begins to set put into a wetted mould or moulds and chill.

Before turning out on to a dish, dip in hot water for a few seconds to loosen the jelly. You can decorate with whipped cream and glacé cherries if you wish for a festive occasion. Use pineapple juice or any other juice you fancy for this pudding. Good with orange but needs a bit more sugar. Test for sweetness before cooking.

Ukrainian cherries

serves 4

400 g (1 lb) dessert cherries
200 g (8 oz) 1 cup sugar
250 ml (½ pt) 1¼ cups sour cream

Wash and remove stalks and stones from cherries. Cover cherries with sugar and allow to stand for 1 hour. Before serving pour the sour cream over.

Black cherries are best for this dish but as the season is short try fresh strawberries or raspberries. Use only sour cream made at home for this. It gives a richer and smoother flavour.

Ukrainian rice and apple pudding

serves 6

200 g (8 oz) 1 ⅓ cups patna rice
1.75 l (3 pt) 7½ cups water
3 medium cooking apples
125 ml (¼ pt) ⅔ cup sour cream
1 large egg
½ teaspoon powdered cinnamon
1 teaspoon salt
50 g (2 oz) 4 tablespoons butter
50 g (2 oz) 4 tablespoons sugar and 1 extra tablespoon

Boil rice in 1.75 l (3 pt) 7½ cups water with the salt till just ready, ie not more than 20 minutes. Drain in a colander and hold under cold running water till all the starch is washed away. Melt butter. Peel and core apples. Slice thinly. Mix 50 g (2 oz) 4 tablespoons sugar with the cinnamon. Beat the egg. Put the rice back in the saucepan and add the melted butter and the beaten egg and 1 tablespoon sugar. Blend all ingredients. Put half the rice in a buttered pie dish. Cover with the sliced apples. Sprinkle with sugar and cinnamon and cover with the remainder of the rice. Pour over the sour cream and bake for 1 hour at 180°C (350°F) Mark 4.

This pudding can be eaten with more sour cream and castor sugar at the table. It is not very sweet. You will need 250 ml (½ pt) 1¼ cups of sour cream if you serve more at the table. Remember to make the cream at home well in advance (page 148).

Nut and raisin sweetmeat Uzbek dish

200 g (8 oz) 2 cups shelled walnuts
50 g (2 oz) ½ cup icing sugar
50 g (2 oz) ½ cup sweet biscuits or cakecrumbs
300 g (12 oz) 2 cups seedless raisins
1 tablespoon fruit juice (ie orange) or spirit

Put the nuts, raisins and biscuits or cake twice through a mincer. Mix with the orange juice or spirit and form into balls the size of a walnut. Roll in icing sugar. Put into a pretty dish and serve with after dinner coffee or with lemon tea.

The icing sugar does not stick very well so I dredge the remainder of the sugar over the balls and this improves the appearance. The balls should not be too soft. This depends on how dry the raisins are so add the liquid a little at a time till the mixture is the right consistency to form into balls. This quantity makes approximately 600 g (1 lb 8 oz) of this sweetmeat.

Orange compôte

serves 4

4 oranges
50 g (2 oz) 4 tablespoons sugar
125 ml (¼ pt) ⅔ cup water
a little powdered cinnamon
1-2 tablespoons rum

Peel the oranges, removing all pith and slice thinly. If the oranges are large cut into quarters before slicing. Boil the water, sugar and a little cinnamon together for about 20 minutes till the liquid thickens. Test for cinnamon and add more if necessary. Pour the hot syrup over the slices of orange and cool. Add the rum before serving and stir.

If the oranges are very sweet add a little lemon juice to taste.

Bread and walnut pudding

serves 6

4 eggs
200 g (8 oz) 2 cups walnuts
25 g (1 oz) 2 tablespoons melted butter
2 tablespoons dry breadcrumbs

Separate eggs and chill whites. Whip the yolks together with the sugar till white. Add the melted butter gradually. Grind the walnuts. Whip the whites till they stand in peaks and fold in the rest of the ingredients. Transfer to an oiled soufflé dish, well buttered and coated with breadcrumbs. Bake at 200°C (400°F) Mark 6, for 30 minutes.

This makes a change from the usual soufflé. You can if you wish put the mixture into a basin and cover with paper and steam for 1½ hours instead of cooking in the oven. Serve with thin cream or thin fruit kissel in the summer when berries are available.

Drinks

Vishnyovka

1.2 kg (3 lb) morello cherries
1 kg (2½ lb) 5 cups granulated sugar
½ bottle vodka

Wash, stalk and carefully stone the cherries. Put the cherries and sugar in stone jars in alternate layers, ending with a sugar layer. Cover with muslin, and leave for three weeks in a warm place to ferment. When it has stopped fermenting add the vodka, cork the jars firmly and leave for a month or longer. Strain the liquid into bottles and seal. Leave nine months if possible.

The cherries, when discarded, can be dipped in castor sugar and eaten with Russian tea.

You can use honey instead of sugar for this. It should be almost colourless. For a different method called Ukrainian Vishnyovka use vodka thus: Cook the cherries which should have no leaves or stems in the oven. They should not be over cooked but only slightly and in fact still be moist and not dry. Transfer them to a barrel with metal rings round it or a large jar (depending on how much you want to make). Shake the jar or turn the barrel so that they are packed tight. Pour your best vodka over and seal. Keep in a cool place for 10 days. This should not be iced. You can even bury it in the ground! Pour off the liquid formed after ten days and repeat the process for a further 2 weeks. Pour off the liquid again. Cover the cherries a third time with vodka and leave for a further 3 weeks. Strain the liquid off and add to the vishnyovka you already have. Pour into bottles adding from 100 g (4 oz) to 300 g (12 oz) ⅔-1½ cups of sugar to each bottle according to taste. You can drink it in about 3 months.

Krushon

100 g (4 oz) ½ cup sugar
125 ml (¼ pt) ⅔ cup boiling water
1 small tin pineapple
2 bottles medium dry white wine
¼ bottle rum

Dissolve 100 g (4 oz) ½ cup sugar in 125 ml (¼ pt) ⅔ cup boiling water. Chop the pineapple. Put all the ingredients into a large bowl. Ice before serving and serve immediately as it will not keep.

This is an excellent party drink and best given on a hot summer day. See that all the ingredients are chilled so that it will keep cold longer.

Tzar's punch

200 g (8 oz) 1 cup sugar
juice of 6 lemons
1 small tin crushed pineapple
½ bottle rum
juice of 3 oranges
1 bottle champagne

Heat the sugar in a little water over a low heat to

make a syrup. Add the strained lemon juice. A clear syrup will form. Sieve the pineapple into a large bowl and pour in the hot syrup. Add the rum and cool. Add the strained orange juice and champagne. Serve iced.

This is indeed a lovely drink although rather expensive. Make it for special occasions such as weddings, christenings and birthdays. You can of course use sparkling wine instead of champagne. But try and get the French variety since it is so much better. This drink will not keep and should be drunk at once.

Balalaika cocktail

1 part vodka
1 part orange juice (fresh or tinned)
1 part soda water

Mix well and chill. Serve with a thin slice of lemon or orange.

This is a very refreshing drink for a party. It will not keep so it has to be made several times during the evening. Use chilled ingredients so that it will keep cold longer.

Kvass

400 g (1 lb) black bread
3 l (5 pt) 12½ cups boiling water
15 g (½ oz) fresh yeast or 1 packet dried yeast
100 g (4 oz) ½ cup sugar
sprig of mint
200 g (8 oz) 1½ cups sultanas

Cut the bread in cubes and dry in a very slow oven for 1-2 hours. Do not let it burn. Put these rusks in a bowl and pour in the boiling water. Cover with a cloth and leave for 3-4 hours. Strain through muslin and add the yeast, sugar and mint. Cover with a cloth and leave for 5-6 hours. When the kvass starts to foam strain it through muslin again and put it in bottles. Add a few sultanas to each bottle. Soak the corks in boiling water to make them more flexible and cork the bottles very securely. Replace the corks if they pop. Leave the bottles lying down in a cool place. The kvass should be ready in 2-3 days.

Kvass is similar in taste to a weak English beer. It is served with meals and can also be used as a stock for okroshka, borshch and other soups.

This is a very popular Russian drink and very thirst quenching. I well remember the workmen in France when I was staying at the Château de Mosqueros (A Russian Emigré School) at Salies de Bearn having a bottle each as their ration for the day. It was extremely hot and they enjoyed their drink very much. The French chef we had at the time made the kvass. Unfortunately he was always drunk and in the end went mad and had to be taken away by the police! He was an excellent chef however.

HOW TO SERVE VODKA

Vodka should be served in very small glasses as it is drunk in one gulp, never sipped. It is always iced and served with food, either with zakuski (see first section of this book) or with any course of the meal, apart from the sweet. It is excellent with blini (page 108). A few thin slices of lemon or orange peel added several hours before serving give the drink a very special flavour.

Fruit punch

makes 6 glasses

100 g (4 oz) fruit or berries
50 g (2 oz) 4 tablespoons sugar
2 tablespoons brandy
2 wine glasses champagne or white wine
2 wineglasses fresh home-made lemonade
ice

Chop fruit if large such as plums or large strawberries. Sprinkle with sugar and allow to stand for 3 hours or so with the brandy. Transfer to jug and pour over home-made lemonade and white wine or champagne in equal quantities as above. Add two ice cubes.

This was a favourite drink in hot weather in Russia in well-to-do families. Serve on a hot day before lunch in the garden.

Ukrainian plum brandy

Use a large earthenware wide necked jar. Remove stalks and damaged fruit. Fill the jar with ripe plums. Add vodka to cover. Seal. Put in dark place for 4-6 weeks. Strain and set the vodka aside in bottles. Cover the plums in the jar with sugar. You can use sugar syrup if you like: 400 g (1 lb) 2 cups sugar to 150 l (2½ pt) 6¼ cups water. Boil together and cool before using. The sugar draws the alcohol out of the plums. Allow to stand for a further two weeks. Strain. Combine with the strained vodka. Filter and fill bottles. Cork and label. Put in store for 6 months in a cool dark place. The plums may be used for fruit salad or with ice cream.

The climate is not very good in England for making brandy but it is well worth trying for the fun of it. It works better in America.

Strawberry ice punch

400 g (1 lb) strawberries
200 g (8 oz) 1 cup sugar
½ bottle white wine

Remove stalks from strawberries and wash. Dry. Put through a nylon sieve. Mix the purée with the sugar. Dilute with wine and chill. Do not freeze hard, this punch should look like water with snow in it.

Serve in a glass jug on a hot day with ice cubes in tall glasses.

Miscellaneous

Sour milk

Milk should only take about 24 hours to go sour. If it takes longer it will have a bitter taste and can then only be used for baking. Pour the required amount of milk into a bowl and leave in a place in the kitchen where there are plenty of germs. Milk will not ferment in a clinically clean kitchen. When it is ready the sour milk will be like junket. Eat with sugar and black bread or use for making curd cheese.

Sour milk is very refreshing on a hot day. It is a very quick and easy pudding. You can also make it into a cream mould.

Curd cheese

2.50 l (4 pt) 10 cups of milk will make approximately 400 g (1 lb) 2 cups of curd cheese

Make the sour milk (see above) in two bowls as it is then easier to handle. Cut the solid sour milk in four with a knife. This helps it to cook more quickly. The cream which forms on top of the sour milk can be skimmed off and used separately but the cheese will taste much better if it is left. Put the sour milk in a fireproof dish in a slow oven 140-150°C (275-300°F) Mark 1-2 for about 1½ hours until the curds have separated from the whey. Cool. Hang in a muslin bag over a large bowl to dry off.

Sieve, if lumpy, and mix with a tablespoon of washed sultanas and serve with sugar and sour cream, or use for making paskha (page 136 or vatrushka (page 107).

Curd cheese if made at home tastes entirely different from the commercial variety. For one thing it should have some sour cream still in it. You can of course skim off the sour cream beforehand if you wish and use it for cooking or add it to the cheese when ready. It is not at all sour when fresh but goes sour by degrees. Any dish made with home-made cheese requires less sugar and tastes much better. The only time you can really make good cheese or sour milk is when it is really hot. It will not go sour if the weather is cool.

Curd cheese is so popular in Russia it is eaten in most households every day in some form or another.

Yoghurt

500 ml (1 pt) 2½ cups best quality milk
1 tablespoon bought yoghurt

Use only the best quality milk as this has more cream and gives the yoghurt a far better flavour. Boil the milk in a saucepan for a few minutes and then cool to a temperature just above blood heat. Put into a bowl with a tablespoon of bought yoghurt. Cover with a plate and wrap the bowl round with several layers of cloth so that it retains the heat. Leave in a warm place for about 12 hours. It will set when cool. It differs from bought yoghurt in that it has a layer of cream on top. Serve with sugar or jam.

I have taught many people to make yoghurt. It is really worthwhile. Not only because you can make large quantities at a time compared with the little cartons one buys in shops and it is much cheaper and also is infinitely better. It should have a thick layer of cream if made with the best milk and is not nearly as sour as that bought in the supermarket. If you do not succeed the first time try again. The main thing to remember is that the milk should not be too hot or it curdles and that it should cool by degrees and be in a warm place.

Sour cream

Sour cream is not, of course, cream which has gone off. Cream which has gone off has a bitter taste and can only be used for baking. There are two ways of making sour cream:

(1) Add a little lemon juice to fresh cream and stir. It should thicken immediately, but if not leave it to stand for a short time.

(2) Allow the cream to sour naturally. This is very difficult in England since the cream is pasteurized and the weather is rarely very hot. Cream will not go sour in a clinically clean kitchen. If the cream has not thickened in 24 hours add lemon juice; otherwise the cream will go off and taste bitter.

Sour cream will keep for several days in the fridge. A little single cream or top of the milk can be added to prevent it thickening too much.

Sour cream is now universally known and used and can of course be bought quite easily. Do try and make it yourself however. The taste is so much better and you have the real thing. In Russia it is extremely popular since cream would not keep in the summer and this is how it originated. It is much more digestible than fresh cream and not so rich.

Ragenka

500 ml (1 pt) 2½ cups best quality milk
1 tablespoon sour cream

This is similar to yoghurt but richer. Bake a pint of Jersey milk in a slow oven 140-150°C (275-300°F) Mark 1-2 for about 1½-2 hours. The longer it is cooked, the richer the ragenka. A brown skin will form on top as in a milk pudding. Take out of the oven and cool to just above blood heat. Put a tablespoon of sour cream under the skin and leave in a warm place to set. Eat when cold. Serve with sugar, jam or black bread.

Ragenka is a creamy form of sour milk. When baked the milk goes a golden colour and it is much richer than ordinary milk. It is extremely tasty and refreshing if served chilled and considered quite a treat. Makes a good and quick summer pudding.

Salted cabbage

2 medium hard white cabbages
25 g (1 oz) common salt
6 peppercorns

Wash and drain the cabbage and remove the stalk and outer leaves. Cut the cabbage in quarters. Line the bottom of an earthenware jar with some of the whole cabbage leaves. Shred the rest of the cabbage finely and sprinkle with the salt. Pack it tightly in the jar together with the peppercorns. Cover with some whole leaves. Tie a muslin cloth over the top of the jar and cover this with a small plate. The cabbage will go bad unless it remains covered all the time. Store in a fairly warm place. In a few days, when the cabbage starts to ferment, a foam will appear on the surface. When this disappears, after about a week, the cabbage is ready for use and can be stored in a cool, dry place until required. The muslin may need washing during fermentation. If so, rinse it well in cold water and replace.

A variation on plain salted cabbage can be achieved by adding slices of a peeled apple and carrot and a tablespoon of cleaned cranberries. If these are included an extra teaspooon of salt will be needed. Serve with meat or poultry.

This method of preserving cabbage retains its vitamins and improves the quality. Another method is to use sweet white wine (a half bottle of wine per large cabbage) leave to mature as above. Bilberries may also be added to the cabbage and a layer of rye flour at the bottom of the jar to help fermentation. For a less salty type of cabbage pour boiling water over the cabbage and then rinse in cold water. Salt as above. The cabbage will be ready in 5-6 days.

Pickled mushrooms

400 g (1 lb) mushrooms	3 peppercorns
60 ml ($\frac{1}{8}$ pt) ¼ cup wine vinegar	1 bayleaf
125 ml (¼ pt) $\frac{2}{3}$ cup water	2 cloves
¾ tablespoon common salt	

Use only one variety of mushrooms. They should be freshly picked, if possible. Discard the stalks and any unsound parts. Wash, drain well and peel. Cut in quarters if they are large; otherwise leave whole. Put the wine vinegar and water in a saucepan. Add the mushrooms and bring to the boil. Remove any scum and add the salt, peppercorns, bayleaf and cloves and simmer for about 20 minutes, stirring all the time. When the mushrooms settle on the bottom of the saucepan remove it from the heat. Cool, transfer to jars and seal. Serve as zakuski with vodka (page 144).

A good time to preserve mushrooms is when you have picked too many to eat. The best time to pick mushrooms is in August or September early in the morning. Cut the stem with a knife and do not pull out by the roots. This ensures that another mushroom will grow in its place. Mushrooms spoil easily so use them within 5-6 hours of picking. To the recipe above you can add a little dried dill if you have it. These pickled mushrooms are excellent before a meal and make an original hors d'oeuvre.

Slightly salted cucumbers

1.2 kg (3 lb) cucumbers	1 clove garlic
oak, blackcurrant, cherry or vine leaves	2 heaped tablespoons common salt
4 sprigs dill	1.25 l (2 pt) 5 cups water
4 peppercorns	

Use firm ripe ridge cucumbers about 7.5 cm (3 in.) long. Line the bottom of an earthenware jar with the leaves. Wash the cucumbers and stand them upright in the jar. Add the dill, peppercorns and garlic. Bring the saline solution to the boil. Be careful not to exceed the quantity of salt stated as too much will ruin this recipe. Cool and pour over the cucumbers and cover with a few more leaves. To make sure that the cucumbers remain immersed in the liquid all the time and do not float up, tie a muslin cloth over the top of the jar and put a saucer or plate on top. The leaves are important in this recipe as they help to prevent the cucumbers from going soft.

The cucumbers will be ready to eat in about a week. Serve as zakuski with vodka (page 144).

Small cucumbers suitable to be salted are in season in the summer. Remember to choose those of equal size otherwise some will be ready before others. Salted cucumbers are often used as a garnish for cotletti or steak. Can also garnish fried fish. These cannot be bought in shops and so are considered a delicacy.

Salted tomatoes

1.2 kg (3 lb) tomatoes	1 clove garlic
oak, blackcurrant, cherry or vine leaves	2 heaped tablespoons common salt
4 sprigs dill	1.25 l (2 pt) 5 cups water
12 peppercorns	

Choose tomatoes of the same size, either small green ones or larger ripe ones. Use the same method as for salted cucumbers, packing them tightly in an earthenware jar. Note, however, that more peppercorns are used. They should be ready to eat in about a week. Serve as zakuski with vodka (page 144).

This is a good way to preserve tomatoes that have not ripened at the end of the summer. The tomatoes should be very tight so shake the jar to see that there are no empty spaces. Fill the jar right to the top. These should be kept in a cool place.

Pickled grapes or plums

400 g (1 lb) grapes or plums	100 g (4 oz) ½ cup sugar
125 ml (¼ pt) $\frac{2}{3}$ cup wine vinegar	2 peppercorns
250 ml (½ pt) 1¼ cups water	1 clove
½ teaspoon salt	

Remove the stalks and wash the grapes or plums.

Put them into earthenware or bottling jars. Put the wine vinegar, water, salt, sugar, peppercorns and clove into a saucepan and bring to the boil. Cool and pour over the fruit. Cover the jars with greaseproof paper tied with string. They should keep for about 6 months in a cool place. Serve as zakuski with vodka (page 144) or with roast meat or poultry.

If you eat cold chicken or turkey often pickled grapes or plums make an original accompaniment. Or they can be kept for Christmas when various cold meats are eaten. This is a useful preservative to make at the end of the summer if you have a plum tree and do not know what to do with the remainder of the plums.

This marinade can also be used for melon. Cut off the outside skin, remove seeds and cut into cubes. The melon should not be over ripe or green but just right. Follow instructions as above.

Dill

Dill is a herb which is widely used in Russia for salads and soups and as garnish for other dishes. It can be grown in the garden in the summer and dried at home for use in the winter. To dry, remove the stalks and leave the dill on clean sheets of paper for about two weeks, turning from time to time. When completely dry, rub gently between the hands and put into sealed jars. (Parsley can be dried and stored in the same way.) Dried dill is also obtainable in delicatessen shops and is sold in jars at most supermarkets now.

Dill goes a long way when dried. Use it to flavour salads, stews and soups.

Vanilla pods and vanilla sugar

Vanilla can be used in two ways:

(1) Cut the pod in half with a sharp knife and remove the seeds. If you are using milk in the recipe, put both the pod and the seeds in the milk and boil for a few minutes.

(2) If you wish to keep the vanilla for future use, cut the pod in half with a knife and remove the seeds. Mix the pod and the seeds with castor sugar: 400 g (1 lb) 2 cups sugar to each pod. Put into an airtight jar and keep in a cool, dry place. The vanilla sugar will be ready to use in about a week. It can be kept for a long time if stored in this way.

If you have never made vanilla sugar, now is the time to try. You will find it excellent to flavour cakes and puddings. If you want a stronger flavour use two large pods per 400 g (1 lb) 2 cups of castor verifine sugar.

Index